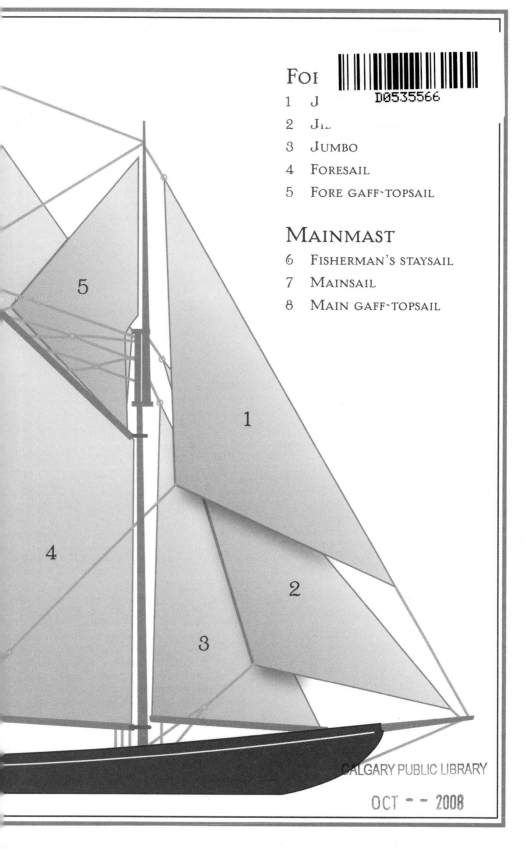

5

1

4

2

3

D0535566

Books of Merit

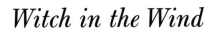

Witch in the Wind

in the Wind

The True Story of the
Legendary Bluenose

Marq de Villiers

Thomas Allen Publishers
Toronto

Library and Archives Canada Cataloguing in Publication

De Villiers, Marq, 1940–
Witch in the wind : the true story of the Bluenose / Marq de Villiers.

Includes bibliographical references and index.
ISBN-13: 978-0-88762-224-3
ISBN-10: 0-88762-224-0

1. Bluenose (Ship)—History.
2. Shipping—Atlantic Provinces—History—20th century.
3. Fisheries—Atlantic Provinces—History—20th century.
4. Atlantic Provinces—Economic conditions—20th century.
5. Atlantic Provinces—Social conditions—20th century.
I. Title.

VM395.B5D48 2007   971.5'03   c2006-906639-6

Editor: Janice Zawerbny
Cover image: Library and Archives Canada

Published by Thomas Allen Publishers,
a division of Thomas Allen & Son Limited,
145 Front Street East, Suite 209,
Toronto, Ontario M5A 1E3 Canada

www.thomas-allen.com

ONTARIO ARTS COUNCIL
CONSEIL DES ARTS DE L'ONTARIO

Canada Council
for the Arts

The publisher gratefully acknowledges the support of
The Ontario Arts Council for its publishing program.

We acknowledge the support of the Canada Council for the Arts, which
last year invested $20.0 million in writing and publishing throughout Canada.

We acknowledge the Government of Ontario through the Ontario
Media Development Corporation's Ontario Book Initiative.

We acknowledge the financial support of the Government of Canada through the Book
Publishing Industry Development Program (BPIDP) for our publishing activities.

11 10 09 08 07   1 2 3 4 5
Printed and bound in Canada

Contents

Acknowledgments and grateful thanks

. . . to Bill Gilkerson, who really does seem to know everything; to Dan Moreland, who told me what the story was about; to Ralph Getson, every Bluenoser's favourite resource; to Kline Falkenham, who has put many a vessel (including *Bluenose II*) together, plank by plank; to Matt Mitchell, who was there; to Martha Keddy Smith and her generous spirit; to Peter Barss, whose pictures are worth much more than a thousand words; to Wayne Walters, who has lived part of the story; and to so many others, including:

Charles Armour, archivist and historian; Brian Backman, a Lunenburger now a long way from the sea, in Switzerland; Dan Conlin, of the Maritime Museum in Halifax; Hugh Corkum, collector of memorabilia; Graham Dennis, publisher of the *Halifax Chronicle Herald*; Tom Gallant, author, raconteur, and sailor; Andy German, author and former curator at the Mystic Seaport Museum; Craig Harding, crew member of *Bluenose II*; Clem Hiltz, crew member of *Bluenose* herself; Ian Mackay, historian at Queen's University; Senator Wilfred Moore, who ran the Bluenose Trust; Susan Pratt and Jane Ritcey, always generous with their many connections; Garry Shutlak of the Nova Scotia Archives; Ron Whynacht, who knows both fish and sailing vessels; and Barbara Zwicker, doyenne of Lunenburg.

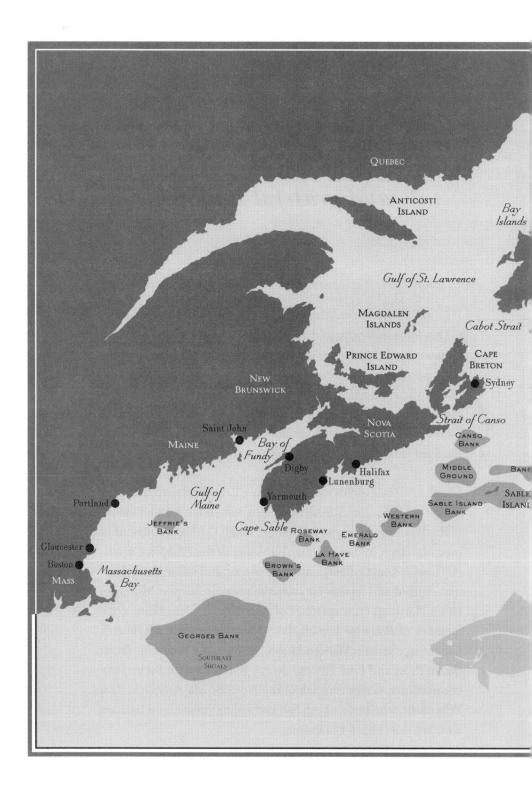

North Atlantic Fishing Banks

NEWFOUNDLAND

St. John's

Cape Broyle

FLEMISH CAP

Placentia Bay

Cape Race

ST. PIERRE & MIQUELON

ST. PIERRE BANK

GREEN BANK

WHALE DEEP

GRAND BANK

SOUTHEAST SHOAL

N

W   E

S

Witch in the Wind

P R O L O G U E

*I*n the night it came on to blow, in the phrase of the coast, and by dawn's thin light it was blustery and wet, white-water shredding off the swells in a southeasterly gale, the early morning sun invisible behind ragged clouds. Hard Atlantic weather, to be sure, but the *Bluenose* shrugged it off in her usual disdainful way and sailed into the fairway of Gloucester, Massachusetts, looking every bit the Queen. It was September 30, 1938, and she was freshly painted in her traditional matte black with gold trim, new sails white as ghosts, spars and booms and wheel and every bit of exposed wood spit'n'polished, apparently ready for the last real challenge of her life, the final reel in her long and eventful drama. Angus Walters, her skipper, was at the wheel, oiled up as the saying went, in full oilskin raingear, and so were the crew.

There were people standing on the rocks at Cape Ann, up early in the bleak New England dawn, watching as she passed, sensing an historic moment; more people lined the wharves in Gloucester harbour, silently staring; a few vessels sounded their horns as the *Bluenose* reefed her sails and prepared for mooring, but neither Angus nor the crew paid them any mind. Little was said. Angus spoke his orders in an ordinary voice, without his customary megaphone, and the men moved to obey in their practised way, but there was little conversation as the town and the harbour and the jetties glided by, for each man was locked into his own thoughts. The

Bluenose was here for the last races of her life, they knew that, and she looked like a queen, they knew that too, but they had felt her riding low and logy in the water through the long night's run from Lunenburg, and some of them were thinking, for the first time and with considerable foreboding, that the old champion might not any longer be up to defending her title.

Thoroughbred royalty, yes, she was still that, but a dowager queen now, older than she should be, and hard used. She had spent a bad few years in the Depression. They had even cut off her topmasts and poked around in her innards to install twin diesels, a terrible indignity there in her bowels; her planking was water-logged and heavy, a few of her ribs softer than was safe. Her top-sails had been taken ashore and stored in lockers, just in case. She was old, that was it. Her skipper knew that better than anyone. He was old too, for a fishing man, closer to sixty than fifty, his wife recently dead; he didn't bend as easily as he used to, and was often weary.

When the challenge came from Gloucester for one more series, another international fishing schooner racing series, perhaps the last ever, he had been reluctant. Oh, he had understood where the Gloucestermen were coming from. The Master Mariners Asso-ciation of that gritty seafaring town had been fired up again by the unexpected success of the MGM movie *Captains Courageous*, based on Kipling's romantic novel, which had rekindled public interest in fishermen and their traditions; the *Gertrude L. Thebaud*, *Bluenose*'s old foe, was still alive; the *Bluenose* herself was aging and battered but still the champion, still a looming presence in the minds of New Englanders. They were the only two such vessels left, but there they were. It didn't take much persuasion to get Newfoundlander–turned–Gloucesterman Ben Pine going again, and he went up to Halifax to issue the challenge. It would be a best-of-five series raced off Gloucester and Boston—Boston had always wanted the races sailed there, and maybe this was their chance, here at the end. Same prize money as before, and the trophy declaring the winner, one more time, the Queen of the Atlantic.

Angus's reluctance was partly for himself. His life was changing. He wasn't going fishing much anymore. He was ready to retire from the sea, and was casting around onshore for a job to do, perhaps as a harbourmaster somewhere. He was involved in union affairs and in the town of Lunenburg, and he wasn't sure he wanted to tear himself away for yet more races that were bound to be acrimonious, their results uncertain. And a good deal of his reluctance was for the old girl herself. He knew that eighteen was very old for a wooden working vessel. He knew she was in poor shape, waterlogged and heavy, her hull soft and a little "hogged," sagging at the bow and stern. She would need new sails and a complete refit, new rigging and blocks and tackles and the rest. Who was to pay for those? He estimated the cost at nearly $10,000, a third of what it cost to build her in the first place. Even were she to win, the prize money would not be nearly enough to cover the costs. He'd been trying to sell her for some time now, after all, for no one would listen to his alternative plan, for a permanent berth somewhere and a memorial. And if she were to lose? After all that time as champion? It didn't bear thinking about.

But his old rival from Gloucester, Ben Pine, the moving force behind so many of the early racing series, was a masterful man and not to be denied. He persuaded his friends in Boston to come up with $8,000 to help refit the *Bluenose*. With the prodding of this Yankee contribution, the Canadian fisheries department came up with $2,500 and the Nova Scotia government another $1,000. This would be enough, and Angus accepted the challenge on behalf of the *Bluenose* company. A Lunenburg boy, Doug Pyke, collected all the newly minted *Bluenose* Canadian dimes he could get, called them "silver engraving souvenirs of the *Bluenose*," and hawked them in Boston for $2 each.[1]

And so she was hauled and scraped and caulked and the too-soft planking removed and new lumber installed. The painters went to work, and in the sail lofts along the wharves and over in

Dauphinee's block shop up the hill in Lunenburg a new suit of sails and rigging were put together. Claude Darrach, who had crewed in all her races and was there for the finish, remembers helping to rummage through the lockers to find the topmasts and other gear that had been struck down when *Bluenose*'s engines were installed three years earlier. And so she was ready, or as ready as she would ever be.

They left Lunenburg on the morning of September 29, heading into the gusty southeaster, riding low not just because she was logy but because Angus had left her engines installed for the run south, suspicious that at the last moment the races would fail to come off and he would have taken them out for nothing. He also loaded an extra 40 tons of ballast, to use when the engines were indeed taken out, and that made her heavier than ever.

By the time they reached Shelburne the wind was 20 knots, and Angus was carrying every sail she had, keeping the crew busy adjusting the lines and halyards and checking the shackles and blocks. By nightfall the wind had picked up some more, and Angus oiled up and advised the crew to do the same; the crew lashed themselves to the vessel with loose bowlines "in case of too much green water." The boat was doing 14 knots in a 25-knot wind, and at last Angus ordered the mainsail reefed and the jib taken in; he was by now less concerned with making good time than keeping his sails in shape for the races. Even so, she made 12 knots the rest of the way, pretty decent going for an old girl.

A little more than 24 hours after leaving Lunenburg, the *Bluenose* entered the Gloucester fairway. As she was going in, she passed the *Thebaud* going out for her sea trials. They exchanged foghorn signals and went on their way.

Onshore, the city fathers issued instructions to the tavern keepers to batten down all the movable furniture and to close tight on time; there had already been fights in the streets and at least one rum-

fuelled melee, and with the national press out in full force Gloucester wanted their town to at least appear squeaky clean; the tourists
might want colourful, but they didn't want brawls. That night, the
Massachusetts governor invited both crews to a pre-race banquet.
Angus Walters, prickly as ever, declined to go. "Let 'em go on all
they want," he said. "I'm here to race, not to jaw."

The press gleefully picked up the salvos Angus fired at all parties. Told that the race committee had organized a short triangular
course so the races could be better seen from shore, he was con-
temptuous, calling it "a merry-go-round course, unfit for real vessels." There were no Canadians on the seven-person committee,
he pointed out; it was insulting. (Ben Pine for his part thought it
equally insulting that there were no Gloucestermen on the committee either.) Even after two Canadians were added and a compromise was reached on the course, Angus was not assuaged. The
head of the committee, Captain Charles Lyons, should go back to
the farm, which is where he really belonged, being unfit to run
anything but a milking stool.

The *Bluenose* had been assigned jettyside storage and a shed,
and into this shed went the engines, one multi-ton component at a
time. She was then hauled out and the recently installed framing
timbers for the engines removed and put ashore, and so were all
shafts and bearings. She was refloated but she was too high in the
water; the Gloucester racing committee sent busybodies around
with measuring story-poles and plumb bobs, and more ballast was
installed. The crew was unhappy. She was now correct at the waterline, but eighteen years of heavy use had hogged her and the cop-
per nails marking the waterline were too high in the middle. The
race committee didn't mind this—all they cared about was overall
length at the waterline, and they were satisfied. But as a consequence, the *Bluenose* was out of trim, and would be harder than
usual to handle.

And so it proved. On October 9 the two boats crossed the Cape
Ann starting line pretty much neck and neck. *Bluenose* was ahead

at the first marker but fell behind on the second—not her fault, Angus was outmanoeuvred by Ben Pine. On the third leg, in a stiff northwesterly wind, her bowsprit cracked and then split, slacking off the jib, but Walters admitted it made no difference. The *Thebaud* was ahead at the time and would have won anyway. He thought Ben had sailed well and all in all it had been a grand race.

Two days later, a brand-new Douglas fir bowsprit in place and the stays tight, the two vessels set off again, but the winds had turned against them. So fitful and light were they that the "race" became nothing more than a drifting match; they only covered 12 miles in three hours. The committee was asked to call off the race and they wavered. At first they refused, but it became more and more clear that neither vessel would finish in anything like the required time and they finally ended it.

On the 13th the second race finally came off, in a decent 18-knot wind and comfortable seas. The *Thebaud* crossed the line first but was quickly overhauled, and the *Bluenose* never thereafter lost the lead, despite ripping her staysail during the third leg. Ben Pine had trouble locating the marker buoys (they looked rather too much like the buoys marking lobster traps), and twice overshot his mark, losing almost five minutes. In the end, the *Bluenose* won by a comfortable eleven minutes. One race each.

There followed a week of . . . nothing very much. One day of fog and light winds followed the next; each crew tinkered with the ballast and trim, stayed away from the taverns as much as they could, and waited. Ben Pine became ill and was replaced at the *Thebaud*'s helm by Cecil Moulton; on the 20th the two vessels headed to the starting line to try again, but it was no use. The committee called off the race at midpoint, to Moulton's fury—*Thebaud* had been slightly in the lead, and he was convinced he could have finished in the requisite six hours.

Finally, on October 22, the fog blew off and a fresh 18-knot southwesterly wind sprang up, perfect conditions for racing. But five minutes before the starting gun the gears of the *Bluenose*'s helm jammed and broke, and the wheel fell off in the captain's hands and crashed to the deck. They were already under way, doing 9 knots and heading for a nasty reef called Norman's Woe, and Angus was forced to do some quick juggling with sheets to force the vessel to the other tack. He hoisted a "Not Under Command" signal and a passing dragger helped push him back to the wharf. Claude Darrach, who was there, called it embarrassing, and so it was. Angus was mortified; he was not a man who liked to look helpless, and to be helped back by something . . . mechanized . . . was too much.

By noon the next day the repairs had been done, a machinist having copied the gear mechanism built by the Lunenburg Foundry eighteen years earlier, and the race was on, under overcast skies in a fresh wind. Both vessels sailed at better than 12 knots, and Angus outduelled Cecil Moulton in a luffing match to come in six and a half minutes ahead. But the *Bluenose* was feeling the strain: under a full press of sail in a good wind, the stress of thousands of feet of canvas hauling at the wood raised the deck amidships by almost 3 inches. "It had settled back to a more normal position by breakfast," Darrach reported, but it was a sign of the *Bluenose*'s age.

They headed off to Boston in thick fog, with *Bluenose* ahead by two races to one. *Thebaud* scraped a rock leaving Gloucester, but made it safely to Boston. She asked for a day off and was hauled out and inspected. The damage turned out to be minimal, and the races could go ahead.

The fourth race was sailed in driving rain and a gusty west-north-west wind, perfect conditions for these vessels.

Before the start, Angus lectured his crew. He'd taken an instant dislike to Cecil Moulton, who was still at *Thebaud*'s helm for this race, and told them to be ready for anything. "For you can never tell what the fellow is up to," he said. "Just don't foul things up."[2]

As it happened, the tricky Moulton had to do nothing but sail well. On the first 9-mile leg both vessels were going all out, burying their lee rails with a great hiss and roar. *Bluenose* averaged 14.15 knots over the leg, at that point a record for an all-sail vessel on a fixed course, and the *Thebaud* wasn't far behind at 13.87 knots. But as they rounded the first mark a gust snapped the *Bluenose*'s foretopmast stay and the crew watched, appalled, as the mast bent like an archer's bow and as Claude Darrach reported, "the man aloft did some gymnastic feats among the flapping canvas and wires." The foretopsail ripped with a great 40-foot tear, and although the crew hustled it down and the rigger, Kenny Spidel, by then sixty-two years old, stitched it together in jig time and it was hauled back up ten minutes later, it was too late: the *Thebaud* ran for home and crossed the finish line a few minutes ahead. The race boat was nowhere to be seen. Seasickness, the *Thebaud* jeered.

Two races each.

The next day dawned a gale, and to the further jeers of both crews the race was cancelled.

Meanwhile, there was still considerable fretting on the *Bluenose*'s part about her trim and her ballast. They even summoned her designer, Bill Roué, from his home in Dartmouth to come down to Boston and give advice, which rather went against Angus's grain—he didn't much like Roué. But so important had this series become for Nova Scotia that the provincial government held up the departure of the Yarmouth–Bar Harbor ferry to await Roué's arrival, and got him to Boston only twenty hours after leaving home. He advised Angus to send a few more tons of equipment ashore, and Angus went along. Rum and tobacco, Roué reported, helped the night hours pass.

And so it came to the final race of the final series, the last race *Bluenose* would ever race, probably the last race between working fishing sailboats ever, a poignant and perhaps melancholy end to sail itself as a working life. Both crews felt this, and so did Gloucester, which to its disappointment was to see this final race take place off Boston. It was to be the end not just of schooner races, but would be a marker that the era of sail, an era that stretched back into the mists of time, had drawn at last to a close. This would be a magnificent end, perhaps, but the age of machines had arrived, and an end it would be. There were smaller anxieties too, of course—for Angus and his crew, some of them soon to retire (Adam Knickle was the oldest at eighty-two, and Sam Shaw seventy) and facing an uncertain future; for the town of Lunenburg, still racked by strikes and wrenching change; for Nova Scotia, the *Bluenose* a reminder of a glorious era now passed, an era in which the province was once important, and now was important no longer; and for Canada, always nigglingly envious of *that place* to the south, and for whom the *Bluenose* was a symbol of high standards never bettered. For Gloucester, too, winning the cup from the legendary *Bluenose* would be some compensation for feeling set adrift on the uneasy tides of history, with no clear harbour in view. It was felt to be true even though the *Thebaud* was a Boston boat, and the finale was to be sailed off Cape Nahant. The local press and public? In Nova Scotia they of course hoped the cup would stay where it had always been in the *Bluenose* era; the Gloucesterites just wanted a winner, and in their view it would be far better that the cup should come "home" to America, to join the others, the America's Cup, the Lipton Cup and more, a whole shelf of ornate silver memories.[3]

This was it, everything on the line. Whether or not you considered the *Bluenose* unbeaten—she lost, after all, to the *Haligonian* in 1930, and again to the *Thebaud* in the Lipton Cup the same year, and she lost individual races to the *Henry Ford* and others—she had never lost where everyone agreed it counted. She was old and weary, but the crew most desperately wanted her to retire with dignity, and not have to run home to the crowing of the Gloucestermen.

The betting men would give odds on neither vessel. It was too close to risk money, in their view.

There is a wonderful photograph of the *Bluenose* and the *Thebaud* neck and neck in the final race, heeling hard under a full press of sail, green water flowing over the rail. Angus can just be made out at the helm, standing with both feet planted, solid and balanced, one hand on the wheel. Cecil Moulton, still at the helm instead of Ben Pine, is hidden in the picture by the main boom, but you can see a solid arm resting on the wheel. Both crews are standing amidships, waiting for orders. A bow wave of whitewater is cutting past both vessels, and astern flows a long wake of foam. In the picture, the *Thebaud* looks to be half a length ahead. The picture is in black and white, of course, but both vessels are breathtakingly elegant, beautiful artifacts at the very pinnacle of boat-building craft, and it's easy to see why they captured the imagination in the way they did, and why they still do, a marvellous snapshot of a more innocent age, when it still seemed possible that mastery of the world could be achieved without fumes and smoke and noxious emissions, when skill and bravery were more important than internal combustion. Beautiful, but already obsolete: in the backdrop of the picture, just passing by as it seems, is a steamer with a high castle at the poop and a large black stack belching smoke. It's so far away it looks like a toy, but it isn't: it is the death knell of the elegant creatures in the foreground, their nemesis.[4]

It was October 26. The weather was cooperating. Cool winds were blowing from the southwest at 18 knots as the gun went off. Cecil Moulton crossed a few seconds after the signal, Angus to his windward, his beloved "black bitch" heeling a little as she caught the wind. By the first marker *Bluenose* was three minutes ahead, but he went a little wide around the buoy and for the next leg it was neck and neck, only yards apart, lee rails buried. Round the second marker and the *Bluenose* surged ahead, and halfway through to the run home into the wind she was almost four minutes in front. With just one short tack left, a foretopmast block broke as she came about, jamming the halyard and leaving the staysail flapping noisily. But it really didn't matter. She was too far in front to be caught. Dipping her bow into the waves, she ran for the finish line, crossing two minutes and fifty seconds ahead of her rival.

It was a thrilling finish, the elegant Queen from Canada putting the pretty little upstart filly from Boston in her place, the "breathtaker," to use Joe Garland's word, at the moment of her ultimate triumph, crossing the line in a great hiss of foam and whitewater, lifting the hearts of her master and crew, who had by now of course not doubted her for a minute, not *really* . . . "The crowd was silent for a moment," author Silver Donald Cameron wrote, years later, "and then the bells and whistles and horns of Boston burst on the air, mingling with the cheers of crew and crowds alike in a thunderous ovation. She had won the regard of a foreign city. She had won the race, the series, and the trophy. And she would keep them forever."[5]

Thus the legend.

Alas, it was not really so simple or so satisfying. As we shall see.

And the conventional *Bluenose* story, the legend of the incomparable Queen and her innumerable triumphs, is too simple, too contrived, with too much left out, a body with neither backbone nor heart. The backbone is the tradition from which the *Bluenose* came—she didn't just spring fully formed from the brilliant inspirations of a few inspired amateurs, or even from the inspirations of a few rustic fishermen. Instead, she grew from an astonishingly fecund industrial background now largely forgotten. And the heart? The heart of the story is the men who sailed her, fished her, raced her, crewed her, captained her. These were tough men in a tough business, with an almost inhuman fortitude in the face of the savage sea. Eastern seaboard fishermen have been romanticized before, as Iron Men in Wooden Ships. Thing is, their stories are true, and without looking at their lives the *Bluenose* is just a pretty legend, just a ship-on-a-dime, a winner without losers, a Queen without rivals, an artifact without context.

CHAPTER ONE

H E R

C O N C E P T I O N

a n d

B I R T H

*T*he *Bluenose* was conceived a good year before she was born.

The seed was planted in the now-famous challenge from Lunenburg/Halifax/Nova Scotia/Canada to Gloucester/ Boston/Massachusetts/New England, but the story of this challenge has been so embellished—the accretions covering up the narrative like barnacles smothering a hull—that the "true" story is rather hard to ascertain.

Most versions agree that it starts with the America's Cup yachting challenge races for 1920. In that year Sir Thomas Lipton, who had sponsored fishermen's schooner races in Gloucester as far back as 1892, was still counting his mountains of tea bags and coveting the America's Cup, which he had so far failed to win three times, with vessels *Shamrock*, *Shamrock II* and *Shamrock III*. So he duly entered *Shamrock IV,* apparently too dim, or at least too stubborn, to have learned that it was a name of ill omen, and of course lost again, to the American defender *Resolute.* The critical thing, however, was not the outcome but the decision of the organizers and the participating skippers to call off the most significant race of the series because of bad weather. Apparently the seas had been a little choppy and the wind a little fresh for the yachtsmen— blowing at 23 knots.

This derisory breeze, a pleasant enough thing to belly out the sails of a true schooner but not enough to disturb a skipper's slumbers or cause him to reef so much as a jib or a tops'l, was received with widespread scorn among . . . well, among whom is one of the questions. Joe Garland in Gloucester gave the conventional version when he wrote that "such chicken heartedness was too much for William Dennis, who regarded with disgust the spectacle of the Mother Country harbour-bound by a little wind."[1] Dennis was the feisty second-generation publisher of the *Halifax Herald,* a newspaper that still publishes under the same family, and a popular version was that Dennis had read the news in the sports pages of an unnamed American newspaper, thought to be the New York *Herald.* Claude Darrach, the *Bluenose* crewman, gives a more democratic version: ". . . Back from the Banks, the schoonermen learned that an America's Cup race had been postponed one fine July morning because there had been a 23 knot breeze, and such news echoed and re-echoed among schooner fishermen from Newfoundland to Boston. Men who lived by wind and sail were not pleased . . ."[2] Silver Donald Cameron, in his even-handed way, butters the bread of credit a little more thickly: "The fishermen followed the America's Cup races with professional interest and patriotic partisanship . . . In 1920 the race was called off because of dangerously high winds, 23 knots . . . Angus Walters heard about it on his way back from the Banks in the *Gilbert B. Walters,* and was not impressed. Nor were Dennis and his cronies." James Connolly, an American writer and romantic (and also America's first medal winner in the modern Olympics—gold for triple jump in 1896), offers a much more prosaic explanation that has nothing to do with the America's Cup and much more to do with simple boosterism: "In 1921 the city of Halifax, seeking a big feature for their carnival week and the legitimate publicity which might spring from the same, staged a race for Canadian fishing schooners. The race was won by the *Delawana* of Lunenburg . . . After the race a Halifax committee challenged the port of Gloucester to a fishing schooner race with the *Delawana*, the winner to be the champion of the world."[3] Since he got the year wrong his version rather lacks credibility, but his notion that publicity-seeking played a role is not entirely misplaced: Dennis, particularly, was an energetic publisher of the old school, always looking for ways of boosting circulation with enterprising stunts (he went to great lengths, for instance, to enable his newspaper to publish the news of the Armistice of 1918 before anyone else) and his patriotism, genuine though it no doubt was, was always tempered with an eye to its commercial exploitation.

And so the conventional story goes that Dennis was having lunch in Halifax with a few of his cronies, among them Reg Corbett, Hugh R. Silver and Harry de Wolf, all of them chortling over this notion of a cancellation in the face of a 23-knot wind, and somewhere between the soup and the port the idea was broached of a "real competition, between real sailors, real fishermen." That much might even be true. But that Dennis then said (as he is widely reported to have said, on very thin evidence) that races between the best of Nova Scotia and the best of Massachusetts "would give a chance for our men in Lunenburg to show their heels to those lily-livered millionaires down there" is almost certainly false. If by the "lily-livered millionaires" he meant Sir Thomas and his American counterparts, he would have known well enough that Gloucester's fishermen could have shown them their heels in vigorous weather just as easily. And he most certainly knew that the fishermen and skippers of Gloucester were no millionaires, lily-livered or not;

he was as aware as anyone that many of them were Nova Scotians anyway, having gone there to make the kind of living they really couldn't achieve at home.

In any case, the real originator of the challenge was not Dennis, nor Walters, nor any of the unnamed fishermen so democratically cited by Claude Darrach. The credit must go to Colin McKay, of Shelburne, grandson of the famous Donald McKay, a shipbuilder of genius who had left Jordan River near Shelburne for New York and become a celebrity in the maritime world for building some of the first-ever Yankee clippers. Colin McKay had been both a sailor and a yachtsman, and it was his letter to the Montreal *Gazette* pouring scorn on the America's Cup and its "millionaires' frolic of fooling round with costly devices," and his subsequent suggestion of a "real race between real fishing schooners" that started the whole thing. McKay himself didn't take credit either, but claimed he was only following the suggestion of the then mayor of Lunenburg, William Duff, who might indeed have been following the yarns of the fishermen of the town, so in that way Darrach's story of its democratic origins might have some basis in truth. In any case, McKay's letter was picked up by Frederick William Wallace, then editor of *The Canadian Fisherman*, and republished with an endorsement in his August 1920 edition, along with a photo of the *Albert J. Lutz*, the winner of a series of fishermen's races in Digby, Nova Scotia, a few years earlier. Wallace's editorial was subsequently picked up by the Halifax papers and William Dennis, with the results we know.

The erratic Connolly did get several things right. William Dennis's first cup offer was for a race during the "sports carnival" in Halifax, not an international series; and he was right too in his assessment of Nova Scotia vessels: "During this period of incoming auxiliary [motor] power in Gloucester, the fishermen of eastern Canada, of Nova Scotia, Cape Breton, Prince Edward Island and Newfoundland, were arriving at the peak of their progress towards fine sailing vessels. The Provincial fishermen had always been a skil-

ful, hardy, courageous company . . . Some of the greatest skippers
that Gloucester ever knew hailed originally from the Canadian
provinces . . . And so it came to pass that some owners in the
Provincial ports, clinging to their all-sail while Gloucester veered
into motor power, sent out vessels they believed were equal to
Gloucester's best."[4] Why not, in that case, set out to see whether
they were not only as good, but better?

And so the challenge was issued: Senator Dennis, as he was
then, formed himself and his friends into a committee to oversee
what was to be formally known as the Halifax Herald North Atlantic Fishermen's International Competition; they raised $4,000 in
prize money and a splendid silver cup, the Halifax Herald Trophy,
universally known in America as the Dennis Cup, to be awarded
to the winner of "the fastest schooner in the Nova Scotia and New
England fishing fleets." The popular press, Dennis's papers in the
vanguard but swiftly followed by papers in Boston and Gloucester,
picked up the theme: the races were going to be entirely unlike
the fooferaw that surrounded the America's Cup, hidebound by
rules and weighed down by foolish yachty custom. They would be
straightforward and unpretentious, like the fishermen themselves.
"As such, they [were to become] symbols of an older, more innocent time. That all-sail fishermen were also becoming obsolete
only added to their romantic appeal. The same public that barely
noticed the advent of the trawlers ten years earlier now adopted the
races as proof that the age of sail was not ended."[5] Thus wrote the
American academic and writer Michael Wayne Santos. Joe Garland adds another piquant American view: "Thus good heartedly
began the nineteen year racing rivalry between Gloucester and
Lunenburg, the United States and Canada. Except that for a couple
of centuries the Canadians had endured the larceny of their mackerel and their herring at the hands of the invading Americans, and
of their best fishermen enticed by the U.S. dollar to Gloucester—
and now, from under their very noses, the grand larceny of what one
and all had been sure was theirs to keep, a Canada's Cup!"[6]

He had that right. Neither Dennis nor anyone in Lunenburg really expected to lose.

The first thing would be to find the Canadian contender, so an elimination race off Halifax was arranged. The course was designed to allow easy watching from spectator boats or, in places, from shore. Much of Halifax harbour could be seen from Citadel Hill looming over downtown Halifax, and a fair-sized crowd gathered to watch the start, many of them staying around for more than the five hours it took the vessels to return. From the starting line just inside Halifax harbour, a mile south of Georges Island, they would sail about 6 miles straight to a marker buoy (rather unromantically called #1 Inner Automatic), then on a triangular course, 10 miles to the Sambro lightship, then 7 miles southeast, then 6 miles back to Buoy #1, and 6 more miles up the harbour to the start–finish line, a total of 35 miles. Depending on the winds, windward tacking could add another 10 miles or so.

Because the organizers wanted to see their contenders in a good breeze, they set a time limit for finishing the course such that anything under a 20-knot breeze would be insufficient. It turned out not to be a problem: the wind was "fresh puffs to 25" in the phrase of Claude Darrach, who was with Tommy Himmelman's *Delawana* this day.

Although they had to forgo almost two weeks of fishing to rig up, reballast and get themselves to Halifax, nine schooners took part, all of them from Nova Scotia's South Shore, mostly Lunenburg, none at all from Digby or the Fundy shore. When busy swarms of Senator Dennis's reporters asked the skippers why they were there, they tended to give unvarying answers: a chance to show the Gloucestermen what they could do. Unstated was the real reason that everyone knew but wouldn't speak for fear of a jinx or "hoodoo": the chance to be top dog, to go back to the Banks having beaten the pants off every other skipper in the fleet, an unparalleled opportunity for pointed and prolonged boasting. And of course it helped that the Dennis committee offered to pay their expenses while they took time out for the contest.

Most of the participants were 120-footers or so, big schooners capable of carrying 175 tons of fish back from the Banks, each with masts nearly 120 feet high and a total sail area of about 9,000 square feet, about a fifth of an acre. The *Delawana*, under skipper Tommy Himmelman, and the *Gilbert B. Walters*, under Angus Walters, were the favourites; in 1919 both had been highliner skippers, bringing back bulging holds with a nice return for the sharesmen, and both were known as daring sailors who knew to the square inch what canvas their vessels could carry. The *Alcala* under Roly Knickle was a crowd favourite; Roly was a gregarious man and a popular skipper who invariably did well by his crew. The others, in wharf-side opinion, were worthy vessels and good skippers, but with not much of a chance of catching the top three, canny sailors all. They were Tommy Himmelman's brother Albert, in the *Independence*; Lemuel Ritchie in the *Mona Marie* and Calvin Lohnes in the *Ruby L. Pentz*, both skippers from LaHave; Danny Zinck in the *Bernice Zinck*; Bill Deal in *Democracy*; and another Himmelman, Alvin, a cousin, in the *Freda Himmelman*, also a LaHave man.

It went pretty much as expected. Roly Knickle's *Alcala* led for the first two legs, but gradually fell behind when it came to beating into the wind. The other two favourites were neck and neck until 5 miles from the finish line; the wind had freshened to a steady 25 knots with gusts to 40, and both boats had their lee rails awash throughout. Both Tommy Himmelman and Angus Walters had the wheel, and crowded on whatever canvas they could. Especially tacking to windward, they were evenly matched, but at last Angus cracked on a little too much sail and snapped his foretopmast in a gust, forcing him to haul in and stow both foretopsail and balloon sail, losing him precious minutes. Tommy won by five minutes and forty-two seconds. Himmelman came in fore and aft, as the saying went, and the last boat to finish was cousin Alvin, in the *Freda Himmelman*, who trailed in thirty-six minutes later.

For the Americans, it wasn't quite so easy. Nor was Dennis's challenge quite as fair as it appeared.

For one thing, the committee's first cut at a Deed of Gift setting up the races specified that competing vessels must be no bigger than 145 feet overall, 112 feet on the waterline, carrying all their ballast inside. The entrants must be working fishermen, with at least one season on the Banks behind them, and must race with their usual complement of working sails—no yachting foolishness with flying jibs was to be tolerated. In form and construction, as well as sail plan and rigging, entrants had to be of the types "customarily used in the fishing industry, and any radical departure therefrom may be regarded as a freak and eliminated," a stipulation that caused endless controversy later, especially when it was read alongside a contrasting wish, also in the Deed, that the races would help improve the breed.

Why was this unfair?

Most of the American vessels were a good deal smaller than 145 feet; fast, yes, but small, since most of them were designed for quick ten-day trips to the Banks for the fresh-fish market. Few Gloucester vessels any longer went saltbanking, spending a full season on the banks catching and salting fish, and so the stipulation that an entrant had to have sailed at least one saltbanking trip automatically eliminated much of the American fleet. There was one sail-only vessel in New England that was big, but she was, alas, just too big. This was the *Elizabeth Howard*, but her 148 feet 8 inches disqualified her, and so did her New York registry. Whether Dennis set the number at 145 feet just to disqualify her is of course disputed, but he would have known of the *Howard* and her speed, and if he didn't do it deliberately it surely was a convenient coincidence.

Also, few Gloucester schooners were any longer pure sailing vessels. Most had long ago abandoned their towering spars and substituted pole masts with a token rig of sail, and were fast only because of their engines; after all, they started putting auxiliaries into Gloucester vessels in 1902, and the last pure sail ever built there was the year after the races started—1921. The pious intention built into the challenge, which was the hope that the races would encourage the building of better and safer sailing vessels for the fishery, had long ago become pointless for Gloucester. Why improve sailing vessels when no business would ever build them again?

There were several other points. Dennis's challenge telegram had set up a Lunenburg–Gloucester axis. It explicitly excluded Boston, New York, Maine or, for that matter, Newfoundland and French Canada or, to cast a wider net, Portugal, so "international" is true but a little misleading. This stipulation, which would also have difficult implications later, though mostly for the Americans, was nevertheless fitting. Lunenburg was the challenger, and not Halifax or St. John's or Digby, because they felt themselves to be essentially the same people as those of Gloucester, cousins who could compete with each other fairly and without rancour because they were so much alike. The "international races" in this sense were then really an intramural event, and only incidentally American and Canadian. Their roots lay in a genuine rivalry between the two towns, which was very much anchored in the history of the fishing schooner races of earlier days, and the experiences the skippers of both towns remembered from the Banks.

So the challenge to Gloucester was natural enough. That Dennis stipulated Lunenburg, however, had an interesting commercial subtext: Dennis badly needed to get back into Lunenburg's good graces, his newspaper having several times during World War I infuriated the burghers of that town by suggesting that their German origins made them suspect, and by repeating the libel that they were giving succour to German submarines by running food out to their crews; not unexpectedly, Dennis's newspaper had been doing poorly in Lunenburg ever since.

The last point that rankled in Gloucester was the peremptory nature of the challenge. When the challenge telegram was received, the Americans were given only one week to accept and to select their vessel; and it had to arrive in Halifax within 10 days to start the race.

Still, they couldn't turn down the challenge, could they? No Gloucesterman wanted any Lunenburger to crow that they couldn't find a vessel fast enough. A racing committee was hastily assembled that included the legendary skipper Charlie Harty. Alas, when the racing committee looked around, there were no suitable vessels in sight. There were boats at every wharf, but they all had motors. The rest of the fleet was at sea, doing what they were paid to do, fishing.

As luck would have it, the schooner *Esperanto* sailed into port the following day, having been at sea for ten hard weeks, her holds stuffed with 275,000 pounds of hake and cod and haddock. She was fourteen years old and in parlous shape, her sails torn and patched, the hull battered from dories in high seas, salt-encrusted and slimy with marine growth. She was a little thing, too, only 107 feet long. But underneath all this was a solidly built Gloucesterman, made all of oak with a slightly curved bow, long bowsprit and moderate run that made her pleasing to the eye, and Charlie Harty, no fool, recognized her merits beneath the shabby exterior. Charlie had been her first skipper, and he remembered her. "There's our vessel," he shouted. "It's the *Esperanto*, she could run and she could reach and she could go to windward when I had her. Get her in trim and she'll sail again." Besides, there wasn't anything else.[7]

Claude Darrach remembered later only that "the [American] elimination race was run over the Cape Ann triangle off Gloucester. The *Esperanto* won, with Captain Marty Welch at the wheel."[8] But this wasn't really true. There was no race. It was *Esperanto* or nothing.

Benjamin Smith of the Gorton-Pew Fish Company, a yachting man interested in racing, assented to diverting his vessel for the contest. The fish were packed out, her bilges cleaned and reballasted, she was hauled out, polished and scrubbed and painted, and as Claude Darrach described her, "with a new suit of sails and glistening new rigging . . . she looked splendid, as though newly launched. Her cabin house, hatches and bulwark rails glistened white, her sleek black sides swept with the conventional fore and aft yellow stripe, showing off the graceful curve of the sheerline."9

Darrach was right about Marty Welch being at the helm. This was Captain Martin Leander Welch, born in Digby fifty-six years earlier, who had been a fisherman since he was fourteen and a captain for thirty-three years. He was known in Gloucester as an unflappable sailor with excellent judgment. Gloucester approved: here was a good sail carrier who knew how to wring an extra knot from a set of canvas and wouldn't be put off by the ballyhoo ricocheting down from Halifax. As to his Nova Scotian origins, no one thought it would influence his judgment. If anything, a Digby man racing against Lunenburgers would add an extra ounce of probably unneeded determination to his racing. (The somewhat folksy Welch family Web site is these days at pains to point out that Marty was "a naturalized citizen," and that two of his children served with distinction in the U.S. armed forces, but none of this is really necessary: everyone agreed Marty was the man for the job.)

Boston's mayor, swallowing his inborn anti-Gloucester sentiments, sent a telegram wishing *Esperanto* well. "Thank you," Marty fired back. "We are off to win the cup or blow the sticks out of her."

With Marty at the wheel (the first time he had actually sailed her), *Esperanto* left Gloucester on October 25, as a flag-waving, horn-tooting crowd lined the harbour. Aboard was a crew of volunteers, seven of them other fishing skippers; ordinary fishermen were already being ignored, although the races were ostensibly for them. As Michael Wayne Santos points out, only one of the seven captains on board had ever sailed *Esperanto* before. Dominated as it was by Gloucester's elite, "the American Race Committee was content to let the spotlight fall on the master mariner. The workers, a rougher crowd who caroused and drank, were hardly considered."[10] Because these races were going to be good for the tourist industry, the *Esperanto* also carried one writer, James Connolly, to tell her story and exploit her expected victory for the delectation of the American public. From Halifax he telegraphed: "All well. Sailed well in light winds and stiff breeze."

All, indeed, was well for Marty, for *Esperanto* and for Gloucester.

The first race took place on the morning of October 30, the two vessels lining up at the start, an even more spectator-friendly place than the Canadian eliminations had been, the breakwater at the popular Point Pleasant Park. Thence they would travel in an awkward parallelogram back to the start. The day was grey and the clouds lowering, and by the time of the starting gun a fresh breeze was picking up.

Delawana crossed the starting line first by just a few seconds, but *Esperanto* led at the first buoy, increased her lead in the second leg and then, beating up into the wind, showed her clear superiority over her rival, going on to win in a fashion that even Tommy Himmelman said was splendid, making the running for home under full sail, in full sun under sparkling seas. A massive crowd was on hand to cheer the vessels home, the roar hardly faltering when it was clear that the Gloucester boat would be first. The *Delawana* trailed in eighteen minutes later, but in the spirit of the thing immediately led a cheer for her rival. Everyone agreed. This was what racing should be. Alas, for the Canadians, the wrong boat won.

This first contest showed that *Esperanto* was the better boat in a headwind and heavy seas; calm winds the following foggy day made it a much closer affair, and Tommy Himmelman sailed with great skill, leading comfortably around the first two legs after getting a good start, about a minute ahead of Marty Welch. He had taken out 60 tons of ballast, and it showed, for she sailed hull-up in a gentle sea.

This was more in the spirit of it. This was a close race by two wily skippers using whatever advantages they could wrest from the sea, the course, and the wind. Tommy did make one crucial error, missing his mark at Shut-in Island by more than a mile, giving *Esperanto* an opening, and it cost him the lead. On the third leg, when the two boats were neck and neck, Marty Welch's legendary nerve came into play. Tommy Himmelman, holding right-of-way, nudged the *Esperanto* towards the unholy rocks of Devil's Ledge in a "luffing match," each vessel trying to steal the other's wind. The *Esperanto*, closer to shore, drew two more feet of water and as they got closer, the mastheadman, his voice rising to a shriek, called out: "Bottom hoy! Rocks hoy!" He'd seen surf breaking over the jagged ledge. For a while there was less than a foot of green under the keel.

Marty Welch affected not to hear, and they drove ever closer. Himmelman, for his part, was not giving way. A passenger on *Esperanto*, one of the owners, Russell Smith, was so caught up in the excitement that he egged Marty on: "To hell with the kelp and rocks, Marty, keep her to it!" And Marty did.

In the end it was a Halifax harbour pilot on board the *Esperanto* who leaned over the rail, blanched, and yelled across to Tommy Himmelman in the *Delawana*: "Give way! For God's sake, give way!" Tommy, ever the gentleman, complied at once and swung her off, though he knew the move would lose him the weather gage and in the end the race itself. Marty Welch tacked offshore and out of danger, and went on to win. To complete the drama, he crossed the line with lightning crackling about his masthead and deafening peals of thunder, a tumult of Shakespearean proportions.

The Gloucesterman was champion, two races out of three.

To give the city its due, Halifax was generous to the winner. During the races—absent the hysterical presence of 24-hour radio and cable, and absent the now-omnipresent Internet—Haligonians followed the races by watching the outlines of two schooners jerking their way across a wire strung from the *Halifax Herald* offices to an office building across the street, the wires advanced by a copyboy acting on yelled orders from a deskman acting on reports semaphored, yelled, or run in from whatever vantage point was available, not only by an army of reporters but by excited and excitable citizens. When the outline of the *Esperanto* was hauled to the finish first, hundreds of men and women streamed down to the dockside to welcome her ashore, in a show of well-wishing that rather baffled the normally phlegmatic Marty Welch.

That night a banquet was held at Halifax's Green Lantern Club, where Marty pocketed a cheque for $4,000 while the ever-game Tommy Himmelman, keeping a stiff upper lip that he kept tightly buttoned, took away another thousand.

While this was going on, the rival crews slipped away from the formalities and melted into the city's many watering holes. "There was a going ashore and a mingling," as Claude Darrach rather tactfully put it, but since most of the crews were other skippers anyway, the carousing was kept to a minimum.

The next day there was another series of lunches, dinners, and award ceremonies, Dennis and his people milking the occasion for all it was worth; Dennis asserting to all who would listen that the race would be important not just for the winners or the vessels and not just for the fishery but for the way they would help publicize Halifax, which he called "the world's third most important port."

James Connolly added his enthusiastic two cents': "These races are ten times more interesting than the America's Cup," he declared. Marty was presented with the trophy itself, a massive and ostentatiously ornate beaker, as well as a second cup "as a personal tribute" from the operatives of the Colonial Fisheries Company of Boston, which Marty Welch tidily tucked into the bigger vessel. Tommy had to forgo the silverware.

One of the Gloucester race committee insisted on speaking at the luncheon. Arthur J. Millet, who had travelled up from Gloucester for the occasion, said of Captain Marty: "No better man ever sailed out of any harbour in the world. No better man ever walked the deck of a vessel or the streets of a city." The Nova Scotia premier, George Murray, not to be outdone, called it "the greatest sporting event the American continent has ever witnessed," which must surely win some record for hyperbole. No one blushed. Marty Welch, that "no better man," didn't say a word, walking out of the affair without pausing to talk to the premier, the mayor, the publisher or their minions.

On the way home, the Dennis trophy was stowed in the hold. Marty's personal cup was packed away and forgotten. But a broom was lashed to the masthead. The broom was the thing, everything. To the fishermen it was the real symbol of victory, a derisive sweeping of the opposition. No way the broom would be stowed in the hold.

The *Esperanto* arrived back in Gloucester after a sometimes hard 400-mile sail at two in the morning. No one was waiting for them. The crowds had gone home sometime around midnight, leaving a fair amount of patriotic debris dockside. But in the morning word soon spread that the boys had come home, and rapturous crowds swarmed down to the docks to congratulate them. This well-meant and generous feeling persisted no later than lunch, at which time it was overwhelmed by an orgy of patriotic speechmaking that swamped the well-wishing in schmaltz and phoniness. True, there were generous telegrams read out from the premier of

Nova Scotia and Halifax's mayor, John Seakons Parker, but a hundred more people paid $5 for the privilege of making their banal voices heard, and then Gloucester's mayor, Boston's mayor and Massachusetts's governor all outdid each other in laying a thick sludge of patriotism over the proceedings. "The victory," declared the governor, Calvin Coolidge, not yet the president to usher in the Depression, "was a triumph for Americanism and the American way," conveniently forgetting Marty Welch's Digby origins.

After that it was just for the other skippers to find their own vessels, Marty to track down his crew, stow the dories, take on ice and bait and provisions, and head out to the Banks, business as usual.

In this way the 1920 races lived up to the spirit that the Bostonian Tom McManus had envisaged when he set in motion the first series of fishermen's races during the debilitating fishermen's strike of '86, a spirit that William Dennis had hoped to emulate. To attract fishermen, McManus had suggested, the races must be straightforward affairs, with little or no fancy yachting rules and no strictures as to gear or ballast or conduct. They were to be raced by fishermen in from the Banks, and allow the fishermen to return to the Banks with a minimum of fuss; only in that way could they replicate the kinds of impromptu "hook on" races rival skippers would get into on the way home from fishing. These were vessels that could race, sure, but they were built for fishing, and racing was a thing done on the side, when necessary and when the opportunity arose.

That the 1920 contest was in this spirit, that the races were so engagingly simple and unaffected, captured the popular imagination, egged on by Connolly and his fellow romantics. The contest started something which took everyone by surprise, and prolonged by more than a decade the viability, or supposed viability, of the all-sail fishing schooner. The races and their successors showcased the extraordinary skills and grit of the fishermen, and the grace and beauty of the vessels they operated, and exhibited those skills and those vessels for all to see. Before the races were over, twenty-two other elegant schooners had taken part in the various series, vessels crewed by more than five hundred skippers and men, who were thus given an unparalleled and unexpected chance to show off their expertise and their daring. The races were also the prod that would help the building of at least six magnificent new schooners in Nova Scotia, the wondrous *Bluenose* among them, and another half dozen or more in Gloucester and Boston.

And yet, and yet . . . Even at this early stage, the international schooner races were in many ways hollow, just a shell of what might have been.

In its issue following the *Esperanto*'s famous victory, *Yachting* magazine, the bible of America's elite squadrons, declared that the races should become annual and were "surely destined to become a classic." As Michael Wayne Santos says, that this magazine could put it this way was in itself troubling, for it was clear they viewed the possibility of annual races in the same way they viewed the America's Cup, as a chance for a sporting contest utterly divorced from working-class life or from work itself. Sportsmanship and the thrill of a victory was the point; that actual fishermen were involved, showing off their workaday skills, was to the editors entirely un-important.[11] If this seems a stretch, look at it this way: this was the last international race in which workaday vessels were involved. Henceforth, the races would be some kind of sailing equivalent of the arms race, in which each side sought to outdo the other, with hardly anyone looking at what racing would do for the industry, or at who would be racing the vessels, or who owned them, or what the point was. Even the 1920 races, after all, were a fluke, in that *Esperanto* happened into port at exactly the right time. If some other vessel had entered, and had to have its auxiliaries stripped out to fit the conditions, the romantic notion of the pure-sail throwback would have been entirely absent. More than a dozen new vessels were built to contest the races, the *Bluenose* among them, but none were built primarily to fish. They were built to win. And Calvin Coolidge's foolish bombast was a bad sign: even at this early stage friendly competition was no longer the point either. It was, alas, not to be boat versus boat, skipper versus skipper, or even Gloucester versus Lunenburg. It had become flag against flag. Which had never been the plan.

So, with defeat for one side and victory for the other, and in an extravaganza of whipped-up patriotism, began the story of the building of *Bluenose* and her American competitors, and a wonderful and a sorry story it is.

The Canadian side had it easier, in a way, though their path was not without its snares of bile and rancour.

So much patriotic emotion had been invested in the races that *Delawana*'s defeat sent Dennis and his friends into paroxysms of anxiety. Honour would have to be restored, a suitable vessel found, or built, or . . . maybe conjured out of the dense and foggy Nova Scotian air.

The first thing to do was to formalize the rules so everyone knew what was what. (Of course, that this *was* the first thing was another sign that things had already gone a little awry—weren't these supposed to be races between vessels, any vessels, fresh from the Banks?) Dennis and his committee now set about constructing a more formal Deed of Gift for the trophy, a document fussy in its tone and overprecise in its particulars. The overall length was still to be the 145 feet that had excluded the *Elizabeth Howard*, and the waterline length was still 112 feet; but the allowable overall length was mysteriously changed by December to 150 feet, a figure which would have allowed the *Elizabeth Howard* to have competed after all—and she did indeed compete in the American elimination races the following year in 1921, though she didn't do very well.

Another stipulation, which passed by without comment at the time, was that "vessels shall race with the same spars and no greater sail area than used in fishing, but the sail area not to exceed 80 per cent of the square of the waterline length as expressed in square feet." Most people simply passed over this lawyerly phrasing without noticing it, but it was to come back to bite the organizers a year or two later, and cause much rancour of its own.

The Deed of Gift also stipulated how the races were to be organized. The cup would be managed by a committee of nine Canadian trustees, one of them the premier of Nova Scotia, another the mayor of Halifax, the others distributed handily between self-perpetuating nominees controlled by Senator Dennis. The actual races would be run by a five-man committee nominated by each series, consisting of two Canadian members, and two American ones nominated by the governor of Massachusetts. The two members representing the site of the races would pick the chairman, the fifth committee member.

Obviously, the next stage was to find a contender. If the *Esperanto* had beaten the fastest Canadian vessel, then clearly an existing vessel wouldn't do, and a new one would have to be built. And it would have to be done swiftly. One of the stipulations was that a contender had to spend a full season salt fishing on the Banks before racing. That meant whatever boat was built must go down the ways before or by the spring of 1921.

Several things were happening at once. Angus Walters, who many thought would have beaten *Delawana* in the 1920 elimination races but for a broken spar, had turned his own vessel, the *Gilbert B. Walters*, over to one of his brothers, and was already negotiating with the Smith and Rhuland yard in Lunenburg to build him another. This was perfectly normal: highliner skippers usually had no trouble finding investors to built them new boats when they needed one. In this case, though, Angus was keeping an eye on the Deed of Gift stipulations, to make sure that whatever vessel he acquired would indeed be eligible to race. A yard in Shelburne was also making plans for a new, fast vessel, to be launched in time for the new season, and this would no doubt be a competitor in the elimination races. At the same time, William Dennis and his yachting friends were casting about for a way to build a new boat that would be big and strong enough to fish the Banks, and at the same time fast enough to beat anything Gloucester could throw at them—fishing yes, that's important, but fast was the prime stipulation. They found William Roué to design it for them. He was easy enough to find, for he was a fellow member of the Royal Nova Scotia Yacht Squadron in Halifax, and he spent much of his spare time racing yachts. He was a clubhouse chum of the Dennises.

A fair amount of fancy has been invested in the Roué story. The favourite version actually downplays his qualifications, preferring to believe in the brilliant amateur. In this version, he was just a dreamer, a maker of ginger ale whose one brilliant inspiration made him immortal. Like most pretty legends, this was loosely built on fact. Roué did work for a while in his family's "carbonated waters" plant, and he was an amateur, in the sense that he didn't make his living from designing boats, at least not at that point. But he was far from a beginner. He began modelling boats when he was only five, cobbling models together from cedar shingles, based on vessels he saw from his window, which was only a block or two from Halifax harbour. He finished his first full model, a 5-foot sailing yacht, in 1892 when he was thirteen, and before he was old enough to actually become a member of the Yacht Squadron he had become one of the fleet's master skippers. He finally joined five years later, but in the interim he'd studied mechanical drafting, and Frank Bell, a member of the Squadron who had recognized Roué's passion for boats, had given him a copy of Dixon Kemp's *Yacht Architecture*, which he read "over and over, until I could probably check Kemp if he made an error."[12] His first commission was for Bell, a sleek little yacht called *Babette*, which he designed, he said, to be "mathematically calculated"; *Babette* was still sailing out of New York in the

1970s. One of the famous Roué stories is that Bell, having accepted the drawings, showed them to a friend of his, the eminent Boston naval architect Benjamin Crowninshield.

"Who drew these lines?" Crowninshield asked.

"Oh, an amateur who sails with me."

"Go ahead and build, he won't be an amateur long."

Since then Roué had designed a number of yachts, including a racing sloop, the *Zetes*, whose design was the progenitor of *Bluenose* herself. The *Zetes* was built for day sailing and cruising; after she was launched in 1911 she was found to be exceptionally able heading into or close to the wind.

Roué's first design for William Dennis's committee was too big, and would have exceeded the Deed of Gift specifications, and he was sent back to scale it down. He protested that you couldn't just use the same proportions—the whole thing had to be rethought.

So rethink, he was told. The vessel must be allowed to race. That was the point, after all.

Three weeks later, he came back with the design that was to make him famous. This was Roué Design #17. The committee took the plans to Smith and Rhuland's master shipwrights in Lunenburg—it had to be Lunenburg, not Shelburne, if Dennis's circulation department was to benefit. The vessel was to be the yard's Hull #119. She was to be called *Bluenose*.

The drawings show her as lean and sleek, 143 feet and a few inches overall, but only 50 at the keel; she was tapered dramatically at the stern to a narrow afterdeck, just wide enough for the wheel and the mainsheet and a streamlined rudder below. From the forward end of the keel she rises in a long shallow curve to the waterline and beyond, with a slight hook under the bowsprit, giving her a slightly arrogant air. If you're belowdecks standing on the keel, the planking rises almost straight up and then bows sharply outwards, a feature called a tumblehome. Amidships to stern her underbody is almost straight, and the counter stern rises sharply from the water, terminating in a delicately shaped transom. She was 30 feet 6 inches on the beam at deck, and drew 15 feet 4 inches. She carried a main boom 81 feet long, and the height from deck to main topmast was 125 feet 10 inches. *The Rudder* a few years later called her "probably the greatest fishing schooner ever built," with lines "as fine as any schooner yacht." Still, there were dissenting voices, as we shall see.

CHAPTER TWO

HER

LONG

PEDIGREE

Bluenose the breathtaker came out of *somewhere*, obviously, and that somewhere was a deep well of tradition and craftsmanship and of canny business too. She was on the books as Plan #17 to the designer and Hull #119 to her builders, and though they paid her particular attention, she was just one small part of a long, seamless, continuous and surprisingly muscular industry, now largely forgotten. There were other vessels as able as she, others more beautiful, long before her and contemporaneous with her. Not just dozens of them, but hundreds, even thousands, springing from dozens, even hundreds, of shipyards.

All those vessels are gone now, and so have most of the shipyards, disappearing into a tangle of beams and planks and weeds and rotten pilings seen only at low tide, as overcome by time as a pre-Columbian city swallowed by lianas in the Venezuelan jungles, just history, and ill-remembered history at that. To the rest of Canada, the phrases "Maritime Canada" (and Nova Scotia in particular) and "industry" seldom inhabit the same vocabularies. But not so long ago, Nova Scotia was one of the industrial world's global powerhouses, bursting out in an astonishing flowering of entrepreneurial spirit, grit, and skill, caused (like so many powerhouses before and since) partly by accident of timing and place, and in this case partly by the impulses and accidents of imperial politics.

It seemed unlikely, at first.

Sir Charles Whitworth, later the first Earl Whitworth and Britain's exceptionally devious plenipotentiary to the court of the tsars in Petersburg, paid a fleeting visit to the shores of Nova Scotia in 1773, on his way back from the restless and increasingly unruly colonies to the south. He was unimpressed. "From such an unfavourable climate as that of Nova Scotia very little can be expected," he told his journal and, later, his colleagues in the British Parliament. "For seven months the cold is intense and the remaining part of the year the heat becomes as unsupportable as the cold was before and the country is wrapt in a constant gloom of fog. This country is almost one continuous forest and agriculture, though attempted by the English settlers, has hitherto made very little progress. In most parts the soil is thin and barren. The corn it produces is of a shrivled [sic] kind, like rye, and the grass is intermixed with a cold spungy [sic] moss. Not withstanding this general barrenness, the soil in some parts is extremely fertile. It is for the most part well adapted to the produce of Hemp and Flax. The timber is of a fine nature for Ship-building, and produces Pitch and Tar."[1]

Some of this he got wrong, as tourists will. There is fog enough, god knows, but it is usually confined to the spring and early summer. Winters are mild by continental standards, milder even than in New England to the south. (Not for here the St. John's joke that "there are two seasons, winter and yesterday afternoon.") The good earl seems to have sweated in summer in his flannel breeches, but the summers are no more intemperate than the winters. On agriculture he was partly right, though mostly because he confined himself to the perfunctory scrapings of the English settlers; if he had looked south, to where the Germans or "foreign Protestants" had settled, he would have had a more sanguine view; and had his imperial colleagues not recently expelled the Acadians they would have shown him their enormously productive farms in the Annapolis Valley on the other side of the province, Nova Scotia's version of Napa or the Okanagan, in the earl's day still being brought back up to production by the New England "planters" imported to supplant the vanished French.

But yes, there were almost continuous forests, and the timber was, indeed, "of a fine nature for Ship-building."

Fine-natured timber, and a fine place to do it in.

The French built a few boats, in the days when the LaHave River and then Port Royal were the "capitals of New France," but they didn't amount to much. François Greve, or Pontgreve, feeling abandoned at Port Royal by his mentor, Demonts, and failing to see the long-promised supply ships, set out in 1606 to build what were in innocent chauvinism once called "the first vessels ever constructed on the North American continent" (never mind the Virginia colonists and never mind the Mi'kmaq, whose longboats skittered routinely between Nova Scotia and what would become Quebec). He cobbled together a little barque and a littler shallop to carry himself and his fellows east to Canseau [Canso] . . . "where they might fall in with ships bound [for] home."[2]

There, for a while, it rested, while the French went back to France and the British came, and the French came back and were expelled again in their turn. In 1745, Port Royal was Annapolis Royal, where a party unknown caused to be built the *Medford*, a schooner of 20 tons, registered at Boston the same year; and a year or so later, in 1751, the *Osborn Gally*, a brig of 100 tons, was built in Halifax by slave labour. It was owned by one John Gorham, a crony of the Fanieuls and Hancocks of Boston, whose Mohawk Rangers were later notorious in the wars against the French and their Mi'kmag allies for their cruelty and ferocity. On her maiden voyage to England she carried "80 tons of Black Birch timber, 313 oars, 240 hand spikes, 70 spars, 3136 Qt. blubber, 3 tuns pitch pine and 20 Qt. fish."[3] In 1763, a shallop, its name unrecorded, was built at Yarmouth.

This slow pace didn't last. In 1773, the same year Sir Charles was expressing his pique at the province's climate and prospects, a passel of Scottish immigrants sailed into Pictou harbour on the Northumberland shore facing the Gulf of St. Lawrence. There were trees aplenty—they didn't need Sir Charles to point these out to them; towering pines grew right to the water's edge and thick forests of mixed Acadian forest covered the "fields" they needed to farm. A contemporary account called them "dismayed" at the prospect, but on the evidence their chagrin didn't last, for they soon summoned the canniness so often imputed to their culture, and just a few months after they pitched their shelters under the forest canopy they imported a "company of axemen" from nearby Truro to help them out. These doughty foresters, many of them Scots themselves but others imported from the black forests along the Rhine, hacked out farmland, squared the newly cut timber and loaded it into freshly built vessels for shipment to the Old Country. Thus was begun the trade that contributed so much to the prosperity of the region, for soon the Napoleonic Wars and their aftermath cut the Royal Navy off from its traditional woodpatch in the endless forests of the Baltic, and they perforce had to rely on wood from the American colonies.[4]

Politics helped the shipbuilding industry prosper, and so did the American War of Independence. In 1786, a regulation was promulgated that asserted that "no vessel built in the North American colony now called the United States of America [is] allowed to be

registered except those captured and condemned as lawful prizes."
The colonial legislature seized the opportunity and stimulated the
industry by a bounty of ten shillings per ton on all vessels of 40 tons
and upwards, and this was continued for the next three years, and
within a few months a small vessel, albeit below the bounty level at
25 tons, was built in Shelburne.[5]

There were bubbles—the industry briefly collapsed when the
American war was over—but it soon recovered, and the trade grew
quickly: from 1787 to the end of the century, more than 700 vessels
were built in Nova Scotia, and those just the ones their owners registered. As early as 1788 there are records of shipbuilding in Pictou.
The first vessel built there was a small snow by Thomas Copeland;
the first large ship was the *Harriet*, 600 tons, built in 1798.[6]

Well, you can build a boat with wood and a carpenter; but without
wood all you have is a craftsman with nothing to do, and without a
carpenter all you have is forest . . . Anaximenes, a philosopher
who plied his trade in Athens around 600 BC, meant this as a
metaphor for civilization itself, but of course it is also literally true.

A vessel, any vessel from a small skiff to a 1,000-ton ship of the
line, starts with an intention—a builder and a user—and an assembly of raw material. In early New England and Maritime Canada
this raw material was close by, so close in fact that would-be farmers,
like those in Pictou, had first to cut it away to make a place for
crops. The first vessels made use of what was most immediately
available, and in both places the patterns put into place were the
same; the builder, usually a farmer or his sons, would visit his own
backyard and emerge with what he needed, hacking the vessels out
of the forest by hand. The felled trees were hauled to a field in winter, and there cut up. Farmers made some money by felling white
pine for spars and booms, birch and beech and oak for frames and
planking. Many made a little extra money by cutting out the curved

branches or roots, especially those of juniper (or hackmatack, as it was called locally) for use as ship's "knees"—sturdy support brackets for deck planking. There was a steady demand in the navy and the merchant marine for Nova Scotia hackmatack knees.[7]

Knees, and the rest of the tree too. Many of the ships built along the Bay of Fundy were so-called "timber ships"—built merely to be filled with raw timber and sold, cargo and all, on the other end. These ships had bow and stern ports to allow long squared timber into their holds. These ports would be knocked out at the appropriate time and booms and tackle rigged out over bow and stern. "Engaged in this work were expert gangs of timber-stowers, mostly Irish, rough, powerful men who could work like horses throughout the heat of a Canadian summer, and drink and fight with equal ability. These men were variously called timber-swingers, hookers-on, holders, porters and winchers."[8]

Later, professional millers took on the supply of timber, as specialization in the colonies increased. But after a century, the patterns in Nova Scotia and New England began to diverge. The Nova Scotia industry remained highly decentralized, with one-slip yards in every cove, and sawmills that remained relatively small, serving mostly the local community and their own modest customer base. In New England, by contrast, timber barons bought up huge tracts of forestland and prospered by employing the economies of scale.

Within a short time, and for the century that followed, the building of wooden ships was the chief industry of the province. Every little port, and almost every cove, had its shipyard. In the middle of the 1800s an observer remarked that "you could stand on [any] hill . . . and see where fifteen square-rigged vessels were being built at one time." Some of these were those cheaply made vessels filled with timber and sold at the other end, but many more were handsomely put together. The consequences were threefold: money was made, sometimes considerable amounts of it. It also "brought forth a breed of consummate sailors . . . And it turned every little outport into a society of travellers who went to the ends of the earth."9

The first major increase in this commerce was, as suggested, the American War of Independence; this was followed by another boom during the wars with Napoleon. A further increase came about in 1840. Again international events conspired to help maritime shipbuilders: the beginning of free trade between Europe and America in 1844, the California gold rush of 1849, the Crimean War that once again put Baltic forests out of Britain's reach, the discovery of gold in Australia in 1854, and the American civil war in 1861 all resulted in bursts of shipbuilding activity. Nova Scotia did a flourishing trade in coal with eastern United States ports. In the peak year, 1865, more than 660 vessels were built,10 eighty of them more than a thousand tons.

Judge Mather DesBrisay, whose history of Lunenburg County is idiosyncratic, encyclopedic and occasionally erratic all at once, could also wax portentous. Having listed a baker's dozen vessels under construction in Lunenburg town alone, and hinting at the many others recently completed, he added: "If all the vessels above enumerated could be assembled in one of our capacious bays, under sail, in a sort of naval review, what a magnificent marine picture would be presented; and what a splendid representation would it be of the genius and skill of the men who, in this county, have been in the front rank of the shipbuilders of the country! From returns received, it appears that thirteen thousand boats [to 1895]—whalers, dories, skiffs, flat, keel and centre-board boats of all the kinds required—have been built in Lunenburg town [alone]."11

It's fair to say that Lunenburg, populated by "foreign protestants" brought in by the colonial government to act as a countervailing presence against the papist French, was savagely condescended to by polite society in the capital. Here is a Halifax newspaper doing its best to be gracious in 1859: "Why, these despised Dutchmen have done more to for to [sic] foster the art of shipbuilding in

Nova Scotia than any other class of people within our borders . . .
The vessels these people build are marvels of neatness. We verily
believe that they lavish a greater amount of money in ornamenting
their craft—in carving and gilding—than they would be willing to
disburse in decorating their frows [sic] and daughters . . ."[12]

Less than a hundred years after it began, the region had developed a vast shipbuilding industry that during the peak years of the
1860s supplied nearly one-third of all British shipping, and had
captured a huge share of the world's carrying trade, "building
up a reputation for smart ships and native-born seamen that was
a legend in nautical history and fo'c'sle story for many years."[13] By
the end of the century, more than 26,000 vessels had been built
in the Maritimes, some 10,000 between 1847 and 1867. In 1878,
Canada stood fourth (or fifth, or even third, depending on your
authority) on the list of ship-owning countries of the world; 7,469
(or 7,196) vessels were on the registry books,[14] totalling 1,333,000
tons. Seven or eight hundred of these were three and four master
"tern schooners" built for coasting purposes.[15] In a tight little time
period, "a small company of boatbuilders and sailors resident on
the Atlantic coasts of Canada created a mercantile marine which
burst into ocean commerce, made history and drew the admiration of seamen, and thence vanished utterly into the mists of oblivion." Thus Frederick William Wallace, historian, journalist and
romantic.[16]

The most energetic shipbuilder in the region was Captain
George McKenzie (1798–1876), usually referred to in civic histories
as "the father of Nova Scotian shipbuilding." McKenzie himself
built and owned some thirty-four vessels, ranging from 100-ton
schooners to barques and at least one full-rigged ship of 1,465 tons,
the *Magna Charta*.[17]

Joseph Howe had some fun with all this in a famous speech
in 1854, cheerfully tweaking the Mother Country's nose: "Scotland," he thundered, thunder being his normal speaking mode,
". . . Scotland maintains upon the Clyde the greatest manufactory

of ships in the world. Vessels glide up and down that beautiful stream like swallows around a barn, scarcely a day passes but richly laden vessels arrive or depart with domestic manufactures or the products of foreign climes. Go into the factories where the mighty engines of her steamers are wrought and the noise of the fabled Cyclops cave is realized . . . And yet, Sir, the tonnage of Scotland is only a trifle more than that of the North American Provinces. Her whole commercial marine include but 522,222 tons, while in these provinces are shipping amounts to the splendid total of 453,000 tons." And then he got around to working in his friend George McKenzie: "At the time of the Spanish armada (1588) we read in the old chronicles that England then owned but 135 merchant ships. But some were of great size, some four hundred tons with a few reaching 500 tons. If my friend George McKenzie of New Glasgow had dashed into the midst of the Maiden Queen's navy with his one thousand four hundred and forty-ton ships, I fear he would have shaken her nerves and astonished our forefathers . . ."[18]

One of the best-known, not to say notorious, vessels ever built in Maritime Canada was the *Marco Polo*, a substantial vessel 185 feet stem to stern on deck, with three decks with 8-feet clearance, stoutly constructed of hard-pine beams, hackmatack, oak and other woods. As Frederick Wallace put it, "The ship had a clipperish bow but the bilges of a cargo carrier. She was built at Marsh Creek on the Bay of Fundy near Saint John, the most godforsaken hole possibly discovered, considering the fine ships that had been built there. At low tide the place was a marshy creek with little or no water. The *Polo* was so big it was decided to wait until the spring tides to launch her, but the launching went awry and she careened right across the creek and burrowed into the mud on the other side. When the tide went out she fell over, and it was feared she was ruined, but two weeks later after much excavating, she floated off undamaged." She was bought by English interests for the Australian run, and the *Illustrated London News* was gushy: "Her timbering is enormous. Her deck beams are huge balks of pitch-pine. Her timbers are well formed and ponderous. The stem and stern frame are of the choicest material. The hanging and lodging knees are all natural crooks and fitted to the greatest nicety . . . On deck forward of the poop, which is used as a ladies cabin, is a home on deck to be used as a dining cabin. It is ceiled with maple, and the pilasters are panelled with richly ornamented and silvered glass, coins of various countries being a feature of the decorations. . . . A sheet of plate glass with a cleverly painted picturesque view in the centre, with a framework of foliage and scroll in opaque colours and gold. . . . the saloon doors are panelled in stained glass bearing figures of commerce and industry from the designs of Mr. Frank Howard . . ."[19]

But it wasn't just her pilasters that impressed. Her skipper on the Australian run was James Nicol Forbes, the "Bully Forbes" of fo'c'sle legend, who took her into the roaring forties for her "easting," her eastward passage, where she covered 1,344 miles in four days. He was not a man with many scruples. To ensure that his crew wouldn't skip for the Australian gold diggings, he trumped up charges of insubordination against them and clapped them in irons for the duration.

She went out and came back in five months and twenty-one days, and as she lay in the Salthouse Dock in England she flew a banner proclaiming her "The Fastest Ship in the World." Bully Forbes boasted to whoever would listen: "Ladies and gentlemen, last trip I astonished the world with the sailing of this ship. This trip I intend to astonish God Almighty."[20]

Just as before, some vessels were well made, others shoddy enough—war profiteering was not an unknown activity among the more commercial-minded owners. For a while there was a run of cheap softwood vessels purpose-built to be wrecked: unscrupulous shipowners would commission them to go down, thereby collecting on the insurance. This didn't do the province's reputation much good, and the master of the *Dreadnought*, Captain Samuel Samuels, once spoke disparagingly of Nova Scotian vessels. Of a ship called *Leander*, he said ". . . she was a Bluenose, built as they all are in the cheapest and flimsiest manner, of unseasoned timber, iron fastened, in expectation of being sold to the under-writers." (The *Leander* had been built in Tatamagouche in 1841.)[21]

But Frederick Wallace would have none of the naysaying: "In the ports of the Seven Seas and the waters thereof, the terms 'Nova Scotiaman' and 'Bluenose' were known to seamen of all national-ities during the 'sixties. By sheer ability as seamen and aggres-siveness in business, these British North Americans had forced themselves out of the polyglot crowds of maritime nations until they were a factor to conjure with in the world's carrying trade."[22] One can crank out the statistics as much as one likes, but the won-derful thing—the remarkable thing—was that this decentralized, outport- and cove-based industry, run by farmers and at first un-skilled labour, helped bring, in Wallace's words, "the wind-driven ship to the apex of perfection in design and brought out in masters and officers a degree of skill and daring in seamanship which has never been exceeded."[23]

Here's Sterling Hayden, topmastman turned Hollywood actor, who himself raced against *Bluenose* in her final series, on the vessels that were turned out on the Atlantic seaboard. He is writing about Gloucester and Essex, in Massachusetts, but in truth there was no real difference then: "From roughly 1870 . . . [they] brought to life a wondrous swarm of two-masted two-fisted sweet-sheered vessels calculated to do battle with that malevolent wilderness of waters known as the North Atlantic. Their everyday task was to catch fish, but their niche in maritime history is due in no small part to their incomparable ability to battle to windward in the teeth of living gales. To say nothing of their capacity to heave to and ride out some of the most daunting weather and infuriate conditions to be found rampaging around on the surface of the Seven Seas . . . They were also beautiful. Now we're getting down to it. Working craft around the world usually have sea-keeping qualities. But beauty? Soaring, mind boggling beauty? Now that is something else . . ."[24]

They were called "able handsome ladies" in the parlance of the coast. *Able* was for their ability to beat to windward, even in a gale; *handsome* meant the set of the spars, the flawless proportions, the sweep of the hull, the balance of rig and gear; and *ladies*. . . . Well, all vessels were ladies of their kind, able or handsome or not.

The real focus of all this activity, and much of Nova Scotia's early prosperity, had little to do with fishing and almost everything to do with boat-building and trade; Lunenburg's prosperous Old Town, now a UNESCO World Heritage Site, was built on trading money, not fishing, though fishing is what it is remembered for now, partly due to *Bluenose* and the International Fishermen's Races. By 1767, Lunenburg did have six vessels "in the fishery," but just to supply local needs—it wasn't yet a business. Charles Morris, colonial surveyor general, had noted in 1761 that "they had no inclination for the Fishery tho' well situated for that purpose."[25] As a consequence of their trading nature, Lunenburgers were an exceptionally well travelled and cosmopolitan lot, albeit conservative in their outlook; every sea captain's home (and a good many in town belonged to sea captains, active and retired) were filled with artifacts from abroad— conch shells from the Caribbean, bits of trade goods from Africa, Polynesian carvings.

In 1829, Lunenburg had upwards of a hundred vessels already engaged in foreign trade and "coasting." By 1838, the town had as many as seventeen large square-rigged vessels and dozens of top-sail schooners.

Judge DesBrisay noted some of them down, and recounted their adventures: "The schooner *Geneva*, built in Lunenburg by Mr. James Maxner, sailed from Halifax, November 11th, 1890, in charge of Captain H F Sieward. On the 5th day out there was a terrific storm, which lasted twelve hours, with a mountainous sea. The Equator was crossed when thirty-one days out. On January 9th she anchored in San Vincent's Bay, Terra del Fuego, for water and repairs, and left next evening. At noon on January 16th, she was considered to be safely around Cape Horn. The passage from Halifax to Vancouver Island, 14,000 miles, was made in 110 days, including the stop referred to, and broke all sailing records at the latter port. The *Geneva* was called the fastest sailing vessel on the Pacific coast. Captain Sieward's wife was with him on the voyage."

How they did get around! An example of a vessel whose accounts have survived was the Maitland-built *Pegasus*, 1,120 tons, which left Cardiff for Yokohama with a cargo of coal. From there she sailed to the "Chinchas" "in ballast" (without cargo) and picked up a load of guano to take to Antwerp. From Antwerp she crossed back to Cardiff, loaded coal for Montevideo, sailed in ballast around the Chinchas again, and took guano back to Hamburg. From there she sailed to Cardiff, loaded with coals for Hong Kong, and thence to the Philippines to load sugar for Boston. Her books at that point showed she had cleared $82,716 in four years and three months of voyaging. She cost $46,800 to build, so the owner still had the ship and $35,916 in profit.[26]

These voyages didn't always end well: take the full-rigged ship *Milton*, of 1,400 tons, built of spruce in the Bay of Fundy, launched in Maitland at the little yard of Brown and Anthony, in 1879. Her captain was Henry MacArthur, and his wife, Kate, was aboard. (She was a sea captain's daughter, married a sea captain and spent her honeymoon aboard ship; her first voyage was to New Orleans, where their ship burned at the wharf edge.) In August 1881, the *Milton* sailed from Cape Breton with a cargo of coal for San Francisco. There were twenty-three people on board, the captain, his wife, two small children (aged four and two), and seventeen hands before the mast. They had good weather all the way around the Horn, but then, in the Pacific, the cargo of coal was found to be on fire, and they were obliged to take to the boats. Three boats were provisioned and launched; their closest landfall 1,200 miles due north, their course first across the equatorial current, which would carry them eastward, then the counter-equatorial current which would carry them westward, then a long disheartening beat against the northeast trades.

One of the three boats went missing after two days, presumably swamped. On the third day, the second boat went missing, but its occupants were picked up by the British sloop *Cochin* and taken to San Francisco, carrying news of the disaster with them.

By the 18th day the last water in the remaining boat was gone, so the captain built a "condenser" out of a tomato can with a cover, a tube running from it through a second can of cold water, secured to the after-thwart by lashings of marlin. The tube was cut from a tin can in a long strip like apple parings, and wrapped around a pencil and wound with cloth and marlin. The "fireplace" was the cover of Mrs. MacArthur's tin trunk, the fuel was the boat itself—MacArthur literally burned his boat from under him, whittling up all the oars but two, then attacking the planking, the gunwales, the thwarts, every particle of wood that could be spared without weakening the boat. In this way he managed to condense a pint to a quart of water in twenty-four hours, a constant stream of fine hardwood smoke drifting to leeward. "We used to sit around and count the drops, as the condensed water dropped into the tin," said the captain's wife.

The smallest boy died soon thereafter. Finally only a ham remained, then just the bone with shreds of meat on it. On February 6, MacArthur made landfall on St. Roque Island, 500 miles north of Cape St. Lucas, having made 2,619 miles in forty-six days. The survivors were finally rescued by a passing American passenger steamer, the *Newbern*, from San Francisco, bound up the Gulf of California.

On February 16, Mrs. MacArthur gave birth and named the boy Newbern Huntingdon; he later became a physician in California.[27]

This . . . fortitude . . . is another essential thread to help unravel the success of the *Bluenose* and the Nova Scotian Grand Banks fishermen. These were not soft men, and the women were their match in every way. Sure, there was a romance to the sea, and they all felt it at times—the beat to harbour through spumy seas, the deep shadows of a far-off coast; and there was an exhilaration in the afterwards, in the meeting houses and taverns of the safe shore, in remembering the gales that drove out of the dusk, the gusts that tore the crests from towering waves and flung them into the air, the hull slipping like a whisper through the dark o' the sea, the scuppers and then the rail and then the caprail buried; "rail down with a bone in her teeth like the hounds of hell were chasing her, green water to her hatches"[28]; the bow plunging into a sea the size of a house, the mastheadmen yelling with fright, clinging to the ratlines as they swung in violent hundred-foot arcs, sent up to reef a sail that was bucking like a maddened shark . . . Yes, it was exhilarating—afterwards.

Under such circumstances, improvisation and resilience of mind were qualities quite as necessary as courage and strength. Perhaps the most extraordinary story of almost inhuman persistence was that of George Churchill and his brother Aaron, both from Yarmouth, captain and mate respectively on the Yarmouth-built *Research*, 1,459 tons. The vessel departed Quebec on November 10, 1866, bound for Greenock, Scotland, with a cargo of timber. On the 27th, a northwest gale struck, tearing canvas off the yards, and a giant rogue wave slammed into the rudder, parting its chains and shearing two-thirds of it away. To get at what remained, they were forced to change the balance of the ship, lightening her aft by moving the cargo of heavy timber forward, and were able to secure what was left of the rudder by tackles—all this in a full gale. The repair held for two days but was then torn away by another massive sea. A substitute was jury-rigged and installed on December 2, but the gear parted within a day and it was lost. Churchill set his crew to knock down the wheelhouse, and using its boards and a spare topmast, he made a sort of steering oar, which he put over the stern, Viking fashion. It didn't work, and it was brought aboard while the cargo was shifted again, this time to get the stern down. Once more the improvised steering apparatus failed to work, and it was brought aboard and rebuilt. But when the revised version was put overboard, it broke, leaving just enough to keep the vessel into the wind until December 9, when the weather cleared enough for it to be brought on deck, repaired, and installed. The weather turned nasty again, and heavy seas wrecked it once more. The weather prevented anything further being attempted until the 14th, giant seas breaking over the ship in the meantime and destroying the forward house and provision locker. On the morning of the 14th, the new rudder was put over the side during a lull in the continuous gales, but it only lasted a day before it broke. High seas buffeted the *Research* until the 21st, the ship rolling about helplessly, leaking, with one of the two pumps disabled. The weary but undaunted crew hauled what was left of the rudder back aboard and made yet another. It was put over the stern January 2, but it seemed to have no effect, so they turned to and made a second one. This dual system seemed to work, and the ship was more or less under control until January 5, when the second rudder was lost. Heavy weather prevented them trying anything new until January 10, but then the gales let up for a while and Captain Churchill had the main yard brought down from the mast to fashion yet another rudder, which unfortunately failed to work. On January 25, he made another, which was installed two days later but was carried away as soon as it was put to use. They didn't give up, and tried again, installing a new rudder, their 11th, on February 1. This one finally worked, and when the wind turned to their favour at last, they were able to sail into the Firth of Clyde and pick up a tug that towed them up to Greenock. The passage took eighty-eight days.[29] The insurers gave the captain a silver platter, as well they might.

And so it went. Such stories are not uncommon. There are dozens just like them. These were tough ships, and very tough people, *Bluenose*'s people. They made her and sailed her and brought her home, even when the gods said they shouldn't.

CHAPTER THREE

HER

MAGICAL WAYS

i n   t h e

WIND

a n d

WEATHER

The Lunenburg shipyard of Smith and Rhuland seemed like the logical, even inevitable, place to build the new Canadian contender. Partly it was because William Dennis, as we have seen, rather needed to ingratiate himself with the town. Partly it was because Angus Walters, who was to be her skipper, lived in Lunenburg and had dealt with the yard before. And of course Smith and Rhuland had deep roots in the Nova Scotian boat-building industry, and managed a pool of craftsmen whose collective experience, while not unique, was certainly extensive.

Angus Walters had already spoken to the yard about building him a new vessel; he and William Dennis met through the yard, and soon found common cause. Now they needed to settle the actual ownership of the Bluenose Schooner Company, which was to operate the *Bluenose* almost until her demise nearly twenty years later. A common assumption about the schooner, shared by many of the books and records and still widely accepted by townsfolk, is that the vessel had been built by Halifax money. "A group of Halifax businessmen" is the stock phrase that keeps recurring, and though these are never identified, they are assumed to be William Dennis and his friends Hugh Silver, Reg Corbett, and Harry de Wolf. Curiously, the archival records shed little light on the matter. The *Blue-nose* records in the Fisheries Museum of the Atlantic preserve the share certificate book and share stubs, but more than 200 are missing, and those they retain are all attributed to local Lunenburg families. None of the historians I consulted, or the archives, were any more illuminating, not even the papers of Smith and Rhuland or Lunenburg's Zwicker company. In later years, when the ownership became an issue with the race committee in Gloucester, Dennis indignantly denied that she was owned by "a bunch of rich yachtsmen," as the Gloucester papers would have it; she was owned out of Lunenburg, he said. He was right, it turns out. Though not entirely.

By the time the yard received the formal commission to build the *Bluenose*, the company had already been set up and the first annual general meeting had been held. The company was capitalized at $35,000, and 350 shares at $100 each were authorized. A good deal of the seed money did indeed come from Halifax businessmen like Hugh Silver, friends of Dennis's, but these were loans, not investments, and they were quickly repaid. The Bluenose Schooner Company account book from the Lunenburg branch of the Bank of Montreal, for example, shows that Silver had got things going in February 1921 with an initial deposit of $5,680, followed by another cheque for $550; but he was repaid as the shares sold in and around Lunenburg, and he had received all his money back by

November. Smith and Rhuland's bills were fully paid by April 21. The directors were clearly tight with money; in June, the bank statement showed an overdraft of $75.70, rescued by a $100 deposit from one S. Smith. The year-end balance for 1921 was recorded as zero.

The Zwicker brothers of Lunenburg, Arthur H. and E. Fenwick, were given five shares each for agreeing to be on the board of directors, and so was Angus Walters, over and above the shares they purchased. Even this didn't reflect the full investment or, indeed, the full company ownership. Investors, in the Lunenburg way, were made up of a slew of local families, each of whom had bought a share or two—Angus's brother John Walters, various Himmelmans and Hermans and Schnares and Meisners and Knickles, Stewart Hirtle, and then George Rhuland and Richard Smith, whose yard would build the vessel.[1] The first board comprised Angus Walters, and Arthur and Fenwick Zwicker. Captain Adam Knickle and Wallace Knock joined the board shortly afterwards, and so did a member of the Silver family, Captain Richard Silver, who himself sailed from Lunenburg.

The important part, though, was less who paid for the vessel than who controlled it, and that was Angus Walters, who was made managing director of the company; the board explicitly authorized him to act on its behalf, with or without consultation—a clause the Zwickers at least would rue later. Nobody quarrelled with this decision at the time. It was Angus, after all, who would "drive" the vessel, take her fishing—and win a few races. That he had a substantial stake in her only made sense. It remains unclear how many shares Angus actually owned, but it was probably around 90 of the 350 available. He assigned 21 of those to his wife, Maggie.

On March 5, 1921, the board of the company passed the following resolution: "That the Directors may purchase or otherwise acquire from Angus Walters, master mariner, upon such terms and conditions as they see fit, a certain fishing schooner now building in the yard of the firm of Smith and Rhuland." On the 22nd, the board issued a cheque to Angus for $26,500; the balance of the

$35,000 or so she cost represents Angus's own investment plus the shares assigned to George Rhuland and Richard Smith, the vessel's builders.

She was built, naturally enough, in the Lunenburg way.

She lived through many an Atlantic gale in her eventful life, and died a savage death in a tropical squall on a Haitian reef. Which makes it more than a little piquant that a winter storm, one of those violent Atlantic nor'easters that pick away at Maritime nerves twice or thrice a season, had something to do with her birthing too. This may seem a bit of a stretch—it *is* a bit of a stretch—but it's true nevertheless that Maritime boatbuilders of the period used the storms to do some of their work for them. Some of the first-growth oak and beech in the forests of New Germany and the Forties and Simpsons Corner, and in the timber stands of the Davison Lumber Company up in Springfield, halfway across the province, were felled by gales and brought down to Lunenburg on a spur line of the Halifax and South Western Railway, known even then as the Hellish Slow and Wobbly, where they were hauled by oxen to the wharfside yards of the master shipwrights, to be stored until needed.

So it was for the *Bluenose*.

Cutting timber for the boatbuilders had long developed its own peculiar rules. Wood for firewood or for building was usually cut in the late fall and hauled out on sleds in the winter because it was quicker to season with the sap out of it. But the great trees used for ships' spars and booms, and for the major frame members such as the keel or keelson or the ribs, were often "started" in the spring or summer, or at least before the frosts of fall. This "starting" was something other than just a synonym for beginning; it was a technical term meaning felling trees using natural weather patterns as an ally.

It worked this way: the surveyor or crew foreman would blaze the required trees and mark them on a grid. A digging crew would follow, and excavate a pit on the weather-lee side of the required trees. They would dig down until the roots' junction with the tree was exposed. They would then cut the roots, but not too close to the trunk—those junctions of root and tree were immensely strong natural right angles and so of considerable value, often fetching premium prices as "ships' knees," the braces on which the deck beams were supported. Then they would go away and wait for a gale to do the actual felling which, this being Atlantic America, it would inevitably do. The trees would then be limbed and hauled out with teams of horses or oxen; the Canadian provinces tended to use oxen, the New Englanders horses.

This process has an old provenance in Nova Scotia. Indeed, one of its early governors, Sir John Wentworth, had been the royal surveyor in both Maine and Nova Scotia in his earlier years, and used to tramp the woods himself, blazing the great trees he wanted with a royal marque as a sign to others that they were reserved for Royal Navy use. By *Bluenose*'s time the process had been long privatized; boatbuilders had contracts with any number of private woodlot owners, millers, and lumber companies. Smith and Rhuland, the contracting yard for the *Bluenose*, had sheds full of birch and beech, spruce and hemlock and pine, red and white oak and maple, tamarack, and a pile of Oregon pine and American white pine for spars and booms from small millers all over Lunenburg County, Annapolis County, and Queens.

Some of it was from trees felled in a violent late-summer gale in 1920, and another deep into winter. Those trees were hauled out and taken to the mills, where they were squared off on bandsaws. The millers separated the resulting timbers into piles: lumber for export was usually stacked for it to season—shipping green lumber was possible, but it was heavier and thus each vessel would have a smaller payload, so they were usually left for at least a year, and preferably two. Boatbuilders didn't demand seasoned lumber.

Green would do fine, and was in some ways desirable, since green wood was easier to bend in a steam press.

Smith and Rhuland were used to working with wood right off the stump. Wood destined for the *Bluenose* was used at once because its owners were in a hurry—she had to go fishing early in 1921, or she would miss a key deadline that would make her ineligible to race against the Gloucestermen in October. The shipwrights were comfortable with the given timetable. From tree to sea, from living thing to new-built living thing, from laying the keel to slipping down the ways into the harbour, would take just a hundred days. That was their promise.

There was still frost in the heartwood when the shipwrights started their work.

First they laid down her lines on the floor in the largest shed they had. George Rhuland and his foreman had the designer's half model in front of them, and his plans, drawn to a scale of 1:48, or a quarter inch to the foot. The plans were not really necessary; like all Nova Scotian shipwrights, Smith and Rhuland was used to simply scaling up from the sleek softwood lines of a small model, whittled to size and shape in the mind's eye of the man who conceived her. It was the way most vessels were built up and down the coast, at least until the 1880s; but by the turn of the century, New Englanders particularly had become used to the designs of famous naval architects like Benjamin Crowninshield, Tom McManus, and the Burgess family, and except for the participants in the very first race, all the contenders for the Halifax Herald Trophy that *Bluenose* so triumphantly held were built by architects. Before that, most of what designing there was had been done by the foreman in charge of the shipyard.

To scale up from a half model, the foreman would take the model apart and measure the size and shape of each frame and beam. The half model would even show the waterline. The nature of the timbers and the number of board feet required were extrapolated from the model.

Often, alas, the model turned out a vessel that, for some reason or another, just didn't work. Sometimes this was obvious at launch ("Oh, she's not a bad-looking boat if you cut 2 feet off her bow and put a real stern onto her.") And sometimes it only became obvious at work. Some vessels looked fine but were unaccountably dogs, as Joe Garland put it, "if not downright Jonahs, hoodoos." An old fisherman from Tancook said not long ago of a boat lying at the government wharf: ". . . reminds me of the fellow from Lunenburg, must have gone through a dozen boats, said he was going to do just one more and name her *Just Right*. Well, he got her and she wasn't just right . . ."[2] And sometimes the vessel was fine but something else was awry. Some, Garland once wrote, "were mackerel killers but couldn't seem to touch a haddock and vice versa. It depended on who modelled her and who put her together, whether for speed or stability, year-round fishing or Sunday sailing, who her skipper was and who her crew, what kind of grub and what kind of bait and as much as anything on plain luck."[3] Successful half models were widely copied; the cranks were discarded and forgotten.

From the plans scaled up and drawn on the shed floor, they built templates for each of the *Bluenose*'s framing members from soft pine. In the nature of a boat's hull, with its double-ended taper fore and aft and its arcing curved ribs, each one was different from all the others. These rib templates are critical because from them everything flows, the shape of the hull, the construction of the ribs, the very size of the keel, the finished planking, everything. Then the foreman went to his woodpile to mark and pull out what was needed. The *Bluenose* was winter-started, and though it hadn't yet snowed there was ice in the pile, and many of the logs had stuck together from the frost. Workmen separated them with great mauls and hauled them into a stack. They worked with what they had, a jumble of spruce, hemlock, beech, some maple, red oak. The keel wood was white American oak from the States (the native red oak was too porous for the purpose), imported from New York State via barge, railway and then barge again; the rest from Lunenburg County, "up the river, around Hebbville and New Germany and thereabouts," some of it storm-felled as described.

The first stage was to lay out the keel blocks along the "ways" where the vessel was to grow; these were simply massive timber props on which the equally massive keel would rest. "The keel is always first except when it's not," Kline Falkenham (who was yard foreman for the building of *Bluenose II* and whose father had helped build *Bluenose* herself) told me, by which he meant that you should lay the keel down first and construct the framing members on it, but sometimes good lumber for this most critical part wasn't in the yard, in which case the rib-frames were constructed separately first and fitted later, after the keel had arrived.

Meanwhile, the shipwrights and the building crew were assembling. For smaller vessels, a small group of jacks-of-all-trades would do. For larger vessels like the *Bluenose*, specialists were more common, though even then there was a fair amount of fluidity in the trades, and neither unions nor union rules existed. Kline Falkenham started as a labourer but became an adzeman, caulker, carpenter, and rigger before becoming foreman. American and Canadian organizational patterns somewhat diverged in the boatyard, just as they did in the timber and lumbering business. In the Maritime provinces model, a small group of versatile workers tended to stay with one yard, their fortunes fluctuating as the yard's did, and so it was with Smith and Rhuland. The New Englanders, by contrast, developed an early version of the production line. Every worker was a specialist whose loyalty was to his gang, not the yard; segments of these gangs moved from yard to yard as their particular skills were needed. This model meant that the workers were seldom un- or underemployed. Both models could turn out vessels very quickly, but the Massachusetts system, "a triumph," as Joe Garland put it, "of community effort and discipline,"4 was at once less secure for the workers and somewhat more flexible for the yardmasters.

In whatever place, the bigger the yard, the more specialized the trades. There were men whose sole job it was to drill holes in the massive timbers for bolting; they would work for a penny a hole, and some days could make $3—300 holes through 14-inch timbers in a working day, a hole every two minutes, using hand-turned auger bits—these were very strong men. Most workers toiled for $2 a day for a ten-hour day, six days a week, and felt themselves lucky. There were hole drillers, caulkers and painters, riggers, mast and spar men; the rudder or rudder set guys were a different trade from the rudder port guys; there were men for the planking, sawpit men, bandsaw and steambox men, framers, treenail ("trunnel") setters, sailmakers, blacksmiths, joiners, block and tackle makers, cordage men for the rope and rigging, specialists in anchors or "bowers." Most boat-building towns had businesses for these trades spread across the waterfront. Boston's sailmakers were famous; the McManus family, from which the designer Tom McManus came, were primarily sailmakers, and their sail loft became the hangout for skippers between voyages, yachting people who felt the romance of the Merchant Marine, and tradespeople looking for work.

Smaller towns like Lunenburg had their sail lofts too, and buildings for other trades. Some of them became famous wherever vessels were built; Arthur Dauphinee of Lunenburg ("A. Dauphinee and Son") shipped orders to Hong Kong, Rio, Nassau, Taiwan, wherever anyone wanted "blocks and tackles," which is what marine people call a system of pulleys. In the 1980s my wife and I almost bought the Dauphinee building in Lunenburg when Arthur put it up for sale, having moved his diminished business out of town. It would have made an interesting conversion to a dwelling space, for the uppermost floor had a 30-degree list on it, and there were still remnants of the machinery Dauphinee used to crank out his wares, including some ancient belt-driven lathes and saws. A few of the old blocks were still hanging in the shop, but only a few and not representative of their best work. Silver Donald Cameron described them, these Rolls-Royces of the blocks business: ". . . regular works of art, turned and shaped out of mahogany, ash, or lignum vitae, according to the order, glowing and glistening in the sunlight with the deep rich grains of the wood under many coats of varnish . . . Blocks, single blocks, doubles, triples; blocks with beckets and twisted shackles; blocks with ring-bolts and screw eyes; turning blocks, cheek blocks, snatch blocks. Rows upon rows of them, hanging above the heavy, glue-lumpy [benches], or lining the window sill and gleaming in the sunlight." The blocks on *Bluenose* and *Bluenose II* came from Dauphinee's.[5]

Construction starts once the keel props are in place. The *Bluenose*'s American white oak keel was a substantial thing, three layers of 12 x 12 oak, bolted together every 2½ feet. The keel was 50 feet long, pieced together from shorter lengths and then joined together with lap joints, or "scarfed," in the jargon of the trade, and then bolted. The hole-driller lines up the bolt holes, driving his auger through almost a yard of hard oak (*Bluenose II* was drilled by power drills, but even those took considerable skill to keep plumb).

Midway along the *Bluenose* keel a symbolic and functionally useless golden spike was driven, an early signal that this was not to be merely another fishing boat. It was driven by the Governor General come down from Ottawa for the occasion. (Not that the dignitary concerned, the Duke of Devonshire, was that successful. He performed with aplomb, but the rumours were that he'd fallen into convivial company too early, which did not improve his eye, and he swung and missed several times before someone rescued him by wresting the maul away and pounding the spike home.)

The foreman then marked on the keel the location of the stem and stern post and the various frames or ribs, which were already being constructed in other parts of the yard. In a small boat, the frames or ribs are one piece, steamed and bent into shape, but in a large vessel like *Bluenose* they were built up of several lengths, sawed or adzed into the necessary shapes and joined together with dowels and treenails, or trunnels.

For *Bluenose*, these ribs, the framing skeleton, were themselves substantial. Each frame was made double, twin ribs of 9 inch timber, bolted side by side to make a single rib 18 inches thick, their depth tapered from 10 inches at the base to about 8 at the top. Each frame has a different bevel, transferred from the plan-derived templates and then run through the massive bandsaws in the yard. They were made of a combination of woods, pine and spruce, birch, some hardwood maple. Each frame was pieced together from half a dozen smaller timbers, butted with lap joints and fastened with screw bolts.

There were sixty-three sets of ribs, set on 21-inch centres, raised and set in place with blocks and poles. Each was held in place with stays, lined up properly and "ribboned out fair with battens and scarfed in"—scarfing in, wrapping the whole in a "scarf" of timber, was the next stage. But before that began, the stem and sternposts were raised and fitted to the keel by aprons and other pieces of solid timber designed to hold everything together as strongly as possible, then bolted through. The skeleton of the vessel erected, she was said to be "in frame."

To lock the frames to the keel was like constructing a gigantic vise. The feet of the frames that lay on the keel were overlaid with a timber almost as massive as the keel itself. This was a heavy beam of spruce called the keelson, which lay on top of the frames, which now had become the filling in a huge wood sandwich—keel on the bottom, frame filling, keelson on top. On *Bluenose* there were also side keelsons called rather prosaically assistant keelsons, and to the side of those, assistant assistant keelsons, cut from spruce, a long-fibred wood that bends relatively easily.

Holes were then bored through the keelson and its assistants, through the frames and, finally, through the keel itself and out the bottom. Then massive steel bolts more than 6 feet long were punched down through the holes, heavy nuts were fitted at each end, and everything tightened down, bearing the keelson onto the frames and the whole thing onto the keel, clamping the frames in an iron grip. The process made a skeleton that was incredibly strong.

The planking and ceiling were next. The ceiling is not what you think—not the thing overhead, or the underside of the deck. The ceiling in a vessel is the interior planking, attached directly to the frames.

The planking was birch and oak below the waterline, and West Coast Douglas fir for the top five "strakes" of freeboard. This inside and outside planking gives the vessel a double skin, and since each skin is 2½ inches thick, it adds a bracing of heavy timber fully 5 inches through, "making a fabric that knitted together keel, keelsons, frames, bow-stem and sternpost to form a ship's body of terrific strength and rigidity."[6] The longest plank on the *Bluenose*'s 143-foot frame was about 30 feet. They tapered, somewhere around 12 inches amidships, down to 7 inches at the bow and stern. They were bent in the steam box before fastening.

These planks were neither bolted nor nailed but fastened with trunnels. A hole is bored through the plank, through the frame and clear through the ceiling plank opposite the frame, and then a trunnel is bashed in with a maul. These trunnels are hackmatack or juniper dowels just slightly thicker than the hole and are driven in until they stick out on the other side. They are then cut off flush, the ends split with a blunt iron chisel, and oak wedges driven in. Nothing on earth could move those trunnels when they were set.

A 100-foot wooden schooner would use about 15,000 trunnels. Better than 19,000 were used on *Bluenose*. There were workers whose entire workaday life was to set trunnels.

When she was "ceiled up" to the height of the deck, the shelf and clamp timbers were bolted on. These timbers would carry the heavy deck beams, and needed to be sturdy; on *Bluenose* they consisted of two layers of 6 x 6 timber fastened with trunnels through to the outside. They were cambered and scarfed together to form a horizontal strake running the whole length of the ship, about 6 inches wide. On *Bluenose* they were spruce, coped to fit. The deck beams were then laid on the shelf, and heavy knees, essentially huge shelf brackets, saved as described from fallen trees, were fitted for extra support.

A deck of clear pine planks, 3 inches thick and 4¾ inches wide, was laid on top of the deck beams, tightly butted together with a V groove cut into the seams for the caulkers to work with. Openings were cut out for housings, the deckhouse, companionways, hatch coamings, stanchions and, of course, masts. Most of the superstructure was made of mahogany, all of it imported. The rudder was then fitted to the sternpost. The rudderpost was a substantial piece of timber, 12 inches on a side, made of birch. The rudder itself was made of seventeen pieces of pine laminated and rabbeted together.

The planks were still rough after fitting. They had come from the sawmills with only a single pass through a plane, and there was still rough wood to cut and smooth. This was among the most skilled of the shipwright's tasks; the men used an adze and a spokeshave, a sort of oversize drawknife, to make them true, and finished the job with a plane and multiple grades of sandpaper. A skilled man with a clumsy-looking but razor-sharp adze could finish the wood to a degree that would satisfy anyone but a cabinetmaker, and the plane would only be used to clean up imperfections invisible to the outsider.

As soon as the planking and decking was finished, the caulkers moved in. This was dirty work, and tough; wielding a 16-inch caulking hammer for ten hours at a stretch called for stamina and strength, and caulkers were usually paid a premium. Smith and Rhuland caulkers used hammers with a groove in the blade end, which muted the noise the hammering made and lessened the number of workers who went deaf, a hazard of their trade. A first layer of oakum was driven far into the seams with what they called a "horse iron"; then a second layer was driven in over that, a process called, for no apparent reason, beetling. The two layers of oakum were then covered with putty and the whole with pitch. When the caulkers were done, water was pumped into the hull and wherever a leak was noticed it was chalk-marked for attention and recaulked.

The railings were installed next, birch and oak timbers roughly shaped at the mill but smoothed to a satin finish on site; all the necessary blacksmith work was done, such as channel plates, staybolts and more, and the vessel was then ready for painting: a prime coat, more sanding, then the blue-black finish coat and the gilded trimwork.

The vessel was ready for launching. *Bluenose* was conventionally made, sent into the water as a completed hull, and sparred and rigged after she was afloat. The practice varied. Some ships had all their masts and spars in place and were fully rigged at launching; others were launched with only the lower masts in place.

On launch day, the launching ways under her bottom was greased, the hull was raised off the keel blocks, and blocks and shores were knocked out until the vessel rested on its carrying cradle. When high water arrived, twenty-one-year-old Audrey Smith, Angus Walters's niece, swung a bottle of champagne against her hull, the cradle was released, and the hull slipped down into the water.

From tree to sea, from green wood to racing down the stays with a triumphant splash—ninety-seven days. Not a record, but not too slow either, and three days better than their deadline. Smith and

Rhuland averaged some seven such vessels a year. Other yards did more, some fewer. Business goes as business is.

"Fitting out the sticks"—the poles, the spars, the masts—was done onshore while the shipwrights were busy elsewhere. Few things seem as magical to the untutored eye as this process of shaping a 90-foot behemoth of timber, a square more than 2 feet on a side, into a perfectly tapered cylinder, all done by eye and by adze, spokeshave and plane. The Douglas fir logs were so heavy that despite their massiveness they needed to be jacked up and braced at intervals, or they would have sagged and twisted.

First, the top two corners were "fetched up," turning the monster into a six-sided pole. The whole thing was then rolled over, and the same thing was done to the other two corners, resulting in an octagon. The foot of the mast, to about 6 inches above the deckline, was left octagonal to allow the mast to be stepped through a hole in the decking of the same shape and dimensions. About 10 feet from the top, a flat surface was cut out for attaching the topmasts. The rest of the mast was then rendered first into a 16-sided shape, then a 32-sided shape, and finally all the edges were rounded with adze and plane, the foreman directing the work by squinting down the length of the spar to spot minute imperfections, indentations, and protrusions.

The mainmast, foremast, topmasts, booms, gaffs, and bowsprit were all installed after launch, by the riggers. A few coins were placed under each mast for luck, they were carefully lifted into place, and the stays installed and tightened to secure them.[7]

The rigging of sailing ships has few variations and the pattern for every mast is about the same. Every rope and block has a purpose, every coil has its place. The rig of a sailing ship is the epitome of order and function. A ship has two kinds of rigging. Standing rigging, which holds fast or "stays" the masts and transmits the power of the sails to the hull, is permanent. It includes the heavy shrouds that stop the masts from falling sideways and come down to the rails of the ship; the shrouds are fitted with horizontal ropes, called ratlines, which provide a ladder for the crew to go aloft. Running rigging is the complex system of adjustable chains, wires, and ropes by which the sails are set and trimmed to the wind. Sailors working aloft never use the running rigging for handholds because it could suddenly run out or flail in the wind. On square-rigged vessels the sails hang from horizontal spars called yards; and on every mast the entire trembling edifice of canvas is rotated by hauling on long ropes called braces. Like bridles, these lead to the ends of each yard and come down to massive belaying pins on each side of the deck.[8] Except for topsail schooners, which have a small square-rigged topsail, schooners have no yards, only gaffs and booms, each secured with its own running rigging. The main boom on the *Bluenose* was 81 feet long, housed in a crutch on deck when not in use. A fully rigged schooner like *Bluenose* had about thirty halyards with sheets and downhauls secured to belaying pins, and every crew member must know each one and its purpose, and be ready to go aloft at any time.[9]

After launch, the standing rigging is installed, the running rigging left dangling until the sails themselves are on board; Charlie Hebb, the town's best-known sailmaker, was in charge of those.

She had on board a primitive make-and-break engine for the winches and cargo hoists; the invoice from the Lunenburg Foundry was for $100, plus $12.40 for an "oil dryer."

All this time Angus Walters had been hanging about the yard, making sure that everything was done to his exacting specifications. He hadn't much liked the name assigned the boat—there had been a number of *Bluenose*s before, dating back to the *Blue Nose* built in 1839 in New Brunswick, and another built by Elkanah Zwicker in Mahone Bay, Nova Scotia, in 1850, and of course "Bluenose" had long been a shorthand way of saying "Nova Scotian" (which is why the Halifax interests pushed for it), but Angus thought the name a joke, and that a family member should have been honoured instead, which would have been more traditional in the Lunenburg fishery. He didn't dispute the name though, as long as he could have some say in how she was put together.

She went into the water pretty much as Roué had designed her. Yard foreman Fred Rhuland was asked once whether he had made any changes in her specs, and he answered a little huffily, his yard's reputation for probity clearly on the line: "No reputable yard-master would dare to make any change without confirming it in advance with the owners. The *Bluenose* was definitely no freak." His colleague, Richard Smith, was asked his thoughts: "I don't think nothin' of her," he said. "She's different from any vessel we ever built. We built her as close to the Roué lines as we know how. If she's a success, he gets the praise. If she's a failure, he gets the blame."

In fact, one change had been made to the vessel, though at the insistence of Angus Walters himself, so Rhuland's assertion of probity remained true. Angus had been looking the plans over with a professional eye; he wanted to win races, but he also wanted a vessel that wouldn't risk his safety and that of his men before she ever got a chance to race. He was concerned that she was too "sharp," that her yachty lines would give her speed but make her vulnerable in high seas, and make her broach too easily. Roué had never designed a fishing schooner, but he knew the work of the great naval architects, Crowninshield, Burgess, and above all Tom McManus in Massachusetts, and he knew his design had to have as low a centre of gravity as possible. By Roué's own assertion, she was to be "a combination of the Gloucester and Nova Scotia vessels, having the depth of the former and the breadth of the latter." Angus had no quarrel with any of this, but he still insisted on raising her freeboard forward, raising the fore deckline above the fo'c'sle by 18 inches. Apart from this one change, the vessel was all Roué.

Some versions of the *Bluenose* legend maintain that the change was made after the carcass was under construction, forcing the yard to send a burly yardman into the ribs with a gigantic sledge-hammer to shift a few of the main timbers farther apart, causing a good deal of head-shaking among the gaffers and gawkers who were following her raising. But actually Roué had already accepted Walters's suggestion, and it was incorporated when he drew up her final profile. The change was controversial, though; it had the effect of altering Roué's first elegant lines, giving the *Bluenose* a slightly lumpy appearance that made her not as pretty a vessel as some of those that followed her, the *Canadia* and the *Haligonian* in Canada, the *Puritan*, the *Mayflower*, the sublime *Columbia*, and the delightful little filly the *Gertrude L. Thebaud* in the U.S. Some of the yachting writers were unkind. Harlan Trott of Boston called her "an ungainly herring-choker, with a great homely bow."

Pretty well all the published accounts say Angus made the change to give the fo'c'sle hands more headroom; the fore part of the vessel was where they'd spend their time off watch, and taking care of his crew, making sure they are content, is obviously in a skipper's interests. Claude Darrach gave the orthodox account when he wrote, "Men who dress in oilskins go over the side in dories at 0600. At 2200 or sixteen hours later they are still at work, gutting and splitting fish. They deserve and need a well ventilated and spacious accommodation in which to eat and sleep. [Angus] Walters decided to raise the forecastle 18 inches, and several frames were taken out and reset. If this did anything to slow her down no one will ever know." But this explanation makes no sense. If you look at the plans, or if you visit the *Theresa E. Connor*, a similar vessel now at the wharf of the fisheries museum in Lunenburg, you can plainly see that the only people it would really benefit would be the ship's boys and the most junior hands, whose bunks are always tucked as much for'ard as possible. That Angus Walters, a notoriously chilly personality who wouldn't dream of doing such a thing for his own family, would alter the profile of his vessel for a few junior hands, simply beggars belief. He was both ferociously competitive and ferociously parsimonious, and if he thought it would affect his boat's performance by a quarter knot he wouldn't consider it for a moment.

So why did he do it, and how did he persuade Bill Roué to go along?

The "how" is not hard to see; Roué's was a diffident personality, Walters's was, well, not. He just bullied the designer until he saw the light.

The "why" isn't really so hard either, once you discard the notion of Angus's solicitousness to his crew. The real reason was buoyancy in heavy seas—to make her a drier boat. "The bow was upswept because she would be drier in good seas," Captain Dan Moreland says. "This was definitely about buoyancy forward, because he knew the boat as designed would be too pointy for the Banks."

If this is true—and I liked a ship captain's judicious use of the technical term "pointy"—it worked. It caused her, in another piece of nice boatspeak, to become knees-up in wet weather. A writer for the old *Toronto Telegram* put it this way: "When the helmsman was up to his knees on the lee side of other fishermen's wheels, in *Bluenose* he was working dryshod. *Bluenose* would go along just scuppering it, her lee rail out, the tumblehome and tuck-in of her long tapering quarters keeping everything dry."

Many schooners, in short, will bury their bows and drag water, too much green water tumbling about on deck. *Bluenose* was different. Her bow would split the crest of the swells, displacing the water out and under, lifting the bow. Claude Darrach once spent twenty minutes at the end of the bowsprit with another crew member, Kenny Spidel, replacing a strained shackle, and described what he saw: "*Bluenose* was doing about 10 knots. Under the lee bow at water line the bow wave rolled out, down and inboard, making an air tunnel of less than 18 inches in diameter. There was a constant roaring sound . . . We took our time returning inboard. It was a fascinating sight to see 10,000 square feet of wind-filled white canvas, the long black hull laying over to a 12 degree angle and pushing a huge bow wave of white foam. We had a full view of the entire vessel, from 18 feet beyond the stem."[10]

The changed profile meant, in writer Feenie Ziner's phrase, that the *Bluenose* was a witch to windward. She was good in a light wind, but best of all to windward, even in a heavy blow. Hove to, under gale force conditions and under foresail only, she would range ahead, responding to the rudder, making headway where other vessels couldn't. It was perhaps this that made her different.

Of course, even *Bluenose* buried sometimes, and if you were on the bowsprit you'd be waist deep in green before she'd rise up again. An old seaman who sailed on the *Bluenose* told a National Film Board crew, "a ship, a wessel as they say here, to me she . . . well you might say she's not flesh and blood but she has a life. *Bluenose* had good sense, she was a good sailor, she used to do things no other ship ever done. Normal, when a ship raises up on a sea and she falls down she falls off [that is, downwind], but whatever made the *Bluenose* do it I can't tell you but every time she fell down she cut the wind off, she'd move against the wind as she cut into it. And that's why she was always windward of 'er mark. I used to watch that lots of time up the masthead, you could actually see that, that cut . . . if you didn't watch yourself she'd throw you off that masthead pretty quick. I was up there one time when we cracked the masthead, it didn't take me very long to get on deck, I tell you . . . the staging coming down around me neck . . . But the rougher it got, the faster she went. It seemed the further she got over on her side, the faster she went. She was a good old ship."

The *Bluenose* cost $35,580.76 to build, which was expensive, about a third more than the cost of a conventional schooner to that date. The designer got 3 per cent of the cost of construction, about $900. The wood cost Smith and Rhuland twice that. Labour costs were better than $26,584, not including rigging, which came to $1331.95, split between two companies. Dories and gear cost $815, ballast $352.40, sails $1,003, foundry work $760, anchor and chain $660, and "rope and duck" from the Zwicker company $622.11. The 19,000 trunnels cost almost $200. Whew! It all adds up.

There was a testy footnote to the commissioning of the *Bluenose.* On December 19, 1920—a full three months before she was even launched—a stiff note was delivered to the Bluenose Schooner Company from Bill Roué, the designer. He'd not been paid. "If there is any reason why I should not be paid for my work, I should like to know what it is," he demanded.

There was no reply. *Bluenose* was duly launched on March 26, and Roué went down for the ceremony, and visited the Zwickers, ship's chandlers, and *Bluenose* co-owners, in their waterfront offices, without result. (Except a letter now in the fisheries museum in Lunenburg from the Zwickers to Hugh Silver in Halifax, suggesting he might want to pay the bill; after all, he'd been in the group that had hired Roué in the first place. Silver declined the honour.) In the fall of that year, by the time the *Bluenose* had won its first series against the American challengers, and still no money had gone Roué's way, the designer got himself a lawyer, and an even more indignant note on heavy lawyer's vellum paper followed.

The designer's work had "obviously" (the lawyer said with pointed irony) "given some satisfaction," the vessel having won as intended, and having proven seaworthy, fast and very able. His client's fee was supposed to be 3 per cent of the price of construction, plus expenses, and these were detailed in an addendum (ten trips from Halifax to Lunenburg, total cost $152.20, cumulative train trips at $2.50 each, hotels at $4.50 and assorted meals averaging $1.75 for dinner—Roué was clearly not a high liver). The total bill was $1,052.20. It was another year before he got a cheque. He and Angus Walters disliked each other for the rest of their lives.

After she was launched and the riggers were done she came to be unmoored for the first time and backed away from the wharf, turning into the sun (never away, for that would be bad luck), set for Battery Point and beyond, Angus Walters with his hand on the wheel. No one can know what he was thinking, for he never said; but he did recall that the start to *Bluenose*'s life at sea was auspicious, for outside the harbour the fog had burned off to a sunny day with the glass steady, winds southwesterly at 20 knots, enough to carry a good press of sail. By the time they passed the point the foresail and jumbo were up with the mainsail sheeted home, then as they hit the crosswise groundswell beyond the headland she headed down the wind, and immediately the tone of the rigging—the sounds of the creaking blocks, the straining cords, and squeaking sailcloth—rose a note or two. As the deck moved on the breathing swells, his hand on the wheel would have felt the schooner's living essence, a subtle vibration transmitted up from the water to the keel and the rudder and the deck itself and down from the thrumming of the rigging, "feeling the wheel's kick and the wind's song," as the poet John Masefield put it. Course east-north-east, all hands on deck to raise the foretop, maintop, and jib, then after half an hour the lead went over and the report came back: speed 12 knots, sir, no bottom at 40 fathoms . . . Starboard were the fish shacks of Feltzen South and First South, as the shore southwest of Lunenburg was prosaically called; larboard was the village of Blue Rocks; around the point the intricate channels of Black Rocks, called

Stonehurst; ahead and around Cross Island was open sea, where he could put his beauty through her paces.

In the next couple of days of sea trials the skipper came to know some of the things *Bluenose* could do. He ran her before the wind and beat up into it, he reefed her and held her to a drogue, "jogging in place," he ran her with just the jumbo and a storms'l, and though he hadn't yet put her to the test of a real Atlantic gale he already knew she was capable, fast and able both, for he'd had her rail-down in a brisk breeze, with that exhilarating hissing along the scuppers, she rising to it like the thoroughbred she clearly was, keeping her knees-up and her deck dry.

If he'd been in church the previous Sunday—far from sure, for he was not generally a churchgoing man—he would have heard the little prayer that was standard for Lunenburg preachers in fishing season . . .

Lord ere we go to thee we trust our all
Thy sea is mighty and our boats are small

. . . but generally the fishing skippers thought prayer was for funerals and weddings, for a real skipper trusted his men and the hull he stood on and the rig he controlled and his own very considerable skills.

Which he got to use, oh yes: not very long after her sea trials, before her first trip to Burin for baitin' and the Banks, he took her up the coast from Lunenburg to Halifax. In the nostalgic memory of a now-old fisherman who was with him ". . . the wind was coming from the north and it blowed, it blowed like the old devil, and we went inside of Sambro Island, an' the *Bluenose* was laying over, rail under, and all the wind that she could carry, Lord was she ever tearin' boy, and after we was down through the ledges, Angus [Walters] woke up, he come up [on deck], she was going over, heeling over, and the rail was going under, and Angus would yell,

'Don't let her come up! Don't let her come up!' He [already] knew nobody and nothin' could beat her, see, when she was rail down in a rough sea . . ."

By this time people on both sides of the border had taken the measure of the "sleek whale"; Angus had measured her in all conditions and knew intimately what she could do. The codgers all agreed she was incomparable beating to windward, making do with one tack where other vessels needed two. And she was fast, no doubting that . . . There were dozens of reasons given why *Bluenose* was so fast. Many of them were fanciful.

One popular story was that the timbers froze when they were framing her up, which somehow made her fast. The story was sometimes attributed to "an old shipwright" who had worked on her: ". . . and it was always my thought that it was what the weather done to her ribs. See, we got her ribs up around the fall of the year. Now, the first frost commenced right about then and one morning in partic'lar it hit her pretty hard. Now, I think it might have set her beams, set 'em like as no man could ever do. Why you know very well that something made her faster'n any other ship as came out of Lunenburg."[11] It's true that *Bluenose* was framed up in an exceptionally cold fall and winter, and the meteorological records do show a few days when the temperatures plunged to zero Fahrenheit (unusual in Lunenburg in winter, and especially that early in winter), but there is no credible reason why this would have made a difference or would have "set her beams" in any way that changed her performance. The raised fo'c'sle was also offered as an explanation, but no one could explain why it should have made a difference, or if it did, why it wouldn't rather have slowed the vessel down some.

Another theory is that her speed lay in the setup of her rigging, but no one could explain what the differences were, or why they would have happened. And the chief rigger himself, Morris Allen (known in Lunenburg by the macabre nickname "Rigger Morris," pronounced rather more like rigor mortis than it looks), was always skeptical. "Rigged her up like all the rest," was all he'd say.

Bill Roué, when asked his opinion, said rather disingenuously, "I only wish I knew." Angus Walters's own theory was that the setting of her masts perfectly balanced the vessel. Rather ungenerously, he didn't think this was Roué's doing. "If the rest of her is good, a vessel's spars will pretty well tell what she will do. Somehow the *Bluenose*'s spars was stepped mathematically perfect, in a way that no man could do. I think that was it, I don't feel as though there was a vessel that ever came out of Lunenburg that had her sticks stepped that perfect."[12] In later years, sometime in the 1950s, Angus told a young doctor in town, Dr. Bruce Keddy (who had had the confident boldness to invite the famous skipper out for a sail on his little 20-foot schooner, *Foggy*), that the real reason she won so often was not so much speed as her ability to head a quarter mile into the wind after each tack before falling over; a quarter mile gained at every tack added up to a lot of sea miles.[13]

Others have attributed her speed to the sailing ability of her skipper. Angus Walters wasn't a popular man, but no one ever doubted his sailing ability, and no one but Angus was ever at the helm when *Bluenose* raced.

But the real reason was probably much simpler than that: she was fast because she was designed to be fast. In this view, Roué was a very good designer but not a genius, and his boat far from revolutionary—he just did as he was asked, drawing on the experience of many others who had gone before him. The naval historian George Owen was dismissive of the "amount of claptrap" written about the *Bluenose*. "There is no mystery of her performance. She is a superlatively good adaptation of the well-known laws governing naval architecture. Look at her beautiful entrance and long clean run." The *Bluenose* was designed to be what she was. She wasn't designed as a fisherman who could be fast. She was designed as a speedster who could also fish. She not only could but should beat regular fishermen; just as a schooner yacht, put up against the *Bluenose*, should win every time, because the *Bluenose* was a compromise between speed and cargo, and yachts didn't have to do anything but race. In the end, the *Bluenose* never did get to race against some of the other vessels designed the way she was, for speed. She was fast, but so were *Puritan*, *Mayflower*, and many others, and her experience against *Columbia* was, at best, a wash.

This is not to denigrate *Bluenose*, or Roué. It's easy enough to design a fast boat, but not so easy to design one that is fast and capable too, and *Bluenose* was certainly that. (The dainty little *Gertrude L. Thebaud* beat *Bluenose* several times in races, but she was what Lunenburgers call a "tender vessel," and not good in rough weather, and she was a hopeless fisherman, constantly losing money for her owners.)

The thing to remember is that *Bluenose* wasn't just another vessel abuildin' at the Smith and Rhuland yard. She may have been on their books as Hull #119, but she was treated differently from the start. She cost more than an ordinary fisherman, for one thing— $35,000 was regarded as an extravagant sum to pay for a boat in 1920. She was designed by an architect, and not just put together by her builders and owners. William Dennis always indignantly dismissed accusations that the *Bluenose* was really a yacht masquerading as a fisherman (charges relayed from Gloucester, mostly). But he did admit it was not exactly usual for a fishing schooner to be finished with trim in brass, or to carry sail covers, electric lights, and an electric signal bell system, not to mention a brass bed for the skipper. And why did the Governor General make a special trip down from Ottawa to drive home, or attempt to drive home, the first symbolic bolt? How many ordinary fishing vessels rated the presence of the Governor General?[14]

Whatever the reasons, *Bluenose* was fast, there's no doubting that. She could do 12 knots in a decent breeze, but was several times clocked at better than 14 knots and once passed a U.S. Coast

Guard vessel doing 16 knots. The rest of it is anecdotes and admiring sound bites: Willis Rhodenizer, a former cook aboard *Bluenose*, once said she sailed like a wild horse, a quote that has been reproduced in a dozen films, books, and articles. A sweet story published in the *Shelburne Gazette and Coast Guard* has the smell of apocrypha but gives the flavour: Once Captain Walters was asked if *Bluenose* could really sail as fast as was claimed. "Can she sail?" queried the Captain. "Man, she can sail like a comet. Did I ever tell you how she beat the Dog Star in a race across the sky? 'Twas a fine night and a boy was at the wheel. He hadn't very much experience and needed a bit of watching, so as I was going below for a while I said to him, 'Boy, keep her head on the Dog Star there and ye'll be all right.' 'Aye Aye sir,' says he. Being down below for a while I left the boy to his own devices and presently he hailed with a trace of excitement: 'Hi skipper, come up and find me another star . . . I've passed that one.'"[15]

CHAPTER FOUR

H E R

M A S T E R

a n d

M E N

*L*ate spring, 1921, the *Bluenose* at wharfside, taking on supplies. Her maiden voyage, first trip to the Banks, first to Burin or the Magdalens for bait, then to catch what she can. She needed to do this, for so many reasons. Pre-eminent among them was that she wouldn't be allowed to race unless she had been to the Banks at least once, for a full season. The whole point of the races, after all, was that they be between regular fishing vessels, crewed by regular fishermen. Without that, they were meaningless—might as well be another America's Cup. And of course while racing was important, she would still need the money—the shareholders wouldn't carry her forever, even should she consistently win. Her first voyage would likely be what they called a "shacking trip," filling the holds with a mix of whatever she found, a little cod, or haddock, or hake, cusk, pollock, whatever,

maybe some halibut; or if they got lucky, just with sleek cod, some
marketed fresh, the rest salted down for later "making," or curing,
their pungent oil filling up the puncheons on deck, oil "enough to
turn the men yeller," as young Matt Mitchell said (of course, he was
only eight in 1921, too young even for a flunky's job on board, and
his memories of these matters are from later voyages). Undecided:
the master will make up his mind on the Banks where and when to
set the dories adrift.

In all justice the sun should have been shining that day, for the
beginning of the commercial life of the future Queen, but this was
Lunenburg and the eastern seaboard and it was foggy inshore, it
almost always being foggy in June. The high hill of the town, covered with improbable houses painted in improbable colours, each
bump and dormer and corbel and piece of gingerbread tricked out
like a Portuguese wedding or a gypsy carousel, this high hill was
hidden from view. Only the chandlers' buildings and the lofts along
the shore, already old wooden warehouses painted in red ochre
and fish oil, would have loomed up in the mist. Lunenburg wasn't
like her rival Gloucester down in Massachusetts, a tough port, grey
and girdled with wharves, a wintry port built by a wintry breed
on the scarred New England shore;[1] this was a softer place, gayer
even, and bucolic to look at, though tough enough in its way; the
Lunenburg taverns were hard places for hard men, and many a face
got battered and bone broken after the black rum went down.

The familiar odour would have been there on the wharves, tar
and pungent salt fish on the flakes and the smell of smokehouses and
the weedy rot of the pilings at half tide, woodsmoke and drying
canvas and hemp cords, and mud. Stacks of dun-yellow dories on
the wharves, marine gear, ocean-going debris, old masts and new,
piles of rigging, hawsers, blocks, buoys, kegs, and all the arcane
gear of the fishery. The wharves slippery with wet garbage, bits of
ox dung not yet swept into the sea, fish bits, spilled oil. Half a
dozen other schooners clinging to the wharves, waiting, some of
them brilliantly turned out in the traditional black-and-gold trim,

others hard-luck boats stalked by the insurers, bilges stinking with fish guts and slime and meals that wouldn't stay down and god knows what sloshing around on a ballast of shifting "pobble rocks" from the beaches around the county, badly in need of a paint-pot and new rigging. Onshore, warehouses full of ropes, lofts for the sailmakers and the block makers and the rigging people, great baulks of caulk, oakum by the hundredweight, stacked in piles behind the blacksmith's shop. Hands going aboard, their "kit" in wooden chests, boots and spare clothing and oilskins, over the rail along with oars and thole pins for the dories, from piles stacked on the wharf, put there by the schooner's owners. Wharves crowded with carts and animals and deliverymen, fishermen and idlers and spare hands looking for a berth, maybe knowing that down the wharf is a schooner that came back a few hands short, flag at half mast, a signal to the widows to start grieving. The master of the *Bluenose* was nowhere to be seen, maybe below.

The cook, on some vessels still called the doctor in the naval way, would watch the barrels come aboard and supervise their stowing, a more or less standard menu that varied only slightly port by port: six barrels of "salt junk" (mixed pork and beef), a barrel of pickled pork, a tub of stewbones, knuckles and shanks with a few pigs' ears thrown in for flavour, hogsheads of white and red beans, bushels of potatoes, carrots, onions, barrels of flour, tubs of sugar and molasses brought in from the West Indias, as Jamaica and Puerto Rico were collectively called in Lunenburg, lard by the hundredweight, half a hundredweight of coffee and tea. And the spices, great jars of salt and cloves and nutmeg, sacks of raisins, and a barrel of hardtack biscuit, these days without the previously inevitable weevils. (Joke: "Which of these two biscuits will you have, with the large weevils or the smaller?" "I always believe in the lesser of two weevils . . ."[2]) Lunenburg beef and pork were renowned in the fisheries, fresh from the pickling sheds of "dutchy" farmers schooled in the traditions brought in from Schwabia and Montbelliard a hundred and fifty years earlier; elsewhere in the older days in other ports both could be years old, the beef "so hard you could carve ornamental boxes from it."3

The cook was always chosen by the master himself; it was too important a post to leave to the mate. A cook must be cheerful, always ready, strong as an ox, a good seaman (he must help the skipper with the vessel when the dories are all out), and a man who needs little sleep—he must be ready to serve breakfast any time after midnight, and dinner any time before. Breakfast was often sausage and scouse—a kind of potato soup with corned beef—and hot biscuits. The coffee and teapots must be ready at all times for mug-up, and he must know his way around breads and "dough-balls," or "doughboys," elsewhere called "duff," a version of the figgy-dowdy of the Royal Navy, great dumplings boiled with pig's grease, yeast, and molasses, and dumped into soups and stews to fatten 'em up. "Oh my," said a former Bluenoser, "we had one fellow, Clarrie Allen from Lunenburg, I tell you he could make good soup. When we were on the Banks we had pies and beans and hash and that kind of stuff, soups, kraut, one time we had a cook from up river there took a big piece of salt beef and I don't know how long he soaked it out and soaked it out and you didn't know you wasn't eating fresh meat roast beef. . ." A meal will take no more than twenty minutes at sea, if that, the men wolfing down great mugs of tea or coffee, vegetable soup with doughballs in it, stewed beef with potatoes and carrots, dessert of tapioca, massive chunks of bread and butter, doughnuts and ginger cakes. The meal is fast, but it must be copious and very good; the men will tolerate much at sea, but not a cook who is sour of face and a meagre hand with the spice jar. Good cooks earn their money and then some, and are paid whether the trip is a bonanza or a failure.

The master and mate and probably the second hand have already inspected the masts and gaffs and booms and stays and shrouds and running rigging, and have watched the crew as they furled and unfurled each of the suit of sails (nearly 11,000 square feet of canvas, now neatly stowed again), have watched the ballast rigged, the salt put in its bins, the ice from the icehouses on shore hauled aboard from their ox-driven boxes and dropped into its pens. Paperwork is done, crew lists and logbooks to hand, crew signed up—no need to scour the taverns for *Bluenose* sharesmen, for the skipper had been highliner, or most prolific fisherman, the year before and the word is out that *Bluenose* is going fishing just to get her ready to thump the Gloucestermen in the fall, and everyone wanted a piece of that.

She pulled away from Lunenburg April 22, 1921.

She paused in Halifax for a few days on the way north. Just as well: Angus had forgotten his charts at home, and he needed them to get around and among the Magdalens, where he figured he would bait up. They were hurriedly brought up from Lunenburg, and she slipped away.

The skipper's job was to get her there, find the fish, and get her back, a formula easy enough to state but ferociously difficult to execute. How he did that, well or ill, decided whether he was a potential highliner, as Angus Walters consistently was, making steady money for himself, his crew, and the vessel's owners, or whether he'd be better off ashore, in some chandlery, or plodding along a stony field behind a team of oxen.

Like all good captains, Angus wanted his vessel well trimmed, well rigged, well sailed. He couldn't do much about the hull—although he had influenced her shape, somewhat, and hence her performance—but he could adjust the trim by shifting ballast and cargo, and the rigging and sails were in a way one and the same: that intricate web of mast, gaff, boom, bowsprit, canvas, and rigging was infinitely adjustable, and the wind and the weather were infinitely variable, and keeping the two systems in harmony required deep technical skill and an intuitive feel for the "tuning" of the whole; this was Angus's great skill, the "feeling" he had for his boat and how she behaved, and was the reason he was so hard to beat in races, where there was no time for reflection, only reaction. Everyone who watched him acknowledged the speed of his reactions to minute changes in weather and sea, and they called it intuition, but it was really sensitivity in the service of deep knowledge and a quick intelligence. The crew, his hands, were his mechanical system, the capricious perpetual-motion machine of the wind his motive power, and how he used the two fixed his reputation in the taverns and meeting houses.

Fishing skippers were not like captains in the Merchant Marine. In Maritime lore, and to some degree in Maritime law, the captain of a sailing vessel was "master of everything but the weather, second in command only to god." But fishing schooners were more democratic affairs than merchant navies—the hands could leave when they wanted to, after all, though without pay. The skipper was rather first among equals, and both in fishing and handling the vessel, the crew obeyed his commands voluntarily, partly because they admired him and his reputation, and partly because they knew their livelihoods depended on their own good performance. If the skipper didn't find them fish, they'd not be paid that trip. The best skippers were therefore people with multiple virtues—not just fine sailors and intuitive pilots and skilled vessel handlers, but also fair men, with something of the diplomat in them. Fair but tough, and with guts: indecision at sea is soon found out and indecisive skippers never attracted skilled men.

Skippers like Angus were always attuned to the weather, watching the slightest move in the barometer and the signs of change indicated by wind and sky; a good skipper must know the run of tides and currents and how to find good winds and where.[4] He could "crack on" sail until the masts thrummed with the pressure, but he should know how much they could take and the best sailors seldom lost a spar: oversailing cost time and money, and in the worst cases lives and the vessel itself.

A hard-driving man without the necessary skills—a man who

couldn't catch enough fish often enough—would find his men impossible to handle. The fishing fleet was not the navy or even the Merchant Marine; when the men were recalcitrant, there was little a skipper could do. Of course, this being a rough living made by sometimes rough people, skippers could be found who were brutal men, and ruthless, and occasionally there were men who wished their skippers would not return to shore and on rare occasions made it so. Occasionally in the small outports and more isolated communities, Banks schooner masters and their owners would shamelessly exploit the fishermen, "becoming little lords of creation keeping the fishermen in deep debt that sometimes lasted for generations."[5] On the coasting schooners it was often much worse. The really hard-case skippers would make life so miserable for the crew that they'd desert before they got any money.

But none of this worked with the fishermen; skippers needed their skills, which could not be coerced.

The skippers found their way to the fishing grounds by chart, by dead reckoning, by the stars and the sun, and by "feel." Many were skilled but untutored, and didn't always understand what their charts were telling them, sometimes taking appalling chances with their vessels, their men, and themselves. Sometimes they missed their landfalls by a dozen miles or more, even a hundred miles. But their intuition was often superb. At least one old skipper navigated around an inshore island in a thick fog by hushing his crew, hallooing, and steering by the sound of dogs barking. As for charts—another skipper rushed to sea with his rolled-up linen chart but it turned out to be one of his wife's roller blinds instead. "Not to worry, he navigated to the Banks and back with it, only commenting on the flyspecks that seemed to cover the fishing grounds."[6]

What pulled them through, as Frederick Wallace put it, was their marvellous seamanship and uncanny intuition about where fish were to be found—they seemed to be able to sense them somehow, a dozen miles away and a hundred fathoms down. Their sense of location, of tidal and current sets, of wind, was guided by compass and chart and a continual plotting and replotting of courses and fixing of positions, all of it coupled with an intimate knowledge of what is underneath the ocean surface in depth of water and character of the bottom and habits of fish. Joe Garland recounts the Gloucester story of the "all time dead reckoner chap" Joseph P. Mesquita, an Azorean operating out of Gloucester. "[He] was once stopped by an ocean liner with its gear off that wanted to know where they were. He heaved the lead, he squinted at the muck that came up, rubbed it between his finger, put it to his lips, checked the current and his chart, gave the liner his coordinates and went back to fishing. He was half a mile off in 3,000."[7]

This deep-sea sounding lead was the captain's spare eye. Using it was sometimes called flying the blue pigeon. For calm weather on shoal water the lead was a 7-pound weight, in rougher seas it could weigh as much as 18 pounds. It wasn't so much a lead weight but a sort of cup, with the hollow at the bottom. The sounding hand filled the hollow with tallow or cold butter or whatever grease was to hand, because what was wanted was not so much the depth—though that was important too—but samples of the ocean floor. They "wanted bottom." The tallow or butter would thump down on the floor and pick up whatever it struck—sand, shells, sludge, mud and weed, or whatever it night be. "The captain would smell it and finger it and give judgment, using it to move pieces blindfold on his gigantic chessboard."[8] Different species of fish liked different bottom at different seasons—halibut only liked gravel, codfish a clean or sandy bottom, other species liked rocks or weed—and it was part of the skipper's job to take his boat to where the fish were feeding. "The skipper feels his way across the bottom with the canniness of a crab and the sensitivity of a blind man's cane."[9] Ervin Langille, a fisherman from Tancook Island, fished with half a dozen skippers in his time. Each had his favourite spot. "You'd generally go to the same place every time. You'd always tow a log and when you got there you'd sound for a hard bottom. If it were mud you'd

only get hake but if it were hard you'd have cod. Down around
Quero you'd have to set in fairly deep water, 60 to 70 fathom, to get
big cod. But around Sable you'd always have shoal water."[10]

Sometimes a captain on his way home would hit heavy fog or a
driving rain close to shore; a lee shore in a sailing boat was greatly
feared, and captains hated not knowing where they were. Many a
skipper cheered up his crew by taking a sounding, even in heavy
seas, and the information he brought up would tell him instantly
where in the ocean he was.

Once, a crew put garden soil in the tallow to confound their
skipper, but he wasn't fooled for a moment. "Glory be, boys, Nantucket's sunk and we're right over Mar'm Hacket's garden! Ready
about!"[11]

No fishing skipper could have become a member of a fancy yacht
club, Michael Wayne Santos wrote once. "But then none of them
wanted to either. They were members of their own fraternity and
no yachtsmen need apply. They strongly felt their superiority to
yachts in heavy weather."[12] It was a sentiment that influenced the
challenge that led to the International Fishermen's Races, and thus
directly to the *Bluenose*.

Santos was writing about Gloucester, where the class system
was much more entrenched than it ever became in Lunenburg, but
at least part of his assessment––that part that spoke to their superiority in seamanship—applied in Nova Scotia as well: fishing skippers thought of yachts as toys, not real vessels, and had small
regard for their "tenderness" or for yachtsmen's wariness of heavy
weather. Consequently, yarns about skippers were always current
in the waterfront taverns, where tales of derring-do to the point of
stupidity were the common currency of sailor's talk.

In the Yarmouth skippers' club, a famous hangout for Nova
Scotian fishing captains, endless stories were told of all the famous

fish killers, most of them from Gloucester but many of those Nova Scotians, the international boundary "being but thinly drawn": John Apt, Peter Dunsky, Angus Walters, Tommy Himmelman, Sol Jacobs, Tommie Bohlin, Marty Welch, Moyle Crouse, Judd Thomas, the Coalfleet brothers, Joe Silva, Charlie Harty, Clayton Morrissey, Maurice Whalen.[13]

Digby's John Apt was said to have been born in a breeze, for he could find wind when everyone else was becalmed, and he could use even tricky little onshore zephyrs that no one else even noticed. Hiram Coalfleet was known for running into harbour at 10 knots under full sail, dropping all canvas at the last possible second and coasting gently up to his berth with never a second look—he'd gone below by then. Peter Dunsky could find fish when nobody else caught a single one, and was utterly fearless in a gale; Charlie Harty could pick his way home in a thick fog through tricky channels with just a lead and his nose. Gloucester's Joe Silva was once challenged by Maurice Whalen to a race in a "fisherman's breeze," a moderate gale, and nonchalant Joe was said to be so confident he just chalked a mark on the gunnels a foot from the rail and went below to snooze, saying, "Call me when she rolls down to there . . .", for which he was ever afterwards known as Roll Down Joe.[14]

Whalen was famously unflappable. Once a man came bouncing down from forward to announce that the men in the windward fo'c'sle bunks had been washed out, "rinsed right off their bunks."

"The planks in a couple of 'em are 'most wide enough apart to let a good-sized flounder float in, skipper!"

"I guess maybe they is a little loose for'ard," said Maurice.

"A wonder they wouldn't fresh caulk her," the man said.

"No owner is putting a vessel up on the ways in Lent," said Maurice blandly. "Price o' fish too high."[15]

Another time Maurice, then only nineteen and a new captain, found the cabin run (the space under the floor) filled with water. He dropped down and located the leak: some caulking had been driven out below the waterline. He stopped the leak by stuffing his own woollen shirt and drawers into the open seam with the cook's hatchet . . . But he knew another storm would drive it out again, so he and the crew shifted tons of ballast and sailed back to Gloucester with her stern sharply in the air and her bow almost buried in the water, to keep the leak dry. "They put in some exciting hours, but they made Gloucester."[16]

The American writer James Connolly took a trip with Maurice once to Georges Bank, in winter. Maurice had an old vessel then, and was constantly fiddling with its gear to get it right. One day when the crew were out in the dories he decided to overhaul her steering gear, and took it all apart. "There we were," Connolly wrote, "a winter's day on Georges Shoals, one of the roughest spots of fishing water in all the world, a winter day on Georges, a cloud-cast day with a hint of snow, the dories away from the vessel, miles away some of them, yet here was this man dismantling the steering-gear of his vessel. I took a peek at the sky. 'Suppose it comes on to blow or snow,' I said, 'before you can put all those gadgets together again?' 'It won't,' he said calmly. It did not; but late that night it came a howler . . ."

Clayton Morrissey raced against *Bluenose* several times, and lost. But like the rest of them he was a famous sail carrier—a man who cracked on whatever sail he could whenever he could, and be damned if any man would make him reef the main or drop the jib. "Not the sort of dragger who carries spars away and bursts canvas just to show the other fellow how his vessel can fly when it airs," wrote the Boston *Sunday Herald* in 1912. "Oh no. He hangs the duds aloft until it pipes and pipes but lowers away and furls in the nick of time and fools the gale."[17]

Tommie Bohlin was another who pushed his vessel to the ultimate without quite sliding over the edge. Of his schooner, the *Nannie C. Bohlin*, he said, "I drove her an' I drove her. Could I make her quit? The man never lived who could make the *Nannie* quit."[18]

Captain Alden Geele, a native of Shelburne, Nova Scotia, was yet another, regarded as the greatest of handline dory skippers, landing more big trips of salt fish than any other skipper this side of the Atlantic.[19]

And then there was George Mackenzie, a beloved skipper from New Glasgow on the other side of the province, one of those who stayed in Nova Scotia throughout his career. Mackenzie was a colourful character even in a colourful crowd; he notoriously refused to take his sails in ahead of a falling glass, preferring to hang out his canvas until the last minute, and drive his ship under all it could carry. He never lost a man overboard, though he once leaped into the water to hold a man afloat, despite being a non-swimmer himself; and when his brother died on one voyage, he pickled the body in rum until it could be decently buried at home.[20]

The *Bluenose*'s Angus Walters . . . men told no great tales of Angus, but they all wanted to sail with him, for they knew he'd get 'em there and get 'em back "with his salt wet and his holds full." The men would follow him because he was a fish killer with the best of them—he was skilful without being reckless, a man who seemed intuitively to understand his vessel's capabilities—and their shares were always better than they could have been. But, as mentioned earlier, they regarded him with little affection.

The American naval historian Howard Chapelle, writing of the *Bluenose* in the aftermath of the international races, said she was "a powerful vessel, well able to carry sail in the hands of her captain, who was an aggressive, unsportsmanlike and abusive man, but a prime sailor." This "unsportsmanlike" notion was ridiculous, though it cropped up time and again from American writers. Angus took part in the races because he wanted to win. He was intensely competitive, and his notion of racing was the one the fishermen had always used—it was his boat, he'd do what he liked with it, there was no need for rules, and the first boat to cross the finish line was the winner, to take home the cash and a cup for his wife to keep flowers in. He cared more about winning than about how he played the game, as long as no one got hurt. It would never have occurred to him that this was "sport."

Still, the rest of Chapelle's assessment can stand. Angus Walters was aggressive and abusive, no question about it. He was a small man, but intense, with cold eyes, and his tongue was his sharpest weapon; many a burly bucko cringed under Angus's scathing tirades. He wouldn't tolerate disorder or indiscipline, and if you did something at sea he didn't like, you'd hear about it often, loudly, and at length. His means of command was the megaphone, and he had a fine vocabulary of abuse. He was not an exploiter of men—all acknowledged his fairness—but he was a cold man with a sharp tongue, and not at all lovable. Dory gear sloppily stored—he'd bawl you out. Not quick enough over the side—he'd bawl you out. Slow to reef a sail—the bawlin' would get louder.

It was the same ashore. He was not, to put it politely, a man comfortable in society, or even in the bosom of his family. The most generous assessment I found came from Wayne Walters, Angus's grandson, who said, "People always ask, do you remember your grandfather? Well of course I remember my grandfather. He was my grandfather—what's not to remember? But I was just a kid, and he was not a family man. The warmest thing my grandfather ever said to me was after I joined the navy. He said, come up to the house and have a drink of rum, boy." Other members of the family were far less generous, especially Angus's sons, who sometimes felt neglected and unloved. Several people recounted to me the story once told by Bernard, usually known as Spike, who was town clerk of Lunenburg for an astonishing forty-two years: "If my father had to choose between his house on fire, with his family in it, and the *Bluenose*, and he could only save one, he'd choose the boat every time." The story was always told in supposed humour, its intent to show how much Angus loved his boat, but it has a bitter undertone. For years it was a truism around Lunenburg that Angus had bullied everyone he met, and most of all his family.

By the summer of 2006 there were only four survivors from the *Bluenose*'s crew, and they were all in their nineties. Clem Hiltz, Matt Mitchell, John Carter, and Merrill Tanner all had vivid memories of the "old man"—and all of them are yarners of the old school. Clem is perhaps the most garrulous, but he was only thirteen when he served as a boy on the *Bluenose*, and only went out for one season as a throater, a man who slits the fish open so its guts can be easily flicked out. Mostly Walters ignored him—a boy is beneath the dignity of a skipper; the mate does whatever dealing with him is necessary. But Clem does remember how he was once ordered into a dory, "in white water, I didn't want to do that, so I told the captain I was going below to fetch my mittens, and I made sure not to come back up until the last dory was gone. He was some mad. At first he said nothin', but then he ordered me below again, to his cabin, told me to clean the thing out till he told me to stop. Well, the men was all back and the fish salted away before he came back down, looked around, told me to go. That was after nine at night. I'd been cleaning all day, had a longer day than the men in the dories did."

The others are circumspect these days, not wishing to tamper with a Lunenburg legend more than they have to, but they all recall at one time or another attracting Angus's wintry gaze; he could express his fury and contempt without saying a word, ruin a man's day without trying. Nevertheless, they all acknowledged his skills, and occasionally, when one of them won one of his still-chilly smiles, it could make them feel good for months. In 1928, for example, crewman Lloyd Heisler made his first run on the *Bluenose* as a "boy." He'd grown up in Mahone Bay and knew its waters well, and once during a run from Lunenburg to Halifax in the fog, Walters sent him aloft to see what might be visible. "I saw the Feather lighthouse on Pearl Island. I knew the Feather right well, I'd been out there lots of times with my father, so I sung out and told him. 'Aaah, the Feather,' said Angus, 'you don't see the Feather, you see your old man's dung heap.' Well, good enough. I know what I seen, but I came back on deck. After a while the skipper goes up aloft himself. By now we were pretty close to the island, headin' right for it. He didn't have the binoculars to his eyes too long before he called out, 'Haul her off! Haul her off!' When he got down on deck,

I said, 'What's the matter old man? Smell the shit?' He didn't say a thing—just spun around and walked away. But then he turned and he had a big grin on his face. After that we got along pretty well."[21]

Occasionally a crewman could be found who both disliked and disrespected Angus. One of those was Sam Whynacht, who grew up in Heckmans Island near Lunenburg, and sailed as "second hand" with *Bluenose* to the Banks on many a trip. He grew to dislike Angus a great deal, and in later years would relish telling stories about him that cast the old man in a negative light. One of the stories involved an argument he'd had with Angus about a somewhat cheap-looking anchor cable, which Angus refused to replace. It got them into some trouble in a 1926 storm, as we shall see.

Most of the stories about Angus, though, deal with his feel for the sea and for what his boat could and could not do. In many a storm, crewmen reported, Angus would stay below when it was not his watch. He could tell from the thunder of the water, the hisses and roars and creaking, the pitching and rolling, what was happening to his vessel, and he was confident enough that he not only stayed below, but snoozed until his watch was due. If she wasn't laying over properly, though, he'd know it at once.

Claude Darrach, who sailed in all the *Bluenose* races, used to talk about Angus's feeling for the vessel. "When his hand was on the wheel, he could feel the ship's impulse and would act upon it. He had a natural aptitude to recognize any uncoordinated situation and how to correct it. He showed this flair long before he commanded *Bluenose*."[22] All the ship's systems—the ballast, her trim, her rigging and her gear, the belly of the canvas and the way the wind strained her spars—he could feel in the vibrations of her wheel, and he would act with that sailor's instinct, born of intimate knowledge and deep experience.

"The key thing is that he was married to that boat," Dan Moreland says. "Sure he was competitive, a real fisherman, a real sailor, but so were many of the other skippers, and their boats really weren't all that different. But they'd spend a season or two with a boat and then move on, and they'd be racing against Angus Walters who had been on his boat winter and summer for five years, ten years, eighteen by the end of it, and he knew his boat intuitively, from the keel up."

Most of the excuses trotted out to explain Angus Walters's abrasiveness seem to mention the hardscrabble background from which he sprang. But as an explanation of anything at all it rather lacks plausibility. Angus's father, Elias, was not a layabout but master of his own fishing vessel, and as such would have earned a decent living; indeed, he was regarded as one of the best skippers fishing out of Lunenburg. Angus went to sea with his father on his schooner, the *Nyanza*, not because he was "drug into it," in the phrase of the county, but because he couldn't stay away. He'd been hanging around the wharves as long as he could remember. "My father rowed me out here [into the harbour] when I was a little boy, and I was aboard a schooner as soon as I could walk, and I went in her when I was seven years old, he put me aboard and I went from there . . . I knew nothing else in the world, that was the only thing for me to do." And even if he had been "drug," that was the way of the fishing world in those days. You did what your father did and his father before him; it was natural, and there was a pride in doing it well. No one felt exploited.

In any case, his brothers and sisters were from the same parentage, and none of them showed Angus's acid sense of the world. His brother John, another schooner captain, was from all accounts a gentle fellow without any of Angus's cold anger.

Elias was himself the son of a fisherman, Johan Walters, whose father had immigrated from Germany. Elias was at sea when Angus James was born, but that, too, was normal. It was June 9, 1881, and the fleet was at sea for the spring trip, as it usually was at that season. Fishermen's women generally made their own way in the world, and they sometimes felt their men were a sporadic presence in their lives, looming about in the backdrop rather like bad weather on the horizon, only showing up as occasional squalls with busyness and constant demands, to be tolerated before the familial gales subsided and the men went back to the Banks. The Walters family was like that.

Angus got what little schooling he had at the Lunenburg Academy, but went to sea for real in 1895, at the age of thirteen. He was a "boy" on his father's vessel, and started his life as a throater. The only other event that he remembered from that maiden voyage was a sudden squall in which the cook got washed overboard just after the dories were set on the water; the dorymen sent to look for him saw his hat, an English-style affair with a tight brim and bowl shape, floating on the water. "To everyone's surprise, the cook was still attached," and brought aboard.[23]

After two trips Angus became a header, the man to behead the fish, and graduated, again in the normal progression of these things, from guts to liver; he was in charge of the liver butt and its noisome rendering into oil. The following season, for the first time, he fished from a dory with dorymate Ben McLaughlin, an experienced hand who'd been with Elias for a dozen seasons. Angus was fifteen.

He went out on his first trawl in a dead calm—Elias didn't treat his sons any better or worse than the other hands, but seems to have made sure that the first time out would go smoothly. Instead, they went adrift in a dense fog, and they slept uneasily in the dory until midmorning, when the fog lifted and the *Nyanza* hove into view.

The *Nyanza* was wrecked in 1897, holed by an iceberg, but the crew took to the dories and made the comfortable row over to Entry Island, one of the Magdalens, which was only 2 miles away. The vessel was taken over by the wreckers and was a complete write-off.

After that his career proceeded as it should, with no hint of the fame to come. There were a few highlights: on his first run on his brother John's boat to the Caribbean, the skipper was washed overboard. Angus, as mate, took charge, had a boat lowered, and

John was fished back aboard. By the time he was twenty-four he was master of his own vessel, the *Minnie M. Cook*, but this was not particularly precocious; the *Minnie* was a small schooner from the Smith and Rhuland yard, and Angus took her to Puerto Rico and Turk's Island on her maiden run to pick up salt and molasses, his first chance to really carry a full press of sail, and he apparently made the most of it. He made enough money, and was successful enough, that he had little trouble finding backers to build a vessel of his own, and the *Muriel B. Walters*, named for his youngest sister, came down the ways at Smith and Rhuland a year or so later. Her maiden voyage was a seven-month charter to Nice and Marseilles in the Mediterranean. He skippered the *Muriel B.* for eight years, and was several times highliner, once bringing into port the largest catch ever landed in Lunenburg.

Meanwhile he married, for the first time, the nineteen-year-old Maggie (Margaret Alberta) Tanner, who bore four sons, three of whom survived into adulthood: Bernard Murray, born the year they were married, 1908; Gilbert Lowell (1910); Bernard James (Spike, born 1911); and Stewart M. (Stewie, born 1915, the father of Wayne Walters, himself a master mariner and for a time skipper of *Bluenose II*, the replica that still sails out of Lunenburg). The year Stewie was born, Angus and Maggie built a house for the family at the head of Lunenburg Bay, now the Captain Angus Walters Museum.

A year after Stewie's birth, Angus sold the *Muriel B.* and bought the *Donald Silver*, which he sailed until the war's end. Then he felt the need for a larger ship and went back to Smith and Rhuland to build the 170-ton *Gilbert B. Walters*, named for two of his sons. It was in the *Gilbert B.* that Angus challenged *Delawana* and eight other fast schooners in the first of the Dennis Cup's elimination races in 1920, losing only because he lost his foretopmast in the last few miles.

Outsiders have often looked on fishermen and the fishing life in the days of sail with uncomprehending admiration. John Quincy Adams, the Bostonian whose political territory took in the greatest fishing fleets of New England, was among the most effusive: "There's something in the very occupation of fishermen," he said in a speech in Massachusetts, "not only beneficent in itself but noble and exalted in the qualities of which it requires the habitual exercise. In common with the cultivators of the soil, their labours contribute to the subsistence of mankind, and they have the merit of continual exposure to danger, superadded to that of increasing toil. Industry, frugality, patience, perseverance, fortitude, intrepidity, souls insured to perpetual conflict with the elements, and bodies steeled with unremitting action, ever grappling with danger and familiar with death—these are the qualities which are called forth by the daily labours of the fisherman's life."[24] To a modern ear, this is over-florid and sentimental, particularly that "merit" of continual exposure to danger; a more modern rendering is the old Tancook saying "Fishermen have only two guarantees: a tired back and a wet arse."[25]

Fishing crews led different lives from their captains. Skippers tended to live in fine houses, and while they seldom became wealthy they usually made a good living. They had their own clubs, in Yarmouth and Gloucester especially, and were occasionally courted by yachtsmen who found the skippers' lives romantic and their vessels worthy of scrutiny. They had little polish but a great deal of capacity; and the Gloucester legend of the "Bluenose bucko mate [with] a roaring voice, blue jawed, cold eyed broad shouldered thug dexterous at throwing belaying pins and cracking skulls, full of picturesque oaths,"[26] was grotesquely overdrawn.

Most of the men were of similar character, but some were harder cases altogether. In the second half of the nineteenth century every fishing port from Quebec to Halifax, Halifax to Yarmouth, Yarmouth to Boston had more grog shops than groceries, and hard-eyed waterfront harpies were two-a-penny, sometimes almost literally;

seaman's pox was rife among the crews and every second house along Front Street in Gloucester seemed to be a whorehouse. Fishermen were generally exempt from the "crimping" (kidnapping) that was still a common way of rounding out crews for the windjammers of the transocean trade, but they would have seen it happen (a notorious Quebec City "crimp" once shipped a dead man aboard and the mate didn't realize it until he rousted out the hands to set sail).

When the greater part of the fleet was in, the fishing towns tended to batten down and ready for trouble. An executive of the fishing company Gorton-Pew in Gloucester told the writer Russell Bourne that "it was a disgrace . . . they closed the shutters of the city as thousands of brawling Canadians and off-the-boat immigrants roamed the street . . . If that's your 'golden heyday,' you can have it."[27] The sailors' dances at the Shelburne Odd Fellows Hall were notorious up and down the eastern seaboard as far as Boston for their brawls and hard drinking, using "rum that could be leaned on, rum to congeal the blood." And ugly on occasion: one night in Yarmouth word got around the fleet that "coloured youths" from a nearby settlement ". . . came into town at night exhibiting a degree of arrogance towards the white people," and the fishermen were asked to help run them out of town. Doryload after doryload came ashore with belaying pins and clubs and roamed the street, but not a coloured person did they see.[28]

Shorebound ways sometimes spilled over to the sea. Frederick Wallace once travelled from Portland, Maine, to Yarmouth aboard the *Effie M. Morrissey*, leaving a trail of long-neck rum bottles in the wake behind them. He wrote a ditty about it, prudently changing the name of the vessel to the *Mary L. Mackay*, just in case his former shipmates turned nasty. The last verse read:

> *From Portland, Maine to Yarmouth Sound, two hundred miles we ran*
> *In nineteen hours, my bully boys, and beat that if you can!*

The gang, they said, "'Twas seamanship!" The skipper he
　　was mum,
For he knew that Mary *travelled on the power of bootleg rum!* [29]

Fishermen, like all sailors, tended to be superstitious, a legacy of
the days when the gods themselves were as capricious as the sea.
This went far beyond not sailing on the 13th, not wearing coloured
mittens on a schooner, or avoiding certain words or deeds sure to
bring bad luck. Even onshore, two men walking together would be
careful to pass an obstacle in their way on the same side—splitting
up to pass it would inevitably mean a jinxed voyage. Some men,
to their chagrin, became known as "jinkers," men who bring bad
luck; once you became known as a jinker your life as a fisherman
was over. No one would hire you, or if someone did (maybe you're
the skipper's brother), the crews would melt away and stubbornly
refuse to sail, even when they badly needed the work.

Canadians, Nova Scotians . . . "To call a Gloucesterman a
Nova Scotian or Novy is not at all well received," Kipling wrote in
Captains Courageous, having picked up waterfront gossip in the
course of his research. And Frederick Wallace recounts, or possibly invents, a conversation between a British Merchant Marine
captain and one of his hands, Wallace, a Canadian himself, putting
the best possible gloss on the matter:

"Hard packets these Bluenose ships, worse than the Yankees,
they say," said the captain.

"Well sir, they have that name, but for a man what is a sailor and
knows his book there's nothing better nor a Bluenose to sail aboard
of. For bums, hoboes and sojers [slackers], sir, they're a floatin'
hell. They stand for no shenanigans aboard them packets, sir. One
bit o' slack lip or a black look and the mates'll have yer knocked stiff
and lookin' forty ways for Sunday."[30]

A "Nova Scotia tow" in Gloucester meant a skipper too cheap
to pay for a tug; instead, he'd unload his dories and have the men
warp the vessel from the wharf.

Sometimes the toughness was greatly admired. In 1909, the story of the Nova Scotian Hilton Acker was going the rounds of the taverns. He was a crewman on the *John Hays Hammond*, fishing on Quero Bank, when he was swept overboard by a rogue wave, dislocating his shoulder when it banged on the gunnels. He was dressed in full oilskins and boots and swept a hundred yards from the vessel, but managed to swim back, grab hold of the lee rail as she dipped, and drag himself aboard, boots and banged-up shoulder and all. He was taken to Louisbourg for hospital treatment; they bound him up and he rejoined the vessel the next day—couldn't haul fish, but could dress fish, couldn't he?[31]

Every year the "rip fishermen" would come down from Yarmouth to do a job so dangerous no one else would tackle it—fish for mackerel along the riptides of Cape Cod. They were poor and thrifty and honest and tough as nails. When they were in port they would send one man with a dime to a movie, and he would come back to recount the whole affair to the rest. When they wrote home, all letters went in one envelope to save postage.[32]

Yarmouth was tough, Shelburne was tough, Digby was tough, and they all for a time looked down on Lunenburg. The Digby people called them "summertime salt fishermen" who didn't dare the winters. "If a Lunenburger ever was to go winter haddocking and making flying sets he'd probably lose all his gang, all his dories and all his gear."[33] And on the Banks, Lunenburgers developed a reputation for tightfistedness that dogs the town to this day. No Lunenburg boat would ever loan another vessel so much as a half barrel of salt. (In the town's defence, this was more superstition than penny-pinching: to give away your vessel's goods in the middle of a cruise was well known to be horrible bad luck.)[34]

Men went fishing for a thousand reasons. It could be mostly because they had been hanging around the fishing wharves since

they were boys (in the fishing ports youngsters learned to check
the weather first, get dressed later), clambering into dories, rowing
about the harbour and sometimes beyond, learning the ways of fish
and fishing from the yarns that were told whenever two or more
men got together. Fishing was a family business, and a small operation would represent a hundred or more years of family experience;
skippers would commonly go out with a brother or two, a cousin
and a nephew as crew. Or it could be that they were told to go fishing by their fathers, who had been told by their fathers in turn,
because they knew nothing else. Or it could be because they had
no option, there was nothing else to do. You'd quit school as soon
as you were good for the fishery—there was nothing to be educated
for. "I had to do something, didn't I? Something for a living. Then
once I got married I had two, three and then four children, and
after a while it came to nine that we raised. I had to make money,
and that [last] summer I made $700, that was a lot of money."[35] Or
they went on a gamble, because their mates did. Or to escape from
a job that ground them down, or to escape a mounting tide of debt,
or to flee their families, or "because they knew not why."[36] And
they stayed fishing because they developed the skills for it, skills
that were useless anywhere else, and because they were their own
men, and because of the comradeship, force-fed by danger just the
way it is in time of war, and because life on the fearful sea was a rush
of adrenalin they could get no other way. It was why they loved their
schooners and they loved the sailing, because the vessel and the sea
could transform them from men with mundane worries into men
who could confront and triumphantly transcend a good blow, a
"breeze o' wint," a hurricane. Which is perhaps why, as Angus Walters once put it, even hard-bitten skippers "could get kinda sentimental about their vessels."[37] It was even more true for skippers
than for crew: "The vessel was an extension of the skipper's bone
and sinew; the hazards of the sea were a test of his personal character . . . Small wonder, then, that the love which often bloomed
between a master and his vessel could be as deep and abiding as

the love of a man for a woman. And that was the way it was between Angus Walters and the *Bluenose*. She never let me down, he used to say."[38]

To the men, it was a tough life, and a dangerous one, though not one without its compensations. It still beat working in the grimy factories to which their industrial compatriots ashore were consigned. The men were strong, the sea air healthy, and their "factories," not to mince words, were quite simply beautiful.

"They are all great seamen," James Connolly wrote of his beloved Gloucestermen. "All the greater, possibly, because they do not themselves know how truly great they are . . . They are also natural adventurers . . . A fisherman sails out not knowing whether he will come home sharing enough to make him feel like throwing five dollar bills to the wind, or whether he will make so little he will have to go in debt for tobacco and oilskins. Men who choose that way of living may be lost, as many of them expect to be lost; but be sure they will never die of fright for thinking about it beforehand."[39] And again: "The equal of that all-sail fleet and their hard-driving captains will never be seen again, out of Gloucester or any other port whatever; not because men will cease to be equal to the supreme demand . . . It is that the need which created those vessels and captains is ceasing to exist."[40] Overwrought, maybe, but Connolly understood something profound about the fishermen of the East Coast, whether Lunenburg or Gloucester, Maine or Newfoundland—they possessed an independence of mind that was the natural outcome of the way they passed their lives, as their fathers had before them, and their fathers' fathers.

It's true that many, perhaps most, fishermen learned to fear the sea, and sometimes to loathe it. When things were going badly every trip could be a fight, men against the sea, but the fight was hopelessly unequal, "for human nature was seldom prepared for the sea's unmitigated treachery: the squall that beat hissing and roaring out of the night; the uncharted reef avoided only because a bleary lookout happened to sight a spurt of spume tossed into the wind; the harrowing landfall made in a gale when a ship narrowly escaped being cast up on the shores of home."[41] As Norman Duncan put it in his writing from Newfoundland: "Eternal in might and malignance is the sea . . . and it shall endure until the wreck of the world."

A fishing vessel didn't have the formal port and starboard watches of the transoceanic freighters or the clippers. There were smaller watches, and lookouts at the masthead, and of course the helmsman, but fishing was their job, not getting themselves there and back. Still, when sails are to be set or reefed or furled everyone rolls out to help, no matter the time and no matter what watch. "Never take all your clothes off in a vessel," Frederick Wallace was told on his first voyage out, "you never know when you have to turn out in a hurry. And always keep your boots, coat and oilskins ready to pull on."[42] It was an integral part of the egalitarian nature of the Lunenburg fisheries that all hands rousted out whenever a job needed to be done that the man on watch couldn't manage himself. Even if it was only the stowing of a jib, a task that needed three men, not sixteen, all hands were called and all went up on deck. That way, they could be sure that no person was unduly favoured by being permitted to sleep in, or remain below—no favouritism, no rankings, no hierarchy. Except the cook, of course—the cook's work was too important to be interrupted by mundane matters like trying to save the vessel in a storm—many a time the cook's stewpot would be on the hot stove even in a bad gale, the cook holding on with one hand and stirring with the other, and often when a schooner went over on her beam ends, scalding water and live coals would scatter across the fo'c'sle (though soon put out by the water that would inevitably come down the hatchway).

Fishermen had to trust each other. There was no other course, and so slackers and idlers were not tolerated. Youngsters had to clue in fast. The old-timers would show them how to do something, but they'd only show it once. "After that, they learned or stayed home. 'You wanted to be as good as the other guy.' They could find out in no time at all whether you knew your business. If you did, it mattered not whence you came."[43] And, "At sea, any window dressing or dry rot in a person's character is quickly exposed."[44]

It is why you can believe Angus Walters when he said, "I never wanted to be better than any other man. I just wanted to be as good."

In 1922, *The Atlantic Fisherman* unselfconsciously published a poem, true to the spirit:

> *The rules whut there is are fair and square*
> *Each man is expected to do his share*
> *Ef he don't wa'al sumbody parts his hair*
> *Fer that is the fisherman's way*

> *They don't stop to figger out which is worst*
> *To swamp or go down or die of thirst*
> *but say damn the man thet gives in first*
> *Fer that is the fisherman's way.*[45]

At sea, the fishermen had a set of skills that were necessary, unique, and a source of immense pride. Onshore, they frequently couldn't cope. Onshore, these skills had no value, and the men seemed merely crude. Dockside harlots easily parted them from their money, and so did the tavern keepers and the grifters who hung around the wharves waiting for the hands to be paid off. They "survived the sea only to drown on shore."[46] In the end, they might have no choice but to sign on again with another skipper, and go back to sea.

It was why the advent of motor vessels, which threatened to turn them from skilled workmen with a sturdy independence into unskilled and expendable hired labour, were such a threat. It was why the monopoly capitalists and the rise of the corporations brought out their deepest dismay and anger. It was why they so easily bought into the stories that appeared so regularly from James Connolly and Frederick Wallace and others—because the life was what it was, the fishermen came to believe in their own legends, and tried to live up to them, cherishing every comparison between themselves and the free-ranging cowboys of the already vanished West. It was also why Lunenburg and Gloucester and the other fishing towns so eagerly embraced the International Fishermen's Races, which turned them in a time of high anxiety into celebrities, celebrated for their high daring and great skill.

Just as those great skills were not really needed anymore.

H E R

F I R S T

R I V A L S

*T*he *Bluenose* wasn't the only Canadian challenger under
construction in 1921. Even before she was conceived,
Shelburne's mayor, Amos Pentz, one of the most prolific vessel designers in Canada and a man with close ties to New
England, came up with the notion of building the "best boat
Canada ever had" to challenge for the Dennis Cup. It would be
built entirely with local materials (in this case "local" being defined
as Shelburne County, two counties down the south shore from
Lunenburg), would be constructed at the McGill Company's yard
in Shelburne, and would be skippered by a Shelburne fisherman,
Captain Josiah Conrad. The only thing not local about her would
be her name. She'd not be called *Shelburne* but *Canadia*, a nice
burst of national feeling on Pentz's part.

Pentz was not a yachting man but a fisherman, and the design
he came up with was elegant enough, with lines rakish enough for
speed, but nevertheless a sturdy fishing vessel down to her home-
grown keel. He'd taken seriously the notion that the races were to
be for and between real fishermen, and he wanted no truck with a

yachting schooner, later a classic Shelburne knock against *Bluenose*, at least until she'd won enough races to be considered unassailable. The only non-classic thing about *Canadia* was her size: she was much bigger than Pentz's previous designs, coming in at 116 feet at the waterline, in compliance with what Pentz thought to be the revised Deed of Gift's specifications.

She was already ribbed up and her planking started when a copy of the revised and updated Deed of Gift was delivered to her owners. The allowable length was now to be 150 feet on deck, but the maximum waterline length was unchanged at 112 feet. *Canadia* was 4 feet too long.

In vain, Pentz and Conrad protested. They'd built her to the rules they'd been told would be in force at the time, they insisted. The trustees mulled this over for a while, and eventually came up with an awkward compromise: *Canadia* would be eligible to race in the Canadian elimination series, but if she won, she would not be allowed to race against the Americans; in that case, the vessel that lost by the shortest margin would become the contender.

Another Canadian schooner, the *Independence*, was also caught by the new rules. She had actually competed in the 1920 eliminations, and had been handily defeated by *Delawana*. Now she wanted to enter again, but she was too big and the rules forbade it. The trustees came up with the same nonsensical solution: enter, but if you win, you can't race.

As it happened, Angus Walters and *Bluenose* saved them the embarrassment of fielding a champion that couldn't even win at home. The *Bluenose* and her all-skipper crew[1] took on seven other schooners in the elimination run. She was by far the favourite; all through the fishing season people had kept an eye on her, and saw she was manoeuvring well and sailing fast. Whenever she had "fallen into a hook" with other vessels sailing to or from the Banks or to Newfoundland for bait, she had no difficulty outsailing the best of them.

The race was held on October 15, 1921. Eight Lunenburg salt-bankers jostled for position at the start line, which ran between the Royal Nova Scotia Yacht Squadron and Ives Knoll buoy. Apart from the *Bluenose*, the *Canadia*, and the *Independence*, the contestants were the *Delawana* and the *Alcala*, both familiar from the previous year, the *J. Duffy*, the *Uda Corkum*, and the *Donald Cook*. The day dawned with a brisk breeze averaging about 18 knots, conditions that showed both *Bluenose* and *Canadia* to best advantage—both had been designed, after all, for speed. *Bluenose* crossed the finish line four minutes and eight seconds ahead of *Canadia*. Captain Conrad was disgruntled, saying later of his lovely new command that he felt "[he] had a dead thing on [his] hands." Her ballast was all wrong, he thought, and she had handled poorly.[2] *Alcala* and *Delawana* came in third and fourth. Two days later, in a 25-knot breeze, the result was pretty much the same: *Bluenose* came first, followed by *Canadia* and *Delawana*. "She's a good all round vessel, goes to windward well," was Claude Darrach's early verdict, and indeed *Bluenose* proved unbeatable to windward, doing in one tack what many others vessels required two to accomplish.

The American situation was more contentious than a few embarrassingly oversized vessels. This awkwardness had much to do with local politics and community pride, in an industrial context that saw the traditional fishing port of Gloucester being inexorably supplanted by the larger and more muscular port of Boston. The Gloucester view contrasted "real fishermen" (their own), in real working vessels, sailing from a real port, with the industrial capitalists of Boston and their "money syndicates"—syndicates that rumour said were vying to build a "yachting schooner" faster than anything yet afloat. Never mind that the Canadian example of the purpose-built *Bluenose* suggested that the old-fashioned notion of taking a real working fisherman from the Banks and entering her in the races was already obsolete. To Gloucester, at least at that time, Boston was the enemy, not Lunenburg. To them, the *Esperanto*, the hero of 1920, came to represent an ideal not again to be attained.

Gloucester had entered *Esperanto* against Lunenburg's *Delawana* mostly because she happened to be there at the right time—as already recounted, the races she won almost didn't happen. But her victory unleashed an emotion in Gloucester that immediately made her a symbol of everything that was clean and pure; suddenly the races set in motion by Senator Dennis became sacrosanct, a series to be cherished for its purity of motive and authenticity of execution. All of which explains the furious controversy over the Starling Burgess–designed vessel *Mayflower*, whose hull was then being framed up in Boston.

A Boston syndicate, as Gloucester had feared, had hired Burgess to design a vessel to beat whatever contender Gloucester put forward, which would then go on to beat the Canadian challenger. None of this was very different from what had happened in Halifax. Dennis and his people had, after all, hired a yacht designer to build a vessel to win, a vessel that could fish, yes, but whose primary job would be to restore national pride. Boston's attempt was no different. But the storm of protest that followed was.

What was the complaint? No one doubted that the *Mayflower* was a beauty, nor that she was an able vessel: "She was a pretty vessel and smart under sail," as Claude Darrach put it. ". . . [but] fate ruled she was too much a yacht; this was strictly a matter of opinion." Actually, it was not fate at all but seedy politics that made the ruling, egged on by Gloucester and abetted by the Canadians.

The *Mayflower* was different, no doubt about it. She cost $52,000 to build, for one thing—and if the Deed of Gift wanted to encourage the industry to build better schooners, "of the best possible type of craft in pursuit of the industry," then building an extravagantly expensive racing schooner seemed an odd way to go about it. She did look a little different. There were rigging features that were novel for a fishing schooner. She had a yachtlike martingale, upswept spreaders called "whisker spreaders," wire-running rigging and other things, "some very gaudy features," as Dan Moreland put it. Why, she even had 3,000 extra trunnels for strength! She was narrow, deep and fast, with a rakish look.

The squawking from Gloucester (and from Canada) was unremitting. This was not a fishing schooner but a racing yacht in fishermen's clothing, designed for speed and not for fishing. Also, she was a foot too long (true enough, but the designers chopped a foot off before she was finished, which allowed her to comply). The *Halifax Herald* sniffed that "if she were allowed to race, it would mean the spirit of the competition was compromised, and it would become just another America's Cup." The paper called her "a schooner yacht," which they said was the designation written on the drawings of her sailplan. More outrageous yet, she was not owned by fishermen or a fishing company but by a syndicate of wealthy yachtsmen.

The truth was, the *Mayflower* was not at all "a plain and simple yacht," as the *Halifax Herald* called her, and was no more anomalous to the fishing schooners of her day than *Bluenose* was; Thomas McManus's *Fredonia* and *Carrie Phillips* in their day were as much, if not more radically, different, as we shall see, and no one dismissed them as "not real fishermen." The *Fredonia*, one of the most famous (and successful) fishing schooners of all time, had even spent a year as industrialist Malcolm Forbes's yacht, and no one had turned a hair. As to the charge that *Mayflower* was really a yacht and had no cargo capacity for fish, this was false. She could carry 400,000 pounds of fish, a quarter bigger than *Esperanto*'s biggest load, and almost as big as *Bluenose*'s. And she ended up fishing profitably for almost eighteen years.

Nowhere, Boston's *Mayflower* backers pointed out, did the rules talk about a vessel's looks; she didn't have to look like a fishing schooner, only to be one. None of this changed any minds in Gloucester.

The real reason was politics, and Gloucester's resentment of Boston. The races were supposed to be between Lunenburg and Gloucester, after all, the two places in the world with the richest traditions in the industry and the deepest reservoirs of traditional skills. The races should be between traditional fishing schooners, manned by authentic fishermen, from those two towns. Now Boston's money was pushing in where it was not wanted.

Worse, no one in Gloucester believed that any of their vessels would be able to beat the *Mayflower*, and so that lovely boat became a symbol of everything that was going wrong—the growing obsolescence of the all-sail schooner, the emerging dominance of Boston in the industry as symbolized by the Bay State Fishing Company and its monopolistic tendencies; purpose-built racers were a travesty of the spirit of the competition . . . And so on and so on—the list of accusations was long and occasionally ludicrously trivial. Why, *Mayflower* didn't even carry a traditional anchor! There was considerable talk that Gloucester should boycott the races altogether rather than enter a competition in which *Mayflower* had a part.

Just as the uproar was reaching a crescendo, news came that the *Esperanto*, which by now was rapidly becoming the prime symbol of how things should properly be done, had struck the submerged wreckage of the *State of Virginia* off Sable Island, and had sunk. The crew had gotten away in the boat's dories and made it to the island, where they were looked after by the Humane Establishment, set up there for just such a purpose; they were later picked up by a passing Gloucester schooner, the *Elsie*.

This loss was a disaster. Gloucester's hopes had been pinned on banning *Mayflower* and once again racing *Esperanto*, and now *Esperanto* was gone. The first instinct was salvage—perhaps she could be raised and repaired? Several attempts were made, and she was actually floated onto pontoons several times, but each time she got away and slipped back into the shallow waters off Sable Island's treacherous sandbars. The final attempt caused so much damage to the sunken vessel that the salvage crew returned home and reported that nothing further could be done.

Meanwhile the *Mayflower* contretemps was continuing. A huge crowd of cheering Bostonians, as well as Gloucestermen, turned out for her launching in Essex on April 12, 1921, and to Gloucester's intense irritation, Charlie Harty, the man who had "found" *Esperanto* for the 1920 races, declared her "the finest vessel built on this shore."

Then word came that a Canadian delegation had been imported by "the Boston men" to look over *Mayflower* and rule on her eligibility. Among them was Hugh Silver, who was wined and dined at the Parker House Hotel before being taken down to the wharf for a look-see. Silver was, not coincidentally, chairman of the International Committee at this point. He basically told everybody that it was none of his business: "My information is that there is no material difference in the construction of this boat as compared to other United States fishing vessels. Whether she will be eligible as a defender of the international trophy is entirely in the hands of the committee in charge of the United States elimination race . . .just as the Canadian committee will decide what vessels shall enter the elimination race at Halifax."[3]

Gloucester was furious, and more than one reference to Silver's Pontius Pilate–like behaviour made its way into the local newspapers. The town watched *Mayflower*'s leisurely departure for the Banks for the requisite fishing trip with mounting indignation. That *Mayflower* put into Gloucester on the way didn't much help. They followed her progress towards the Banks, and reported on her ports of call along the way—Shelburne and Canso in Nova Scotia, Souris in Prince Edward Island, Port de l'Entreé on the Magdalen Islands, seizing on this leisurely progress as a backdoor way of getting the *Mayflower* disqualified. She had left Boston on

April 28, a couple of days before the Deed of Gift's deadline for eligibility, but her many stops along the way disqualified her, Gloucester maintained: the rules said that she had to have left "her last port of departure" not later than April 30. None of this worked.

So great was the indignation that Gloucester decided to bow out of the elimination races altogether. Better not to race at all than to risk losing to such a travesty. Since none of the Gloucester schooners appeared to race against her, the *Mayflower* was declared the nominee.

The rumour went around both Boston and Gloucester that Angus Walters and the *Bluenose* would boycott the races should *Mayflower* show up as the American defender. This was almost certainly floated by the Gloucester committee under Wilmot Reed and was almost certainly false. Walters later told whoever would listen that he'd seen the *Mayflower* when she'd been hauled out and would have been happy to take her on. "I told the committee that, but they wouldn't listen." He was also quoted as saying, "If that goddamn vessel can beat the *Bluenose* I don't know nothin' about a vessel," and whether he'd actually said this is doubtful, but it would certainly be in character. Abrasive and "unsportsmanlike" he might be, but as Silver Donald Cameron put it, he was never a man to value a cheap victory, and he'd be more likely to want to test his skills and his boat against her than to ban her outright.

He wasn't to get the chance. Wilmot Reed urged the Canadians to lodge "a sufficiently large protest" against the *Mayflower*, and in September his urgings were acceded to when the International Trustees abruptly banned the vessel as a contestant. Hugh Silver, despite his earlier declaration, went along with the decision and, in his capacity as committee chairman, signed the banning order. The Canadians had decided not to risk a contest.

Exactly why they banned *Mayflower* remains a mystery. The committee was not obliged to give their reasons, and they didn't. Speculation centred on the *Mayflower*'s rig and sails; supposedly the crew had admitted the sails were oversized and would be cut down when she went fishing, but this made no sense: *Bluenose*'s total sail area was actually larger than *Mayflower*'s by about 200 square feet. The real reason must be this notion that the *Mayflower* was more yacht than fisherman and was therefore a "freak" under the Deed of Gift. A columnist for the *Halifax Herald* wrote a piece in favour of the ban, saying that the vessel had only been constructed to race, not to fish, "and [this] action of the slick Yankee yacht fanciers is not cricket . . . If they enter *Mayflower* our vessels [should] stay at the wharf." Considering *Bluenose*'s provenance and Roué's Squadron experience, this is almost breathtaking in its hypocrisy.

As Michael Wayne Santos points out, "It is hard to refute the fact that . . . the South Boston Yacht Club and the Eastern Yacht Club [in Gloucester's Eastern Point] were largely responsible for *Mayflower*, [but] it is equally difficult to ignore *Bluenose*'s yachting connections."[4]

Boston, of course, protested, but to no avail. The city's Chamber of Commerce maritime committee issued a declaration that ". . . whereas several public spirited citizens of Boston interested in promoting the fishing industry of New England have built a model fishing schooner with the idea of evolving an economical and workable vessel which shall not need auxiliary power and is strong and sturdy; and whereas this vessel . . . has engaged in salt fishing the past season and is now fresh fishing and will continue in this occupation through the coming winter; be it therefore resolved that the Maritime Association of the Boston Chamber of Commerce declares *Mayflower* to be a genuine fishing vessel built to promote the fishing industry . . ."[5] This declaration contained no small dose of hypocrisy itself (those "public spirited citizens of Boston") but was nevertheless largely true. No one paid any attention. It was written off to Boston jealousy. And so the fact that both *Bluenose* and *Mayflower* were within the spirit of the Deed of Gift was completely missed. The Deed had encouraged the development of the most practical and serviceable type of fishing schooner.

Apart from that passing reference to freaks, it had said nothing about banning innovation. That was left to the racing committees.

All of which left Gloucester scrambling for an entrant.

In the end, five schooners entered the elimination races, all of them working vessels in the *Esperanto* mode: the *Philip P. Manta*, the *Arthur James*, the *Elsie*, the *Elsie G. Silva*, and the *Ralph Brown*. Several of them were more than fifteen years old. The winner was *Elsie*, an eleven-year-old highliner of the Gloucester fleet, under skipper Marty Welch. *Elsie* was small, only 106 feet on the deck, nearly 26 feet shorter than the *Bluenose*, but able enough. There was a nice irony to her selection, too: Marty had been the man to take the Dennis Cup home to America, and *Elsie*, newly back in Gloucester from two years based in Lunenburg, had been the schooner that picked up *Esperanto*'s crew after they were wrecked off Sable Island. (In later years, *Elsie* was the pride of the Newfoundland fleet until she was wrecked in 1935.)

Elsie left Gloucester to the kind of fanfare that had greeted *Esperanto* the previous year; she was escorted to Halifax by a U.S. Navy destroyer, and on the run up, Marty Welch boasted, she'd dragged her lead at 13 knots, not bad for a small old girl.

On her own way to the races in Halifax, the *Bluenose* fell in with none other than the *Mayflower*, which had been haddocking around Cape Sable Island and was taking time out to see one of the races. Angus was putting his boat through her paces, and had both her topsails and her jumbo set. *Mayflower*, on the other hand, had taken her topmasts down for winter sailing and was travelling only with her four lowers. Gradually she fell behind, but the *Bluenose* crew felt she wasn't even trying, so as a "contest" it was meaningless. Equally meaningless was James Connolly's later observation that the *Mayflower* had been taken around the race course on her own "and [that] her manner of out-sailing the *Bluenose* was scandalous to view." He must have known this was nonsensical, but despite Gloucester's animus against Boston, Connolly's pique at the *Bluenose* and her master was greater still.

The 1921 races took place in a fresh 23-knot breeze, and both vessels had all their lowers and topsails set, the mastheadmen swinging in giddy 70-feet gyrations, clinging on as the vessels bucked and heaved in the choppy seas. *Elsie* crossed the start line first, but *Bluenose* took the lead within 3 miles. The two vessels were neck and neck at the first marker. The second leg was beating to windward, and here *Bluenose*'s peculiar genius began to show. The wind had changed to westward at 27 knots with gusts to 35, and great ocean swells 25 feet or more were slapping at the gear. *Bluenose* was pointing higher into the wind and sailing faster under the four lowers, the staysail, and main topsail when Angus risked his "ballooner," a racing sail that was a sort of simplified spinnaker (these days adapted into something called a gennaker or genoa). The spars held and the speed increased and she pulled farther ahead, the boat heeling at nearly 40 degrees, showing half her keel to the spectator boats. Marty Welch matched Angus by hoisting his own ballooner, but the fore topmast failed to take the strain and cracked a few feet above the masthead, dropping the staysail and jib topsail onto the bowsprit, and crew members had to scamper to cut them free. *Elsie* began to bury her bow deeply into the water. It probably didn't matter, but Angus hauled down his own ballooner and clewed up the fore topsail so as to finish the race on more or less equal terms, but everyone agreed *Bluenose* would have won anyway. As it was, she won by thirteen minutes and fifteen seconds.

Angus was triumphant, but generous too, something forgotten by the Gloucestermen in later years. *Elsie* was a fine boat and Marty a great skipper, he said. "The man and boat that want to beat Marty Welch and *Elsie* have a job on their hands," he said.

Two days later the same progression happened. The wind was in the northwest at 12 knots, much more to *Elsie*'s liking, and she crossed the start line a good four lengths ahead. She held her lead for the first two markers, and it seemed she'd have a good shot at holding it to the end. Journalists following on various race and spectator boats reached for their dictionaries of superlatives, for it was a splendid sunny day and the two elegant creatures filled the sky with clouds of sail, tearing through the swells with a great hiss of whitewater. By the time they rounded Sambro Buoy the wind was better than 20 knots, and Angus was only seconds behind the little *Elsie*. As they approached the last buoy, the Outer Automatic, Angus seized his chance and slipped neatly into a small gap between his rival and the buoy itself, leaving C.H.J. ("Jerry") Snider of the *Toronto Telegram* to exclaim that he had shaved that buoy so closely "it must have felt like shrieking for witch-hazel and talcum powder."[6] He missed the buoy by less than a foot, by all accounts, and that was it. They were now heading to windward, and the *Bluenose* pointed closer to the wind than *Elsie* could manage, and crossed the finish line 3 miles in the lead.[7]

The town erupted, the taverns filled, bunting filled the streets, the *Herald* rushed out a special edition, and all was well in the Canadian world. At some point, everyone seems to agree, the *Elsie*'s owners and Marty Welch sent over to the *Bluenose* a crate of champagne. When it was gone, some old salt cried out, "To hell wit' dis apple chuice! Bweak out de rhum an' let's git down to some weal dwinkin'!" and pulled the bung on a barrel of best black Jamaica. Well, it's doubtful. There are many versions of this story, each of them slightly different, but it has the smell of a legend. It's true that most of the "old salts" racing the *Bluenose*, including other skippers, were men hardened to black rum by black nights in winter storms, but it's still doubtful. Makes a pretty story, though.

Less pretty is the nasty little joke allegedly told by a *Bluenose* crewman to Marty Welch's wife after the races.

"*Elsie* would have won today but for something in the water," he said.

"What was that?" she asked innocently.

"The *Bluenose!*"

Even though *Elsie* lost, the feeling in Gloucester was that it had lost honourably. Better to have lost with the genuine article than to have won with *Mayflower*. In Lunenburg there were occasional mutterings that maybe it wasn't fair, to take on the aging little *Elsie* with the sleek whale that was *Bluenose*, spreading 2,000 more feet of canvas. They had a point. *Elsie* was the last genuine working fishing boat, designed just to fish, to compete for the international trophy, and the races weren't even close.

By the end of her first year, the *Bluenose* had done well by her owners, coming in with a gross profit of $6,386.61, although they were obliged to cough up $433.50 to the federal government in income taxes, the finance department having disallowed the declaration of her prize money as a "tax-free gift." The department's reasoning, curiously, paralleled that of *Bluenose*'s opponents in Gloucester: the prize money was income, not a gift, because winning such prizes was one of the reasons the vessel had been built in the first place. In other words, the federal bureaucrats agreed that the boat had been built to win races, not primarily to fish.

Nevertheless, fish she did, and successfully too, bringing in 4,200 quintals of fish, more than 470,000 pounds, and she only just missed being highliner for that season.

Her accounts make interesting reading, the numbers to a modern eye remarkably small: for the Fishing Account, her expenses were $20,452.33, her income $23,314.31, for a profit of $2,496.63. In the Racing Account, she won $5,000 in prize money, and spent $2,496.63, for a profit of $2,503.37. And she made two freighting trips to Puerto Rico, earning a profit of $1,496.16 for the first trip and $1,198.50 for the second.

Among the expenses listed for the spring and summer fishing trips were these:

Spring outfitting	2764.83
Summer outfitting	991.09
Anchors	287.68
Bait	300.00
Salt	348.65
Captain's commission	224.91
Cook's wages summer	500.00
Cook's wages spring	260.00
Flunkey's wages	30.00
Sharesmen spring	2067.48
Sharesmen summer	3538.36
Header and throater	109.83
Fish making and weighing	605.17

For winning the Dennis Cup, Angus himself took home $700, plus $300 paid him to cover expenses.

The whole of the net profit was paid to investors as dividends. A special meeting of the board of directors expressed itself pleased, as well it might.

For their collective $5605.84, a full year's wages, the thirteen sharesmen routinely put in eighteen-hour days, thrice went seventy-two hours without any sleep whatever, once went through a hurricane transitioning into an extra-topical storm, twice more went through intense storms with mountainous seas, losing two dories in the process (but no men), got caught in two ice storms, saw a fellow Banker run aground and broken up on Sable Island, narrowly missed an ice floe or two, and each man caught and hefted on board some 35,000 pounds of fresh fish, and, at the end, professed themselves satisfied with their year's work.

CHAPTER SIX

HER

LIFE ON

THE BANKS

*I*f the men were tough, so was the job.

By the following spring, the *Bluenose* was back on the Banks, where the fish were, or so the old man hoped. The Dennis Cup was on display in Silver's store window in Lunenburg, and there'd be more races in the fall. Races were good, and partly the point, but fish were money.

Depending on the winds and what Angus Walters sniffed in the air, some days they'd slip a loop of rope called a becket over the wheel with just the jumbo up and hauled to the wind, and the vessel would steer itself. Or they'd "go jogging," which is a semi hove-to position in which the jumbo and the mainsail act against each other and cancel each other out, meaning very little headway is maintained and the vessel pretty much stays where it is. Or—Angus's favourite trick when the weather was good—the anchor was allowed to bite on its cable with only a riding sail in place for stability. Then it was said "she'd gone to housekeeping," and the skipper would wait on deck for the dories to go out and come back while the cook baked his bread and his biscuits and brewed up his tea in great black kettles.

On that deck, two nests of six two-man 16-foot dories, enough for the *Bluenose* to cover a dozen square miles of water in one pass. And on the decks also, in apparently untidy heaps but really quite separate and neatly piled, the rest of the gear that had remained standard since the classic dory fishery evolved sometime around the 1860s: for each dory, two pairs of 9-foot oars, wooden thole pins, a pole gaff, a bailing scoop, a wooden roller for hauling in the "trawl," woollen fingerless gloves called nippers, a sharp knife and a dory plug, which is a drain plug with a rope becket on its underside to loop an arm through if the dory overturned, a tin can with grub, a jug of fresh water. If halibut were expected, each dory would also carry a gurdy, a simple winch clamped to the thwarts for hauling in the fish, a killer stick for bashing the halibut on the snout prior to hauling him in, and a gob stick, used to thrust down a halibut's throat to recover the hook—these were big fish, often more than 200 pounds each, and you couldn't just shake them off the hook the way you could a cod. The record halibut was 700 pounds, and 400-pounders were far from uncommon. As *Bluenose* crewman Matt Mitchell put it, "Haddock and cod, yes, just slap 'em off the hook, because the hooks are small, but halibut, especially if they swallow, you'd just break off the hook. So we used this gob stick, a piece of wood with a V notch into it, and shove that down the throat and haul the hook out that way, for you'd never be able to slap a halibut off the hook. God almighty, your arms couldn't stand it, you just couldn't do it."

Each doryman supplied his own gear—oilskins (a full set cost $5 in 1923), his own oars, thole pins, and nippers. He was required to bring his own compass, but hardly ever did. The *Bluenose* supplied the dory.

The key to the whole system were the tubs of trawl. At first these tubs were just barrels sawn in half, but by the *Bluenose*'s time they were heavy baskets (in New England) or purpose-built tubs (in Nova Scotia). The "trawl" was a long line of baited hooks, coiled into the tub and flicked out as the dory rowed over its fishing grounds. This line was heavy tarred cotton, counted in "shots" or "shots o' line" 50 fathoms long, 7 shots per tub, making a continuous string of 350 fathoms, or 2,100 feet. At four tubs per man, that's 1,400 fathoms of line with about 2,700 baited hooks in the water. Multiply that by the number of dories, maybe nine or even a dozen to a vessel, and you could have 24,000 hooks in the water at a time.

The hooks were not inserted directly into the trawl line but into shorter 3-foot lengths of lighter line called "snoods" or "gangings" in Nova Scotia or "gangens" (pronounced gan-jen) in Massachusetts. These gangings were spliced and hitched into the back-line, or ground line, at intervals of between 3 feet to a fathom. The other end of the snood was knotted into a bowline which was inserted through the eye of the hook, looped over it, and hauled taut. In this way broken or rusted hooks could quickly be taken off and new ones slipped on.

The fishermen had to be strong—strong enough to haul a 250-pound halibut on board a small dory—but also deft and nimble-fingered. They cut their own bait on board, squid or capelin or whatever the skipper had been able to find, and baited their own hooks. The most nimble-fingered of all could bait 500 hooks in thirty minutes, but that still meant almost three hours of baiting time before they could even get into the water. And they needed to be even more deft for the next stage, which is to coil hundreds of feet of line, with a sub-line every 6 feet or so and each sub-line hooked at the end, into a neat coil that could be extracted quickly and neatly and flicked over the side into the water. "You had to be careful not to get tangled up. Oh my god, when you get a real snarl only thing to do is take the hooks off, and that's a big job, hours and hours of work. I've seem some skippers wouldn't wait, if your gear got snarled they'd set you out in the dory anyway for you to untangle it there, your gear in two big balls, hey, that was a bad day . . . No fish for you that day."

Matt Mitchell shook his head when he told me this. He remembered some bad tangles, he said.

The second day on the Banks a light breeze was blowing and the swells were regular, no more than 5 or 6 feet, and the dories were put out from the schooner in a flying set, that is, dropped in sequence overboard while the vessel was still under sail, until a long line of them were towed aft, before pulling off one by one to their designated fishing grounds.

"You put 'em over one after t'other, hoisting one dory out and over with tackles. In you'd jump, and your mate would pass down the trawl and gear, in he'd go and you're off while the next is lowered away, and t'one after that till all were in the water in the wake of the vessel. It could get real lively when a sea was running, getting into that dory, I tell you. My oh my."

The dorymen make that vertiginous, perilous drop in any weather but a gale, winter or summer, often at night, wearing thick inner and outer clothing with double-banked oilskins—two suits outside their woollen clothes—and loaded down with heavy boots. "Let them miss the dory, or let the dory capsize as they drop into it, and they would have to be powerful swimmers to stay afloat long enough for a shipmate to gaff them aboard should the tide sweep them away which it likely would do. And the chances are that neither of them can swim."[1]

Sterling Hayden describes what it can be like just before setting out, and he just a boy: "The [vessel] soars now above a hill of a sea. It ceases to rise, pauses and hangs, then drops down into the trough, smashing a hole in the sea only to be quickly flung skyward again. 'Oh now here comes a good one, boys, hang on you sonsabitches, for Jaysus sake hang on.' It's the cook who gives the warning, crouching and watching his stove. The men freeze, to bunkboards, lockers and ladders—whatever comes under their hands. She drops like a roller coaster, the wood protests and the foremast crawls under its wedges, and up on deck a cataract breeches her bows. The kid [Hayden] finds a place at the table. Across from him sits a fiery-faced man with bulging eyes who is wolfing a load of steak and potatoes and cornbread smothered in gravy. 'How you feelin', boy?'

'Okay I guess.'

'Eat up, boy! Eat up! You ain't et enough to keep a canary alive; eat and puke it and eat right away some more.'

'Jack, think we'll fish today?'

'Christ, boy, of course we'll fish today; and every day. Old Ben Pine's [the owner, back in Gloucester] been to the auto show—got his eye hooked on a nice new Buick—so we gotta ketch plenty of fish.'"[2]

Sometimes the crew would protest, usually to no avail. One Newfoundland skipper, told that the sea was too rough and it too windy to put out the dories, had himself slung over in a two-man dory at the end of 100 yards of line. If he could row back to the vessel by himself, it was good enough for fishing; if he had to be hauled in, he'd let them rest that day. He was a big and powerful man, and usually it was just "toss 'em overboard, mate."[3]

In winter they made night sets. As a skipper told Frederick Wallace, "You've got to take advantage of every let up in the weather then, and keep driving. We put the dories over any time after midnight . . . Better early, because if weather sets in the men have daylight ahead of them for fog or thick weather. I'd sooner be caught with my dories astray at four in the morning than at four in the afternoon. More chance of picking 'em up."[4]

Even when the wind was still, or as still as it gets in the open Atlantic, the weather could nevertheless be "t'ick." Sometimes they'd put out at night in what the fishermen call a "black vapour"— heavy black fog. Then the dories would leave the vessel with a lighted flambeau, a great torch with a 2-inch wick. "The flambeaux were for the dories to keep track of each other in the black night.

[Sometimes] the vapour was so thick that even the flare of the big torches could not be seen from one dory to another. The men then had to hulloo from dory to dory so as not to go astray. Hi-oh! Hi-oh-h! Hi-h-h-h! To be standing on the deck of the vessel and not being able to see them—it was as if a lot of dead men had come to life and were calling to each other in some vast graveyard."[5] Thus James Connolly, the romanticizer. Matt Mitchell, who simply did his job on the *Bluenose*, was more matter-of-fact: "When we were soft fishing [that is, fresh as opposed to salt fishing] we'd generally set out in the night. We'd set at night with torches, paraffin torches, we used to burn those all night while we were baiting up too, and that smoke would blow acrost your nose, oh my god what a smell and a smoke . . . Then at daylight you go back and cut your bait and then haul all the gear in. It'd be in the water couple of hours, mostly, depends on how they're bitin', but you never know, let it soak, bring it up, do it again . . . You'd want to run your trawl in the morning before breakfast, that was awful hard work. If you struck a lot of fish, there was no stopping. Start Monday morning don't get in till Thursday. Day time fish and night time dress fish, take 'em all night to clear the decks, then the daylight came again . . ." Sometimes men went for two days and even three without any sleep at all.

Sometimes there was fog, sometimes a squall, sometimes blinding snow. If the wind had backed around, it could mean a very long haul back to the schooner, sometimes making little headway, and in the end the dories might have to be picked up by the schooner itself, a neat trick of seamanship for two or three men, the skipper, the cook, and the idler, to manoeuvre an 80-foot schooner alongside a dory half down to its gunwales with fish in a stiff breeze and a choppy sea.[6]

Fog was bad, and there was almost always some fog out on the Banks. Some dories used a thwart and a killer stick as a primitive drum, to make a noise and keep in touch; others sometimes used a conch shell with the spiral apex drawn off to form a mouthpiece, a device that made a curious hooting, bugling sound that could be heard for miles. Most men just used their voices in long halloos. But the fog was disorienting, deceptive; shifting, smoking floors of water around the vessel, lines that strayed away to nothing, and air that melted on the sea 10 feet from straining eyes.[7]

Commonly, Matt Mitchell said, "You'd have to haul two three or four miles to where you set your trawl. Took an hour or two there, putting them over, then back to the vessel for morning mug-up. You had two of them torches, and if I was in the stern, the first thing I'd do is put the anchor over then I'd tie my line to that, 15 fathoms from the anchor, then you had to row along, but only so fast as you was heaving it or it would tangle or you would run over your own trawl and make a right mess. In the flying setting business you would generally set six or seven tubs a day, three in the morning, mostly every day six or seven, some days eight . . ."

If the fishing was really good, the men would bait on the run, in a process invented by Lunenburg's Ben Anderson called under-running. This called for more than ordinary coordination between dorymates. As the vessel moved forward, the line was pulled up over the bow, the fish knocked off the hooks, and the line moved backwards for rebaiting by the second man in the stern. It could take up to three hours to complete one under-run, but that way trawls could be tended up to four times a day.[8]

In the early spring they'd generally only set one tub of trawl at a time. This is because one tub could be hauled in quickly if a sudden storm or squall hit, which it commonly did. With two or three tubs out, it could take much longer and fishermen were notoriously unwilling to cut loose trawl and make for safety. It was part of the code: rather than reveal any timidity or lack of courage through cutting adrift their lines, they often kept hauling when they should have been pulling for the vessel. Besides, lost gear meant lost income.[9]

Ice in winter was always a terrible hazard. Roy Mason of Tancook Island, near Lunenburg, recalls how "once after a bad storm it took us eleven hours to come in for the five it took to go out.

When we got in the rigging was the size of half barrels with the ice. If we had to come any farther we would have had to stop and pound it off for fear of capsizing. It's not funny when you're outside trying to pound the ice off. It took Gordon and me the whole day to clean her. [But] we had no choice but to go. There was more fish in the winter so you went. We had the boat to pay off and the payments came regular."[10] Sterling Hayden recalls seeing a vessel with "her shrouds [with ice] to the size of a leg in a plaster cast, iced up to the trestletrees . . . ice on the tubed steel masts, ice on the forecastle head, ice on the wheelhouse, ice on the twin iron-hooded toilets that cling to the stern like monks. Black ice in the graveyard watch that lasts from twelve till dawn at last."[11]

"Oh god almighty it was cold!" Matt Mitchell recalls. "Sometimes you'd take a halibut off the hook and place it on the bottom of the dory and it would be right frozen by the time it hit the boards. We wore woollen clothes, everything was wool, wool underwear, wool socks, lots of time you couldn't wear mittens, what would you do baiting up with a mitten on? When you were hauling you were at least in motion, you were keeping yourself warm that way. When it was real cold we'd only haul a line or two and then we'd change over, so the other feller could warm up moving about. He was there settin' 'em in, no strain, and he'd be frozen . . . If it wasn't real cold you could go five lines . . . Sometimes you'd have a thousand pound to haul, and you'd have to haul the whole works up to the dory, all according to the bottom, the feeding grounds you were on. Haddock you'd haul in shallow water, forty-five fathom, fifty fathom. But sometimes halibut would be at a hundred fathoms, and then you'd need the gurdy with a winch head onto it, it would be heavy enough. With halibut, too, the slower you haul the gear with the gurdy the better the fish would bite. We could haul into the dory some pretty good fish, but if you got one as I did once four hundred pounds, you didn't haul those up. You waited for the vessel to haul her up directly. But you could put a pretty nice halibut into the dory. You'd haul it up and put its nose on the gunnel of the dory and give him a right good clip, and he'd curve right into a bow and the tail would flip up and you'd haul and he'd slide right into the dory. That with the killing stick, like a small baseball bat made of hardwood. His tail would curl right up, and in he'd come."

It could be messy getting even a 150-pound or 200-pound halibut into a dory—they were covered with black, gluey slime and alive with sea-lice. And that was a big fish, and if it started thrashing in the boat, it could do a lot of damage, knocking thwarts and oars overboard, getting snarled up in the trawl, almost knocking the fishermen over as they tried to pound it into submission with the club. A halibut heart, notoriously, could beat up to half an hour after the fish was dead, and convulsions took many a man by surprise, with unpleasant consequences.

The men would row back to the vessel when the dory was full, or if their trawl was all pulled even if there was not a full doryload. Dories were sometimes filled to the point of idiocy. One such came back to the vessel loaded with more than a ton of fish, to within a few inches of the gunwales, not more than 2 or 3 inches of freeboard left, and the men were up to their waists in fish. When water slopped in they had to pitch some fish over to make room to bail. The skipper was disgusted: "You goddam fools, that's how men get lost."[12] Another came back to the vessel not only loaded to the gunnels but towing two more large halibut besides. Dorymen were phlegmatic about this. Halibut were broad and flat, and having halibut aboard a dory was considered the same as having a deck—the water would flow right over them and off the other side. "Ye kin load right up to the gunnels with halibut, them big broad fellers, an' ef ye ship any water it slides right over 'em and overboard again without goin' down inside."[13]

The dories come back to the ship one by one. Only the skipper is on board, and the cook, and, rarely, a spare hand. The bowman unships his oars and tosses the painter to the deck; the skipper grabs it and hauls her in, never belaying it but keeping it in his hands—otherwise a sudden jerk of the vessel can cause a man to lose his balance and go over the side. The dory scrapes against the side as the men hand up the tubs of trawl. Then the skipper lets the dory drop back a little towards the wooden pens on deck, into which the dorymates will toss the fish, using a two-tined pitchfork. If they are fishing "by the count" they'll count as they throw them in. When the count is done the hoisting tackles are hooked into the rope beckets, bow and stern, and the dory is lifted out of the water and swung on board, settling into the chocks on deck. Anchors, buoys, and gear are taken out, and seat boards lifted and laid flat on the dory's floor ("racking down" they called it), then the dory plug is pulled free to allow the water that has collected to drain off. The dory is now prepared for nesting.[14]

Getting the fish aboard was only a part of the day's work. The fish would quickly spoil if they weren't dressed right away, and packed in ice. Even with a light catch—maybe one fish per eighteen or twenty hooks, each set would bring in maybe four or five thousand pounds of fish, and cleaning them would eat up much of whatever little time was left before they'd set out again.

The dressing was done on long tables called keelers. There the throaters and gutters would work, a quick deft slash with a sharp knife and the guts were yanked out and either thrown overboard or, if the vessel was by chance in harbour and dumping prohibited, into a bin called a gurry-kid. The gutted fish was then flung into a tub of seawater to rinse, then sorted by species and tossed into the hold.

Cod were treated rather differently. They were separated from their heads, for one thing. The innards were consigned to the sea whence they came, like the other species, but the liver was kept, tossed into a massive liver barrel lashed to the cabin house. When it was nearly full they'd lower a small stove into it and render the livers into oil. As the oil "made out" to the surface of the bilious

(TOP) *Bluenose* was launched March 26, 1921, slipping down the ways at the Smith and Rhuland yard in Lunenburg a mere 97 days after her plans were first laid out and the first maul was taken to the first timber. The harbour was full of vessels: the fleet hadn't yet set out for its summer run to the Banks. Schooners were two a penny, but *Bluenose*'s launch still attracted a substantial crowd; not every launch was a vessel built to beat the Gloucestermen and give bragging rights to the Lunenburg fleet. (BOTTOM LEFT) *Bluenose* was always thrilling to watch, and never more so than when she was leaning into her work and a millrace of white water was scudding the length of her hull, as here in her first race after her first summer's work. Of course, she won. (BOTTOM RIGHT) Gloucester's Ben Pine (with tie), a transplanted Newfoundlander, was Angus Walters's greatest rival. The two men respected each other, but there was no real liking, and by the end the acrimony between them was such that they spoke only through intermediaries.

(ABOVE) Hands making the jib fast in a gale, the canvas thudding and shaking and as hard as iron, a graphic depiction of why work along the bowsprit was called the widowmaker. (BELOW) The schooner *Albert J. Lutz* rail under in heavy weather. But the skipper, the imperturbable John Apt, hadn't yet deigned to take in any canvas.

Keeping lookout in a blow. Neither the name of the vessel nor the crewman on watch was recorded, but Wallace MacAskill has brilliantly captured the stoicism of the fishermen in the teeth of a raging gale. Such gales were common; it was a saying of the coast that a fair breeze was just a weather breeder, with always worse to come.

(ABOVE). Hauling a two hundred or three hundred pound halibut into a dory was rugged work, but if you clubbed the fish just right its tail would spasm upwards and it would, essentially, embark itself. (BELOW). A string of dories towed aft of the vessel prior to heading to their stations to set trawl. Some dories might row three or more kilometers before getting to work.

Hurricanes and "black fog" were bad, but so was freezing spray. Sometimes in winter ropes and cables could be as thick as barrels from the ice; in any kind of blow the crew would turn to with mauls to knock the ice free, or the vessel would risk capsizing. In this picture the winch has iced solid, the reefed mainsail glistens with a sheen of frozen spray and the jib in the background is furled tight.

(TOP) One job of the skipper is to judge how much canvas to carry. In this gale verging on a storm *Bluenose*'s upper sails have been furled and the vessel plows through the sea under the lowers only; in a hurricane most of those would come down too, leaving only a scrap of canvas. (BELOW LEFT) But in a "fishermen's breeze" of 20 or 30 knots or even more, you can crack on all the canvas she can carry; this picture of *Bluenose* shows her at her elegant best, heeling slightly to perfectly capture the wind. (BELOW RIGHT). Angus Walters was a little fellow, but when he was riled up he could seem a giant. This basilisk glare was not unusual; but no one doubted his almost preternatural ability.

(ABOVE) The *Gertrude L. Thebaud* drifting gently in Halifax harbour with a tug steaming grumpily inbound. (BELOW) The *Columbia*, in the foreground, racing *Bluenose* in their first matchup. The sublime *Columbia* was never really tested against *Bluenose*; the only series they raced was called off after an acrimonious dispute midway through, and the following year she was lost at sea.

(ABOVE) Angus Walters posing with the Fishermen's Trophy, which he retained to the end. (BELOW) This is one of the most famous schooner pictures of them all, *Thebaud* and *Bluenose* neck and neck in the final race of the final series, the last real race between working fishing vessels in all the long days of sail. Here, *Thebaud* is slightly ahead, but *Bluenose* was not to be denied and surged through to take the trophy for the last time.

mast in the butt, it was dipped out into water barrels that were stowed below. Back in port the schooners were visited by liver men, with their barrels in their dories, who rowed from vessel to vessel and bought the cod liver oil on the spot. The purified oil was sold to drug firms as a medicinal "lung strengthener"; the heavier residue as industrial tanner's oil.[15]

"Cod heads was some good to eat," Matt Mitchell recalls, "especially the tongues and cheeks, you cut the head open and you got those out they were pretty good. I never could eat the liver, though some people did . . . Mostly the livers went into the liver barrel with its fire, that was the flunky's job, to render out the oil from the livers. These were 90-gallon puncheons. I've seen fellers go to that barrel with a mug and take it and drink it right up, and some people would pop the livers raw, eat them right down. I drank so much of that cod oil when I was a kid it turned the inside of me right yeller. It comes right out your skin sometimes, and I think that was what kept us away from colds all that time, we never had colds. Sometimes it would render without a fire, by itself. Pretty bad smell, you, but the wind would take it right away and we never minded it."

In the hold below, illuminated with candles stuck into special holders called sticky tommies, the men would shave the ice with iron shavers, and lay the fish down, one layer at a time and salted when that was appropriate. By using boards as shelves and vertical divisions the fish were compartmented off and kept from pressing down on the layers below. Stowing and icing fish properly called for care and skill—otherwise a trip of fish could be ruined or its quality impaired.[16]

The fish roe often made its way to Europe, "where they eat that sort of thing"; the sounds, or air bladders of the cod and hake, were generally reduced to pure isinglass, which was used for cooking or for fining wines, again usually in Europe. Whatever was left over mostly went to make fish glue for carpentry.[17]

The first day's work would get done, somehow, and sometime after 9 pm, or 11, they'd turn into their tight, constricted bunks under the fo'c'sle decking, new hands as far forward as possible, older hands closer to the galley. Somewhere around four in the morning the cook would bang a tray or blow sharp blasts on his whistle, scuttling whatever dreams were then being dreamed. As Sterling Hayden put it, "For a moment, twenty men hock and fart. Some of them just lie there, staring out, void of any thought."[18] Then they'd turn out, thrusting their feet directly into their boots, shrugging on their coats, wolfing down a doughnut and a mug of tea and a mess of potatoes and hash and another doughnut and a hunk of bread the size of a small iceberg, washed down with another mug of tea, and up they'd go.

It was always a race to see which vessel could fill its holds first, "to get its salt wet," in the jargon of the trade. First full vessel meant first departed and probably first to port, and first to port meant best prices and thus more money for the skipper and the men. There was a derisive chant:

> *Hih! Yih! Yoho! Send your letters round!*
> *All our salt is wetted an' the anchor's off the ground!*
> *Bend oh bend your mains'l, we're off and homeport bound!*
> *With fifteen hunder' quintal*
> *An' fifteen hunder' quintal*
> *'Teen hunder' toppin' quintal*
> *Twix' old Queereau an' Grand.*[19]

That "send your letters round" was its own triumphant jeer—it meant, if you want to send a note to your loved ones, or to any unloved ones for that matter, we'll take it for you and they'll read it before you ever get under way, because we're there first and you're not. The dories would row around the fleet to see if anyone had anything that needed ferrying home, and they would chortlingly pretend to ignore the irritation their bland questions was causing, just as the irritated ones would valiantly try to pretend good humour.

Even so, there was a great camaraderie on the Banks, as well as a fierce competitiveness. There were forty-odd vessels out of Lunenburg alone on the Banks, and the place would sometimes seem thick as trees, a regular forest of masts. At the height of the season there could be well over 200 vessels on the Grand Banks, and on calm days and Sundays the sea would take on the air of a village, and dories would ply back and forth between vessels, swapping stories and boasts and trading tobacco and rum. Some skippers hated the crowds, and would try to creep away to a fishing ground no one else knew, but usually with no luck, the known fish killers being dogged by unluckier skippers, and even unlucky skippers usually had someone unluckier still to see where they were going. Kipling captured the spirit well: "The schooners rocked and dipped a safe distance away like mother ducks watching their brood, while the dories behaved like mannerless ducklings . . . there is no place for gossip like the Banks fleet . . . Conversation in a confusion of languages, every dialect from Labrador to Long Island, Portuguese, Neapolitan, Lingua Franca, French and Gaelic."[20]

Of course, if two vessels were leaving for home port together, or more or less together, real competitiveness set in and then they "got into a hook," as the saying went. No one could bear to be second. It might be two schooners from Lunenburg or two from Yarmouth, or one from Lunenburg and one from Digby, or one from Boston and one from Gloucester, or maybe Lunenburg and Gloucester, in which case there was the added fillip of international competitiveness. This competitiveness seemed inbuilt through the entire industry. Top dory was top dog. Even headers and throaters competed to see who could throw the most fish into the holds in a given time. Baitin' up was a chore made easier by skill and yarns that amplified the skill (if a nimble-fingered fishermen could bait 500 hooks in thirty minutes, some could do it in twenty-five, and were not shy about the told-you-sos).

And so no two vessels ever swung off for home without a race resulting, "in a fisherman's breeze, everything flying but the cook's drawers . . . How does she ride? Why, she shames the gulls!"[21] No crews ever went ashore without a store of boasts about the sailing qualities of their vessels—the adrenalin rush was authentic, but the real value came in the retelling and reretelling. "[They] would cool off afterwards on religion and politics," as James Connolly put it.[22]

Some of this was grounded in mundane matters of money. True, it was having to make a market that developed fast fishing vessels. True, highliners got the best crews and the best money. True, first man home got the best prices. True, the fact that the men were paid on a share of revenue was a clear incentive to be first. But the intensity of feeling that animated them was much deeper than rivalry caused by money. "Let someone boast of his ability to catch more fish than another skipper, or to sail his vessel better, and a rivalry is created which will cause men to risk their lives, and indulge in superhuman effort, in an attempt to defeat the challenger. This is not the sporting spirit in which landsmen know it. [A real distinction that was to cause the utmost grief in the fishermen's races to come, and cause Angus Walters to be unfairly vilified in the public mind.] Instead, it is a deep and dangerous partisanship, asking no quarter, accepting no excuses, refusing to acknowledge defeat."[23]

In the summer of 1922 the *Bluenose* was the third to leave the Banks with "all salt wet." But she was the first home anyway. *That* was something to crow about.

CHAPTER SEVEN

HER

DANGEROUS

PREDECESSORS

*F*ishing the North Atlantic was a tough job, to be sure—
the point has already been made. But the job was also
deadly, much deadlier than it should have been. In the
years before the building of the *Bluenose* these tough men died at
sea, far too many of them, far too often.

That the *Bluenose* was herself a superb sailor, nimble in a calm
and steady in a gale, was due at least partly to bitter lessons learned
on a sea of drowned men. Bitter lessons about callousness and corporate carelessness on the one hand, and on the other a code that
demanded both bravado and stoic acceptance, sometimes to the
point of idiocy.

Many of those deaths could have been avoided.

❖   ❖   ❖

On her summer trip in 1922, the last trip before the new round of
races, the *Bluenose* reached the Grand Banks on a dirty morning, a
sky of black squalls, heavy thunder and lightning, driving rain, and

still the men went out, for there were fish down there, waiting. There went Angus Heckman and his dorymate over the rail into the sea with fresh squid bait, looking to trawl some cod. The swells were feverish, whitewater whipping by, and they had trouble shipping their oars, the dory was heaving so. "It wasn't fit, wasn't fit to go. He sent us out to make a run—well, he didn't send us out, we went. But he didn't stop us. The second hand got to do wit' that. He thinks it ain't fit to go why he'd go to the master an' say, 'Why, I don't t'ink, old man, it's fit to go.' Well, he didn't stop us from goin' out an' it was too bad to be out. He should'a knowed it. An' the skipper should'a knowed it." But the second hand said nothing and Angus Walters, the old man and the skipper, did nothing, just waited.

Out they went and fished for a while, and with a doryload of cod a hollow sea broke and the dory dove into it. When she came up, half the cod were gone and there was water to the gunnels, and they took the trawl tubs and dumped the line and started bailing. After a while the gunnels came up a little, and the men grabbed the remaining codfish and fired them overboard. "I didn't care if we had one fish in the dory then to go aboard. After a little bit we got up alongside an' got aboard. Why, the old man, the skipper, he come out an' he said, 'What happened?'

"'What happened! What happened! If you want to put a dory out on a night like this you want to keep your eyes around, old man! You want to keep your eyes around in case somethin' does happen that you can do somethin'. . . or somebody can do somethin'. We almost drowned down there! We was all but sunk! We was there 'bout half an hour bailin' and workin' for to get the dory free. An' you fellers up here 'board the vessel didn't look down an' see us . . . nobody to see us.'

"'Oh,' he said, 'that's the way things happen!'"[1]

As the old fisherman said afterwards, deep from the code of stoicism and bravado, "Oh, that's just the way things goes from that . . . you come across some queer ups and downs in fishin'."[2]

And this in the latter days of sail fishing, when safety was—at last!—a factor.

"That's the way things happen," as Angus said. Indeed. The stories accumulated, month by month, year by year. If they'd been written out in fisherman's pencil in a fisherman's looping hand, they would have filled a fo'c'sle with paper, though no one would have read it because everybody knew it. Every fishing family had at last one story that ended in tragedy, a story that left a hole where once there'd been a man.

Everyone preferred the stories where someone survived. Against the odds, and at inhuman cost, but survived.

Matt Mitchell again: "Fog was a problem some days, oh my. I recall how one feller, Jim Knickle from Blue Rocks [a community a few miles from Lunenburg], got away in the fog, and it was real hard weather and I think it was 12 days they was adrift, in the winter time, and they shipped a sea one time and he lost his dorymate, right overboard, and gone. He survived and he's not dead these too many years. One time we picked up two men off a French trawler, on the Grand Banks, they came alongside and we picked them up, and they had been 15 days in a dory, but you know, they wasn't in such bad shape, we didn't have to bring them in. We finished our fishing trip and then brought them in. And I remember some Newfoundland vessel, down around Quero, around Sable Island there, when two men got astray. When that happens the vessel anchors and stays 24 hours, but in the end they had to leave, and when they got back to Burin a telegram was tossed aboard, well not really a telegram, a message, saying as how they had made it, they had beat the vessel back home . . . So they had good going. We've had fellers rowed in from Quero to Sydney or Louisbourg, that's got to be more than sixty miles, from where they were maybe a hundred miles."

In winter if a dory goes astray the men might get picked up by another schooner "or they might pull into Seal Island or maybe they'd manage to rig up a drogue with the anchor and oars and other gear—a sea anchor—and ride it out until it clears and a vessel sees them, or maybe they'll capsize or freeze to death or starve. It ain't the first time it happened."3

Many a man went missing. "Many a time I've had to haul men off from the bottom of [an overturned] dory," Matt Mitchell remembers, "and I was shipmates with many who were drownded. The very last trip I made that happened. I was never in a dory that was upset myself, but I was into many where we had the divil of a job keeping the water out of her. You'd try to keep her head to, you know, but . . . sometimes the only thing that would save you was the fish, she was so full of fish the waves didn't have a chance to get down into the dory." Very few fishermen could swim. The water was too cold, and they felt it pointless to learn.

Nobody liked to talk much about the hazards. "It was quite a thing to be in a boat wit' your brothers an' see a dory bottom up an' go an' pick up the dory and couldn't find the men . . . Back home, you'd be asked, did you have a dirty time, or, how bad was it, but you'll never come home and tell anybody that you have a narrer escape or if you didn't, you didn't tell those things, you forget."4 It was fate, destiny, just something that happened, luck or ill luck. "There was a dory, overturned. Two fellers and this sea came an' fetched 'er o'er. The one feller couldn't swim—an' the sea drug him away from the dory. An the other feller—all he could do was hang on. Just an unlucky sea—an unlucky sea come along. An' see this feller he wasn't lookin' you know—he had his head down lookin' in the tub coilin' the trawl. Just an unlucky sea, nobody's fault."5

Nobody's fault, but when "a man dies on shore, you follow his body to the grave, and a stone marks the spot. You are often prepared for the event. There is always something which helps you to realize it when it happens, and to recall it when it has passed. A man is shot down by your side in battle, and the mangled body remains an object, and a real evidence; but at sea, the man is near you—at your side—you hear his voice, and in an instant he is gone, and nothing but a vacancy shows his loss." Thus Charles Dana in his memoir, *Two Years Before the Mast*. Such a loss can be profoundly shocking, but they learned quickly to shake it off and never to talk about it.

For the families, it was very bad: when a man was lost at sea, swept overboard by a heavy sea, or knocked off deck by a boom, or lost in a dory, or in a dory that swamped, the vessel would come back to port with a flag at half mast, as the *Bluenose* did when Bertie "Boodle" Demone drowned in 1922, or Philip Hanhams was swept overboard on a winter trip in 1938. "Ah, there was a lot of scared times for the folks at home," an old man remembered in Lunenburg after the *Bluenose* had gone. "Times that wasn't nice, you. I 'member a boy of 19 once, an' his dory overturned an' he was lost, an' his mother saw the boat come in with the flag at half mast, but she didn't know who. They come in an' that's terrible hard for the families, they'd come in wit' the flag at half mast an' they'd go down to the wharf an' they'd know someone was gone, but they didn't know who." Some of the old sea captains' houses had a flat platform on the roofline that they called the widow's walk, from which the women could see the sea, where they could watch for the boats coming back home, watching for the flag at half mast. There's a house like that on Pelham Street in Lunenburg, built for a sea captain who never came home to live in it, lost at sea when he took to a dory to rescue a boy, his nephew, and never came back. Mostly the body would be missing, but sometimes not, and then they'd put it in the hold where they iced the fish until it was home for burial, but that didn't affect the selling of the fish—what the buyers didn't know couldn't hurt, could it?

Some survived, some didn't. Nobody's fault, as they said.

"The first vessel I was in was wit' Cap'n George Himmelman— I was wit' him for eighteen years. The one year in January of 1941 we was fishin' out o' Halifax in the *Lila B. Boutillier*. We went out in Emerald Bank for to set out fishin', you know. An' when we got out there, we set out two o'clock in the night wit' torches—twelve dories, 24 men. An' it came down a snowstorm and the Cap'n he changed ends and I didn't know it, an' I got astray in the snowstorm. An' it started to get real dirty then—real nasty, pretty heavy seas runnin'. An' anyway, me and my dory mate got astray. . . . An' we kept astray, like the feller said. They looked for us an' couldn't find us. An' after a while they left for Halifax.

"I said to my dory mate, 'Ernie Mossman's vessel lays there in about four mile to the nor-ward of us. I t'ink I'll see if I can make him.' But when I went there he was gone to Halifax too. I missed him an' I missed Clarence Knickle in the *Theresa E. Connor* an' I missed Forster Corkum. They was all gone in . . . I missed 'em all.

"I was driftin' around for nine days . . . for nine days I was driftin' around the ocean. An' I had nothin' to eat. Twenty-eighth day of January . . . every drop of water froze of ice. We had a fair load of fish but when we went astray I t'rowed 'em all o'erboard except for two haddock.

"So anyway—Wednesday night seven days gone, it was blowin' hard. Right dark . . . an' long nights . . . short days. I said to my dory mate—I hollered to 'im—I couldn't see 'im. He was in the bow of the dory. I said, 'John, I t'ink tomorrow mornin' we'll get picked up.' An' boys it was only about an hour after that a sea struck the side of the dory—it cracked like a pistol, and John went o'erboard. An' he went right under the dory. I grabbed him by the back o' the neck . . . by his oilskins. And I hauled 'im in.

"When he was gone o'erboard he had a pair of paddles rowin' for to keep the dory so she wouldn't get side to it. An' I had two in the aft for to keep her bow to. An' when he went o'erboard, you understand, he lost a pair of paddles. An' when I jumped for to get 'im, I lost my two. So I couldn't row . . . I had not'ing to row wit'. I just had to set there an' take the whole works. The dory was about—I won't say she was half full o' water, but she had a right good junk into her. Pretty near to the risins.

"John, he flopped himself right down into the water. I took my compass bucket for to bail, an' I freed 'er. I saved her . . . got 'er free o' water. That night it was pretty cold, I said to my dory mate, 'How you feelin', John?'

"He said, 'I'm gettin' warmer.'

"Little did I t'ink he was dyin'. I didn't know it. I t'ought his clothes was dryin' on 'im and he was gettin' warmer.

"The next mornin' just about dawn—you could just about see a person, like a shadow—anot'er sea struck 'er. John went o'erboard. An' he was froze, he must have been froze just the same as a rock. I looked o'er my shoulder . . . well I seen him for as far as I could look. An' that was all there was to it."[6]

William Dodge and George Bishop, from the *Lucy Edwina*, went astray for sixteen days, their tins of hardtack and water contaminated. Young Bishop died on the 14th day, but on the 16th Dodge sighted a Portuguese schooner, and was able to row over, where he was strong enough to clamber on board by himself. He attributed his survival for so long to his unshaken faith in getting rescued. Asked if he would go out again, he said, "T'is my way of earnin' a livin'. I'll go out again if I'm able," and he did.[7]

The toughest of all was Howard Blackburn, who was from Barrington, Nova Scotia, and fished out of Gloucester. He and his dorymate, Tom Welch from Newfoundland, were halibuting in January 1883 on the *Grace L. Fears* when they went astray in a snow squall on Burgeo Bank off Newfoundland's east coast. Welch didn't last out the second day, and froze solid. Blackburn kept rowing and bailing and bashing away the ice.

After a while his mittens were frozen solid, and he dropped them into the water in the bottom of the dory to take the ice from them, but they were accidentally bailed overboard. He tried his socks as mittens but that didn't work either. His hands started to freeze, and so he could keep rowing he curled them into claws so they'd freeze and he could still grasp the oars.

"I took to rowing again, and I couldn't manage very well at first. My hands would go knocking against the oar handles and pieces of dead flesh the size of a half dollar would come falling off. . ." After a day or so he was pulling on the oars with his bones bare.

The gale passed, and with the frozen corpse of his dorymate he rowed for five days to the snowbound Newfoundland coast, without any food or water.

There he was found by the Lishman family, near starving themselves, who took him in and nursed him back to health.

"They were poor," Blackburn recalled afterwards, "but my they were good people, very good. They took the wrapping off my hands the right one first, and the little finger dropped off. . . Mrs. Lishman took the scissors to cut away the dead flesh and there was a grown girl in the Lishman family and the tears ran down her face when she first saw her mother dressing my hands and feet. She used to stand behind my back and hold her apron over my face so I couldn't see her mother trimming the flesh away . . . they told me, we have seen many frost-burned men in this country, but you are the worst of all! By all signs you should be dead!"

In the spring he returned to Gloucester and popular acclaim, minus all his fingers, half of each thumb and most of his toes. For years afterwards he ran a saloon, and they came from all over to gawk at him picking up the dimes from the bar.

But he wasn't yet done. In 1897 he organized a Klondike gold expedition, and in 1899 he sailed a 30-foot gaff-rigged sloop to England, single-handed and fingerless. He died in bed in 1932 at the age of seventy-three.

There was one other aspect to his story worth noting: his pay was docked for the days he wasn't on board, on the grounds that he didn't earn his full share. The company paid the crippled and broke sailor a total of $86, some $40 less than his due.[8]

All very well, these stories of fishermen's heroism and dorymen's almost inhuman endurance. But why were they so frequent, or necessary at all? The ocean is hazardous, but does it have to be *that* hazardous? Perhaps, perhaps not. You can romanticize it, as James Connolly did, in the language of his more hero-worshipping time: "And never [again] shall we see the like of those dory men, putting out from their vessels in tiny boats to heave and haul their trawls. Their dories capsize in rough weather; or they go astray in the fog and snow. Five, eight, eleven days they may be away, with no food or drink: and then it is, when they live through it, that we get the stories that tell of human fortitude and courage almost beyond shore-going belief. It is a hard way to make a living; but we can save our pity. Toil is theirs, and suffering and peril: but it is men's work—not boy's or woman's or half made creatures."9

Well, yes—suffering and peril indeed!—but why so much suffering, and why peril so often?

Part of the problem was the dory itself.

Connolly and Wallace and Kipling weren't the only romancers; the eastern seaboard is up to the gunnels with romantic dory stories—a lot of romance, and an equal lot of cant. Some people, even some of the people who used them, considered dories wonderful small craft, stable and almost unsinkable. Except, of course, that many of them did sink, and hundreds more overturned.

The dory itself is a simple thing, put together with a few longitudinal planks overlapped on the flaring sides and with a flat bottom. As already noted, it probably came out of Portuguese beach boats, probably first adapted on this side of the Atlantic by Simeon Lowell of Amesbury in Massachusetts (the Lowell Marine Works is still there, having been founded in 1793). These "broncos of the seas," in Frederick Wallace's phrase, were all heavy and stoutly constructed, built by specialists who turned them out on a mass production basis to a standard size. Traditionally, they were painted a buff yellow for easy visibility, and each had a plug in the bottom with a rope strap on both sides.

So we think of dories and dory trawling as, well, quaint . . . At dory shops in St. John's and Lunenburg and Cape Ann, craftspeople build dories for show or for sale, and while they are real boats generally put to real uses, they are made of wood and nostalgia in equal proportions. Museums in Lunenburg and Mystic and Halifax and Essex and many other places have dories and dory gear on permanent exhibit. Dories are redolent of a romantic way of life, a bygone life that was somehow more authentic than our own. Which is both true and . . . and horribly misleading. For there is also another perspective, which is that dories were one of the by-products of the Industrial Revolution, and have their ugly side; they were not made to be safe, they were made for the convenience of the owners, and the devil take the men who worked in them and sometimes—all too often—drowned in them.

In the early part of the nineteenth century, it was all handline fishing from the ship itself. The crew would line up over the rail with their lines in the water and jig, and they'd catch plenty of fish, for there were plenty to catch in those days. It was productive, but not productive enough; the population was growing, and so was the demand, and the industry needed to grow with it.

More men was the key to productivity, then—obviously, if you catch your fish from a line dangled over the side by a man, the more men you had, the more lines you could put into the water, and the more fish you'd bring home. The pressures were obvious, and before long the decks would be crowded with as many men as possible. In this, fishing schooners were operated completely differently from coasting schooners. A coasting schooner didn't want many men on board—no boat has any more men on board than necessary—but on fishing schooners it was necessary to have lots of men in order to catch lots of fish. For the businessmen back home, the calculus was pretty straightforward: a side effect of having all these men on board is that you could have a big rig, more sails, and could go faster and therefore farther. Dan Moreland, now skipper of the barque *Picton Castle*, puts it this way: "If you have twenty guys on a 60-foot schooner, you can put all the sail up you want. A coasting schooner would have three guys and a boy, or two guys and a dog. But from the 1840s to the *Bluenose* era, the crews got larger, the rigs got bigger, the boats more powerful." Thus the industrialization of fishing.

This didn't help the men much—more men didn't mean more money each, despite catching more fish than ever. But it certainly helped the owners pay for the vessels, and improved their own catch, which they tended to measure in dollars and not quintals.

Soon, even this seemed too slow, and too small. Somewhere around the 1850s someone—no one knows who—had a bright idea: *Why don't I put small boats on board, and I'll launch them, put six guys in each and they can handline over here and over there, and we'll cover more water and we'll catch more fish.* So he did. He loaded a few rowboats on board, and when they got to the fishing grounds the skipper would put them over the side, the men would clamber into them and "fish like hell for six hours," then row back to the vessel. It worked, too: the catch doubled and then tripled.

It still wasn't enough. The answer was not more men—the row-boats were crowded already, and there was no more room on deck for more. Which is when someone—again, no one knows who was first—thought about the dory. Dories were ubiquitous along the shore. They were surf boats with a slightly curved but flat bottom, and that flat bottom was the key. Why, you could stack one into another! You could stack half a dozen on deck in the space taken up by one rowboat! You could easily carry a dozen dories! And so sometime in the 1860s schooners started taking nests of dories to the Banks. One-man dories at first, but then 16-foot two-man dories, a dozen of them, and soon a single schooner could cover a dozen square miles and more at a time with multiple hooks on long lines, in water 60 fathoms deep, and catches once again went up.

Production increased radically. Larger warehouses were built in home ports, which ratcheted up the pressure to maintain and increase catches yet again. Soon the mother ship began to get a lot bigger, because bigger boats meant more dories and thus more men. Within a few years the yards were turning out schooners up to 80 feet, 90, and by the 1880s and 1890s the typical saltbanker was 110 feet long, almost twice as big as they had been just a few decades earlier. It was a self-reinforcing cycle. The market demanded it: more, more, more. It was a classic case, a textbook example, of industrial evolution at work.

With the predictable consequences. Men fished harder and longer, skippers pushed harder and further and faster and more often.

And men died more often.

Dan Moreland, a man who has himself restored a few of the old fishing schooners, puts it this way: ". . . To go paddling out on the ocean in a dory, no question from an industrial point of view, it really worked. It increased production radically. But from a personal safety point of view, this is a very stupid idea. Safety was irrelevant. A 110-foot schooner was almost twice as big as they used to be, its purpose to carry more dories and more men, and with more men you could carry more rig, and more dories. Dories were the classic duplication of process. Fishing this way was incredibly dangerous. Sure, you talk to the old guys, read in the books, that the dory was the greatest boat in the world. Wrong. It was a good boat, and you could put 500 pounds of weight in it, and in the hands of a master it would be safe. But if you're designing a boat to be safe on the sea, it is most certainly not a dory. The dory was a compromise. What a safe boat would have been is a different discussion, but it would definitely not be a dory."

But dories were cheap to build, and trawling from dories brought in a lot of fish and a good deal of profit. If a man drowned, why, you could always hire another. There were lots of men, and they were cheap, in a way even cheaper than dories. You could insure the boats, and get paid back for their loss. You didn't need to insure the men. There were any number of those. Fishing—and shipping—was a heartless business.

It wasn't just dories that were dangerous, though. The vessels that carried them were deeply flawed too. "To Georges to Browns to LaHave to Emerald and Quero to the Grand Banks, [to all these] storm-wracked current-swept shoals have sailed more pinkies and dogboddies, more schooners and draggers than have ever returned."[10] There's an elegiac tone to these laments, but there should have been more anger.

The first boats to ply the shores of what were to become one of the world's most productive fisheries were shallops and ketches. The shallop, a proletarian name for a humble craft, was a little double-ended thing driven by manpower or by a single simple sail. Because they were open to the sea, without any deck, they were only good for close-shore work, and that only when the weather was in a rare good mood; they were not really seaworthy enough for Atlantic waters. The much more versatile ketch, the immediate ancestress of the schooner, was usually rigged with two masts, the larger mainmast forward, and had a single deck and a round stern.[11] They were larger than shallops and a good deal more weatherly. From the ketches came the New England "pinky," a little thing "with her kittiwake-tail stern raised as pertly as a pinky finger." Pinkies were the predominant vessel by the 1830s, and ubiquitous along coastal waters throughout the nineteenth century, and survived as a fisherman into the early twentieth century.[12] Ports in Maine, Massachusetts and Nova Scotia built scores of these popular vessels. During the 1840s the "sharpshooter," a hull with a straighter keel and a modified schooner rig, quickly supplanted the pinkies.

The schooner—the word referred more to the rig than the hull shape—was popularly supposed to have originated in New England around 1700, the name deriving from the Scottish word "scoon" or "scon," meaning to scoot along the water. More probably, the schooner rig came from England, which may in turn have derived it from the Dutch—there are vessels with similar rigs in Dutch engravings from the 1600s. But the schooner did come to its finest flowering in New England and Nova Scotian ports.

It caught on quickly because it was faster than the ketch and held well to windward, and so could jog slowly along the banks when needed—if you lashed the wheel and carried only a small staysail, you could head her up into the wind and she'd move at a walking pace with no man's hand at her helm, a useful thing when the dories are over and out; it was a trick Angus Walters mastered better than almost anyone.[13]

By the middle of the century, as speed to market became increasingly important, the "Essex model schooner" came to dominate the East Coast fishing fleet: "a flat-floored, shallow draft vessel with hardly any drag—reasonably stable to a point, but critically dangerous in squally winds and rough seas and highly susceptible to icing," in the north Atlantic a recipe for disaster,[14] "a bad lot," as Joe Garland put it, "crude, shallow, top heavy, dull to windward and dangerously prone to knockdown."[15]

"In the rush for profit and speed, new sails, of new canvas and even of lighter, more tightly-woven cotton, came into being. Jibs were set out on longer and longer bowsprits [that came to be] called widowmakers with some justification, and topsails were raised above the gaffs on higher and higher topmasts. Fishermen's staysails were devised, vast overlapping sails that spanned the gap between the maintopsail and foretopsail . . . But the ballast remained in bins, and continued to work as a negative force when the schooner was knocked down. The self-righting capabilities of the vessel were reduced to a minimum." The more they rolled, the more they wanted to roll.[16]

If a schooner fell over under the long blast of a gale, or if a great sea broke over the bows and came curling down the decks and pouring over the lee rail and the vessel lurched and hung trembling on her beam ends, it was massively hazardous. Especially if a skipper had carried his mainsail too long, for when the men start to reef or roll her up she can ship a great sea and wash men over the side. In high seas the great boom was especially difficult to handle, and drownings from the boom footropes were lamentably common.

The bowsprit was one of the greatest culprits. The men would need to edge out over the front of the vessel, a dozen feet or more, in heavy seas, often buried to their armpits in water, the gale raging and the canvas heaving like a maddened beast, heavy and stiff with ice; they'd need to punch it down and furl it, doing all this while clinging with one arm, feet balanced on slender rope lines slung below the bowsprit itself, the lines themselves slick with ice and prone to snap in the cold. That any made it back to deck was the real miracle. (They were still doing this in the 1960s, on the *Bluenose II*; Craig Harding, an early crew member, remembers being buried to his waist in roaring green water, "and there were no safety nets underneath then, not like now, only a thin rope to stand on; you clung on with one hand, did your work with the other.")

The dangerously unstable Essex schooner soon evolved into the swifter clipper, longer in hull but without any corresponding depth. They were even more dangerous than their predecessors, and went down at twice the rate.

Two other factors contributed to the deadly toll: winter fishing became the norm, and, as described, dory fishing took over from handlining. Both were "driven by the need for speed to market, paramount in an industry facing the pleasing prospect of a steadily increasing demand."[17]

That the new vessels were more dangerous than the old, and the new modes of fishing more dangerous yet, were never felt by owners or skippers to be valid reasons for not incorporating them. It was the greed for market, expressed by the number of dories on deck, the amount of ice in the holds, and new rail lines to bigger markets that mandated ever-faster ships. Safety never came into it.

In the years of the pinky and the sharpshooter, the New England fleet lost on average 4 schooners a year, in a working fleet of 300. The clippers went down at almost four times that rate, 15 schooners a year. The port of Marblehead lost 11 schooners in a single gale in 1846, with 67 men and boys drowned. The Minot's Light Gale five years later took men and vessels from Boston to Yarmouth; every fishing port on the coast lost at least one man. In 1879 alone, Gloucester lost 29 schooners, very nearly one-tenth of her fleet, and 249 fishermen. Thirteen vessels and 143 men went to the bottom of Georges Bank in a single gale on February 20. In the year 1894, 30 schooners went down. Of their value, $175,000, insurance covered $157,626.[18] The men who were lost counted for nothing, except to their widows.

In the twenty-five years between 1866 and 1890, Gloucester lost 385 schooners, and 2,454 fishermen were drowned, either on those lost schooners or from capsized dories, or having fallen from the rigging or been swept off the widowmaker bowsprit or struck by booms and into the icy sea with broken limbs and heads bleeding.

It's worth noting that of the 5,379 fishermen whose names appear in bronze on the Fishermen's Memorial Cenotaph next to the crudely sentimental "Man at the Wheel" memorial statue in Gloucester, no fewer than 1,596 came from the Canadian Maritimes. The equivalent memorial in Lunenburg is a less sentimental piece of art, a cluster of simple granite pillars inscribed with names; but there are names chiselled into the granite from every year of the Banks fishery, far too many of them.

The owners didn't much like the losses either, of course, but their response was typically brutal. In the 1870s, when the losses were so absolutely staggering and their insurance companies balking, they got together to form an all-season mutual insurance company of their own. The net effect was to push winter fishing even earlier, sometime back to January, in order to be on the grounds when the first shoals of spawning codfish struck in.

As before, the vessels were insured. And as before, the men were paid no attention, and their widows got no compensation.

A second statue on the Gloucester waterfront is a memorial to the fisherwomen, or fishermen's wives, showing a woman staring out to sea, waiting . . . Its passivity is grating to a twenty-first century eye, as though the women had nothing better to do than wait for their men to come home, or not come home, whereas in fact, because of their husbands' schedules, they were much more self-sufficient than that, and ordered their lives without complaint and often with great effectiveness, so much so that on occasion the men returned home feeling excluded and unwanted. But really the statue expresses a truth, because the families had no insurance and usually no other source of income, and there was no welfare to be had, or family support or state emergency care, and the widows did face destitution and hardship.

The men, and their widows, were and remained voiceless. It was left to a master mariner, Captain Joseph W. Collins, and a very few sympathetic industrialists to denounce the old ways and speak up for reform. Collins was a fishing skipper with a blunt manner (he once said that anyone who went winter fishing on Georges Bank was a damn fool[19]), and he developed and maintained close ties to the Republican administration in Washington. He was an admirably trenchant polemicist; his columns appearing in the Cape Ann *Weekly Advertiser* in 1882 under the pseudonym "Skipper" bore the thunderous rubric "When Will the Slaughter Stop?"[20]

Too many vessels were lost, he wrote, for no reason. The perceived need for ever-increasing speed was being used as a licence to build unsafe vessels. Too many men were dying, too many drowned, too many maimed. There were too many widows. Of the men who did survive, too many were used up too early by a life that was insupportably tough. There were also too many men ashore who bore culpability for the slaughter, who could have stopped it but didn't care. Collins knew fishing could be safer. He had been there himself. And it was being done on the other side of the Atlantic. He'd visited the British fleet and was impressed by their fishing cutters, whose deep hulls and balanced rigs could take them to windward in a gale, "and even when hove to they would jog to windward rather than drifting to leeward, going sideways like a crab."

By early in the twentieth century the culpability of the owners in the fisheries' appalling safety record was a matter of well-recorded fact. Collins wasn't the only one to write about it. Rudyard Kipling did so too (though his novel, *Captains Courageous*, further romanticized the fishing life) and so, especially, did James Connolly. For Connolly, the working fisherman was indeed the paragon of sturdy virtues portrayed by Kipling (and later by the MGM movie of the same name, starring Spencer Tracy). Connolly was particularly enamoured of the famous skippers of his time, "sail carriers and fish killers," men who refused to lower sail even in the most atrocious gale, for whom first to market was a badge of honour and reefing a sail a betrayal of the fisherman's code. If there was a fault, he blamed others. Like Joe Garland, he recognized that they were constantly pushed to do more, go faster, carry more sail, by a consortium of "dealers and processors and packers and owners and skippers and bankers and builders," as Garland put it, "who pushed and pushed for the highline, for the top stock, for the fastest vessel, the most reckless crew, forever haranguing for speed, for that press of sail. Drive her, boys! Drive her! Out to the banks and home day and night fair weather and foul first into market for that top dollar, and out again."[21]

Hardly anyone admitted that the skippers were themselves partly to blame. As W.M.P. Dunne writes in his McManus biography, "In an era when hard-bitten masters of clipper ships drove their crews unmercifully to achieve world record ocean crossings, fishing skippers, who were no less desirous of fast passages between fishing grounds and the pier, unmercifully pushed their vessels and their crews to do the same thing. They did so regardless of the widely recognized shortcomings in the design of the clipper schooners, and should have been indicted long before this."[22]

Those "sail carriers and fish killers" were actually part of the problem. They were pushed by forces beyond their control, but like their men they seized on the romances of Kipling and Connolly and Wallace as a way of asserting their resistance to the homogenizing demands of impersonal industrialism; buying into the myth and at the same time trying to live up to it, which led to further stories and even more romance. It was a self-reinforcing cycle; their daring and pride of seamanship became a way of resisting change; their competitiveness a way of showing off their indispensability; but that very daring helped them push their industry to and over the brink of safety. Their fate was in any case hopeless; the advent of engines would make them redundant, no matter how they lived, and later manipulated, the myths. Which is why skippers and men alike seized on the International Fishermen's Races with such desperate eagerness. They would be a last-ditch chance to show everyone what real fishermen could do, and to show why they shouldn't be replaced.

Under the prodding of Joseph Collins the safety record started slowly to improve, with the help of the naval architect Dennison Lawlor and, especially, the genius of Tom McManus, son of a Boston sailmaker who became the most influential designer of fishing vessels in the world.

The McManus family was among the earliest to demand safer schooners, and in the early 1880s tried an experimental vessel, the

Joseph Henry, that was built with a deeper draft than the norm; it turned out to be more stable than her contemporaries and, to the surprise of the conservative industry, a successful fishing vessel.

The Lawlor–Collins collaboration resulted in the experimental deep draft plumb-stemmed schooner *Grampus* in 1886,[23] a vessel that discovered—or rediscovered—depth of keel and a low centre of gravity on the model of the British cutters. It was followed closely by another Lawlor-designed vessel, the *Sarah H. Prior*, an inventive deep draft design built in Boston for John McManus, Tom's father. "She had enough drag in the keel to turn on a dime, and the fishermen appreciated that—tacking quickly in squally weather was a life saving trait. Tom McLaughlin, her first skipper, would often walk down the wharf and stop to admire her: 'What a vessel! What a vessel!' he would mutter to himself."[24]

The *John H. McManus* (named not for Tom's father but for his nephew, son of his brother Charlie) was the successor to the *Sarah H. Prior*, and was followed in short order by the *Carrie E. Phillips*, whose spike bowsprit (instead of the longer jib) perfected a concept introduced into *Grampus* and made her fast to windward and a good sail carrier, and then by the *Nellie Dixon* of 1888 and her sister, the *Fredonia* of 1889.

The McManus-designed Indian Headers, whose distinctive rounded stem was known as "the gripe," were safer yet, but despite his insistence, they generally still carried long bowsprits. He pondered the problem through 1899 to the summer of 1900, when he sketched a curious-looking schooner without a bowsprit at all. The logic of the design, which came to be called a "knockabout" rig, was straightforward: "The jib can be taken in by one man who stands practically on terra firma, and all he had to do was cast off the halyards." It had the added benefit of providing more safe foredeck for the men to work on.[25] The first knockabout fisherman was the *Helen B. Thomas*, one of the most famous two-masted craft ever built. She was built in 1902 at the Oxner and Story yard in Essex for Captain William Thomas.[26] Indian Headers and knockabouts were popular in Canada: the *Albert J. Lutz*, a competitor in the early fishermen's races out of Digby, was a McManus Indian Header. And the second knockabout ever built was launched in Shelburne, Nova Scotia, in 1904—the Canadians were keeping a keen eye on what was happening to the south, and McManus designs were picked up almost as quickly as they were first issued.

Still, Nova Scotian vessels were far from all copies. Massachusetts schooners were generally designed to fish all year, and to carry fish back to port as quickly as possible; Gloucester did some salt-banking but did much more fresh fishing than Nova Scotian vessels. As a result, Massachusetts vessels remained narrower, with heavier ballast, lower in the freeboard. They were fast—generally faster than Maritime vessels, particularly sailing to windward—but they "got wet" in rough weather, and remained less stable and more hazardous.

A few years later the *Mooween* and *Clintonia* followed the *Thomas* with yet another design wrinkle: knockabouts with a small bowsprit. McManus called them round-bow knockabouts, but they came to be called semi-knockabouts.[27] A second *Clintonia* was built at the Smith and Rhuland yard in Lunenburg; and fourteen years later her plans were revived for one of the competitors in the international schooner races, the elegant *Elizabeth Howard*, which came to be known as the White Ghost of the Maine Coast—she was, indeed, white, and could clock 16 knots in a good breeze.[28]

And so came the "breathtakers" of the 1920s, the *Bluenose* and her Canadian and American competitors. Here at last were the fast and able ladies, perfected just as the breed was no longer needed, just as thumping great diesels were making them obsolete. The *Thomas L. Gorton* was the last of the all-sail schooners to go fishing out of Gloucester. She was built in 1905, fifteen years before the *Bluenose* was conceived. She was sold to Arthur Earle of Carbonear, Newfoundland, in 1935, and rebuilt at Dayspring, Nova Scotia, on the LaHave River. She sank after colliding with an iceberg in 1956.[29]

There was a curious *Bluenose* sidelight to this business of improving vessel safety. When Senator Dennis selected a measurement of 145 feet at the deck as the maximum allowed, there were accusations, as we have seen, that the length was selected because it was just shorter than the powerful *Elizabeth Howard*, which measured 148 feet, but there is a counter-argument that the allowed measurement was too big, not too small. Almost all the fishing schooners of the time were a good bit smaller than that. Most of them measured 110 or at most 120 feet on deck, which everyone agreed made a lot of sense. It allowed them to carry a substantial rig, but it wasn't too much for the weather on the Banks, and easy for the crew to handle. Get much above that, 130 or 140 feet, and the rig increases commensurately, until a vessel had to carry, as the *Bluenose* did, a mainsail of more than 4,000 square feet and a total sail area closing in on 11,000 square feet. At this size, no matter how the vessel sails or how cleverly she is tuned as to ballast and rig, they get to be "man-killers," in Dan Moreland's phrase, more dangerous than they should be.

But once the Deed of Gift specified 145 feet (later changed to 150 feet) the designers and builders of the boats that wanted to win were stuck. As Moreland puts it, "The Deed said that a boat could not be 'over' such and such a length. But they didn't take into account human nature. If you tell someone, 'you can't make it any bigger than this table,' the tendency is to make it just as big as the table and not an inch smaller. So the maximum size limit became the actual limit, and locked in for thirty years how big these boats would be. Everyone had to have his boat the same length as the others. It became standard, but it was too long."

One of the intentions of the challenge had been to encourage the building of better, more innovative, and safer boats. But the rules built into the challenge itself made such development unlikely.

CHAPTER EIGHT

HER

RACING

ANTECEDENTS

*I*n some of the earliest true fishermen's races, that entrancing ability to stay upright in a roaring gale was put to almost miraculous use. These races were not the "hook on" affairs that pitted one boastful skipper against another on the way back from the Banks, but more formal contests, real races around a real race course, albeit in fishing schooners and not yachts. At least one of them took place in weather that would have kept any yacht, no matter how seaworthy, firmly lashed to its moorings and any yachtsman, no matter how reckless, in the clubhouse with a hot grog and a thick sweater.

The first such race, an all-Canadian affair, took place in Halifax in 1871, as part of a festival the city fathers called the Great Aquatic Festival. The *Halifax Chronicle* reported the event in a breathless tone that saw the word *splendid* crop up every couple of paragraphs. The race for the under-50-ton class was won by a dainty little schooner called *Flash*, which came in before the winner of the over-50-ton class, although that boat had started a good hour earlier.

The next race that pitted working schooners against each other in formal conditions was a Massachusetts-only affair held in 1886, the stepchild of Tom McManus, fishmonger and boat designer, son of a sailmaker; as usual, Tom McManus had several overlapping reasons for what he did, but the primary drive was still his urgent wish to make vessels better and safer.

Tom's father, John, had been of a similar mind. He was an immigrant who had worked for a while in the Irish fishing fleet of Boston, and he knew in the most personal way how unsafe and unstable the fishing clippers of the day really were. He linked up with naval architect Dennison Lawlor to build a sleek little vessel knowingly and aptly called *Sylph*, a fast boat but stable, and almost impossible to roll over, and though John soon left the sea and turned to sailmaking, the Irish fleet was the better and safer for his efforts. His son Tom never went fishing himself, but his fish wholesale business was a waterfront hangout, and he knew from his father, his customers, and the skippers and sailors who dropped in to yarn just what the problems were with the current fishing fleet.

Tom McManus was that curious American hybrid, a hard-nosed businessman and at the same time an idealist, to the end of his life maintaining an unshakeable conviction that business and ideals could be harnessed in tandem to help make him wealthy and improve everybody's lives at the same time. The outer symbol of his character was his apparently effortless ability to combine profanity with a genuine piety.[1]

In 1886, Boston's dockside workers and fish handlers went out on strike and the fishing fleet was tied up for the duration; with the men and vessels idled, McManus suggested they hold a series of schooner races, to take place on the first of May. For this he was called the Father of the Fishermen's Races, a moniker that irritated him for years afterwards. His notion hadn't been to father anything, but to give the men something to do, and, as a not unimportant corollary, to test the relative merits of two of Boston's most innovative vessels, the John McManus–Lawlor built *Sarah H. Prior*, and the Tom McManus–Lawlor co-production *John H. McManus*. Which boat was faster and better had become a hot topic in master mariner societies and in fishermen's hangouts, and McManus knew it would be good for the fleet and good for his own business to foster the competition. Did the refinements he had introduced into the *John McManus* make the later vessel better? Afterwards he said, making the same point in a more formal and ponderous way, that he had advocated yearly competition "to encourage fishermen to improve on their boats and as the fresh fish industry handles a perishable article of food and the fresher it reaches the consumer the more palatable and the demand increases, so it is essential to that branch of the fisheries to encourage increased speed in the vessels which bring the good to market."[2] He knew the skippers and crews would be unable to resist the challenge.

Tom McManus was well liked among fishermen, but he moved just as easily—possibly more easily by now—among the wealthy yachting elite of Essex County and especially Eastern Point, that bastion of American captains of industry, the nineteenth-century Masters of the Universe. Among his acquaintances was J. Malcolm Forbes, flamboyant industrialist (and father of even more flamboyant magazine publisher and biker Malcolm Forbes Jr.). Forbes summered in Eastern Point, and though his primary passion was horse racing (he owned the mare Nancy Hanks, the model for the horse-and-sulky weathervanes still ubiquitous in New England), he was also a yachtsman of note. He built and skippered the Edward Burgess–designed yacht *Puritan*, which successfully defended the America's Cup in 1885, and subsequently financed three more America's Cup defences by the New York Yacht Club. It seemed logical, therefore, that McManus ask Forbes to sponsor races among the idled vessels of the fishing fleet. It really wasn't as much of a stretch as it might seem. Master mariners were, after all, pillars of the local community, and just as in Lunenburg to the north, everyone in town was either a fisherman, knew a fisherman, or depended on fishermen for a living. The wealthy elites of Eastern Point considered themselves part of this seafaring community, and took a real if rather condescending pride in the sturdy and tough-minded fishermen whose business dominated the town. And Forbes was seaman enough to recognize the considerable merits of the fast and able fishing schooners; others in the Yacht Squadron were too, and many sleek yachts owed their provenance to a working vessel from Gloucester or Boston.

Forbes readily agreed to finance the race, and he and a group of his yachting cronies put up a cup and $1,500 in prize money, a not inconsiderable sum in a period when a sharesman's wages from fishing could be and frequently were less than $300 for a year. Still, none of them took racing that seriously—it was fine, it was fun, but it was not making a living, and when the two things clashed, the fishermen would go off to the Banks without a qualm, and never mind the foolishness of racing for a cup. They left it to the millionaires and the fancy yachtsmen to talk about the spirit of competition and the sporting life; to them those things were a reality only to men who never worked a day in their lives. But in other ways the fishermen liked that first race, for it was raced by fishermen's rules: no fouls were recognized, you could do what you liked with your sails or your ballast, you could carry on deck all your dories or none. In short, there were no real rules except not crossing the start line too early, and though Forbes and his cronies did appoint a "referee" from the Eastern Point Yacht Club, no one paid him any mind, and if he'd tried to interfere they would have brushed him aside. As it happened, this referee did flag a couple of "fouls," at least by yachting standards, and was indeed ignored.

In the end, ten schooners came to the start line: the *John H. McManus* skippered by Johnny O'Brien, the *Sarah H. Prior* under Tom McLaughlin, and eight others, one of them skippered by Bart Whalen, brother of the more famous Maurice. Winds were slight, and the race lacked excitement. The *McManus* pipped the *Prior*, and that, at least in the dockside gossips' minds, settled that. (Though Tom McLaughlin could be heard muttering about waiting for "a real contest in a real wind" that would show people what the *Prior* could do, and he had his supporters in town.)

After a while, the strike was over and the fishermen went back to fishing. There was no racing in 1887; the fleets were busy and McManus felt he had done his duty. But the year after that, Charlie Harty, one of Gloucester's most respected skippers, challenged the *John H. McManus* and its skipper, Johnny O'Brien, to another race; apparently O'Brien had been saying one thing or another about his own natural superiority, and in meeting places and taverns all over town people were sowing doubts about other contenders. At least, that's what Harty felt, and he couldn't stand it.

In the meantime, though, Tom McManus had launched the next in his long series of schooner refinements, the Ned Burgess-designed *Carrie E. Phillips*, which was exceptionally adept at beating to windward, a good sail carrier, and very stable in bad weather.[3] Harty was confident, but not that confident, and his challenge, thrown open to all comers, explicitly excluded the *Phillips*, which he and everyone else admitted would be too fast to make a real race of it. After a while, though, Harty succumbed to pressure, and the *Phillips* was allowed to the start line.

In truth, he had been right to resist the *Phillips*, for she easily won an otherwise hotly contested race, thereby appropriating the entirely unofficial title "Queen of the Fleet"; but Harty took some

comfort in coming second in a five-boat race and soundly defeating Johnny O'Brien's *McManus* and, albeit briefly, silencing that
loquacious champion's most extravagant yarns.

Tom McManus had been right too—the very existence of the
Phillips and her obvious superiority at her work did lead directly
to a new generation of safer, sounder (and faster) schooners that
helped greatly reduce the carnage at sea. Among them was the
Susan R. Stone, whose launch attracted a huge crowd, followed in
due time by McManus's next two vessels, the *Nellie Dixon* of 1888
and the *Fredonia* of 1889, both of them designed by Burgess.

It was the *Fredonia* that was destined to become the most influential of all fishing schooners, directly effecting the building of
dozens of other vessels—known as "*Fredonia*-class vessels"—and
changing forever the shape of the fishing fleet. The "*Fredonia*
schooners" had deep, sharply rising keels; above the waterline their
stems formed graceful overhanging clipperish bows, making them
look sporty and yacht-like while remaining eminently seaworthy.
As recounted, the *Fredonia* had spent a year as J. Malcolm Forbes's
private yacht under the captainship of Charlie Harty, during which
she actually challenged, raced, and thrashed the now-aging *Hesper*.
Harty, in fact, had persuaded Forbes to finance the *Fredonia* for
him; the price was that Forbes was to get use of her for a year first
before Harty could go fishing, and *Fredonia* was launched under
the Eastern Point Yacht Club burgee. Before the long-suffering
skipper could get "his" vessel back, Forbes had himself taken across
the Atlantic to the Azores, where he proposed to the daughter of the
American consul there, Rose Dabney, and took her back to Boston
as a bride. (*Fredonia* sank in a storm on the Grand Banks in 1896.)

The real fisherman's race—the only real fisherman's race, according to the purists—was the contest run off in 1892, an affair to com-
memorate Gloucester's 250th anniversary. It was real because it

was held at a time when the whole fleet was still sail powered, when it was still every skipper's ambition to command a vessel that could stand any weather and beat any other back to market. It was real because it was held in a "real fisherman's breeze," that is, a howling gale just shy of a hurricane, and not by much at that. It was real because it was not subject to foolish yachtsmen's rules—what judging boats showed up were driven to shore, fleeing the gale, and thereafter hadn't a clue who was doing what. It was real because it was run off by plain working vessels sailed by plain working fishermen; there were no fancy yachtsmen in the crew, no ringers in the form of other skippers just there to have fun, as was the case in most of the races the *Bluenose* ran. And it was real because one of the boats came in straight from the fishing grounds and stole the show, to the delight of fo'c'sles and yacht clubs and master mariners' associations everywhere. Kipling or Connolly or later Wallace couldn't have devised a better story had they wanted to write a neat piece of fiction meant to illustrate the daring seamanship of the great skippers, men of whom other skippers would say, *and no man ever made him take his mains'l in . . . once he leaves the Banks he never was known, blow high or blow low, to heave to his vessel . . .* Actually, Connolly did write about the race, though he was not there, and there is more than a hint of suspicion that a little windy embellishment did creep into his version of events. No matter: the race was dramatic enough as it was. And Connolly's name for it stuck. He called it the Race It Blew.

The race was conceived, once again, by the rich folk out at Eastern Point. A friend of Forbes's, Henry Hovey, had acted as one of the judges in 1888, and he put together a regatta committee to organize races for the anniversary. His notion was to have a large vessel race—vessels over 80 feet—and a small-vessel race for anything smaller than that. His own boat, an elegant 108-foot yachting schooner called *Fortuna*, would be the judges' boat. He would entertain his Eastern Point friends aboard, give them a chance to watch the race first-hand.

For weeks prior to the event the town was bubbling over with gossip and speculation. All the great skippers of the fleet would take part, some of them in venerable vessels, some in vessels brand new. The four greatest racing captains were agreed to be Maurice Whalen, master of the *Harry Belden*, Tommie Bohlin of the *Nannie C. Bohlin*, Rube Cameron on the *Joseph Rowe*, and Sol Jacobs of the *Ethel B. Jacobs*. But Charlie Harty was there with a new boat, *Grayling*, and so was Charlie Olsen of the *James S. Steele*. In all, seven schooners entered in the large-vessel category, three in the small-vessel category.

As the day rolled around, everyone was looking at the weather, hoping for a good breeze. "A fast vessel in light air was all right, a pleasing thing to look at, no fault to find with her; but the real vessel after all was the lady that could stand up and go along when it came on to blow."[4]

A strong wind came along for the Wednesday before Friday's race, blowing from the northeast, perfect weather for the practice runs around the 41-mile triangular course, maybe 20 to 30 knots, with bigger gusts, perfect weather for great speed in any seaworthy vessel. On Thursday it was blowing harder, and looking better and better for the following day, for it was agreed this was a blow that would not easily blow itself out. Thursday's winds went up to 30 and then 45 knots, and the seas climbed from large hills into small mountains, smashing against Cape Ann with a monstrous roar. Friday was worse, or better—practically a small hurricane.

It was going to be a race, all right. Tommie Bohlin was fairly dancing with anticipation. This would be a chance, he was heard to say with a certain deliberate arrogance, to show those Boston men how to carry sail.[5]

Most of the vessels were in port all week, tuning up the rigging, hauling out and scraping and painting their bottoms. The cordage was inspected, sheets and halyards replaced where necessary. Everything that could take a coat of paint was painted. Everything was painfully neat; the fishing wharves looked like a yacht club.

Except for Maurice Whalen and the *Harry Belden*. Maurice was nowhere to be found. He'd gone fishing—the mackerel were running and he took seine boats out with him—and he hadn't come back. By Thursday afternoon there was still no sign of him.

He hadn't forgotten—he'd apparently ringed race day on a calendar pinned up on a bulkhead in his cabin—but the fishing was good and he thought he'd have plenty of time. He set the day for return, only to be confronted with a wind from the west, and the next two days dead calm. It was Tuesday night before the wind hauled into the east, to be a living gale by morning, and Maurice swung her off and let her go, 700 miles at 14 knots. "Maurice had her laying right down to her work," Connolly wrote afterwards. "She was lying almost flat on her side, she was sifting through the tumbling seas, making a hissing roar as she went . . . an endless belt of white boiling suds coming over her bow at the lee cat-heads, rushing aft over the nest of dories, over her gurry kids, over her cabin house, over her wheel box and stern rail with a great roar. The cabin roof was half a foot higher than her quarter rail, and the pipe of the cabin stove stuck through the middle of the cabin roof, yet a piece of tarpaulin had to be laid over the stove pipe to keep the water from spilling down through the cabin roof and putting out the fire. The wheel box was buried under the rushing water. Tom White had the wheel and he was standing to his waist in water beside it."[6] It's unclear from all this where the smoke went if there was a tarp over the smokestack and the fire still on, but the basic message is clear: Maurice got her back in time, and tied up in Gloucester late Thursday night, just thirteen hours before race time, much too late to haul her out and scrape her, too late even to unload the mackerel from her holds and still give the crew a decent night's sleep. She even left her mainsail up, to dry out. So she sailed the next day, battered from the gale, deep in the water from her load of fresh fish.

She was a little late to the start line because the towboat that hauled her from the wharf had trouble turning her. They could have turned her away from the sun easily enough with the mainsail up, but everyone knew that would be bad luck, so they hauled the mainsail down, turned her with the sun, hauled the mainsail up again, and she got to the jostling start just as the gun went off.

The wind was blowing 54 miles an hour, at least that's what the official forecast said. At sea, it was blowing harder, the chilly froth coming off the wave tops horizontally and whistling through the shrouds, a "slashing, ominous, chilly broth of rain and fog driven by a mounting gale"—Joe Garland's words.[7]

Despite the wind, despite the mountainous seas, despite the terrible hazards, the three top contenders, the *Belden*, the *Bohlin*, the *Jacobs*, sailed with their halyards lashed aloft. This was a nice piece of provocative bravado. Almost all the hard-driving fishermen on their way in from the Banks had a habit of carrying a sharp knife or a wicked small axe under the quarter rail; the knife and the axe were there to cut the peak halyards in an emergency, when she rolled too low and the only way to get her righted was to slash the halyards so the big mainsail would run down the mast, and so let her come upright again. Lashing the main halyards aloft would prevent that happening. If an over-timid crewman seeking to save himself and his vessel would try to bring the sail down that way, he'd have to go aloft first to do it, and the others would be able to head him off. Charlie Olsen on the *Steele* hadn't lashed his halyards, but he refused to take in any sail even when the crewmen pointed out he'd go faster if he did. "See that boat out there?" Charlie said. "That's the *Ethel Jacobs* . . . if she can carry full sail, so can we."[8] As Connolly put it, no doubt gilding the lily a goodish deal, "All the leading captains sailed out with the firm promise that the only sails coming off that day would be what the Lord took off. And the Lord took off quite a few sails that day."[9]

Crowding the buoy at the first turn, Sol Jacobs broke his main gaff, and for him the race was over. Tommie Bohlin in the *Nannie* had lightened his ballast, expecting light winds, and was having a terrible time of it. He could have taken off some sail and been the better for it, and faster, but of course he couldn't do that. He lashed two men to the wheel and the mastheadman was lashed aloft to prevent himself from being catapulted into the sea from the 70-feet gyrations of the masthead. She was rolling down to her sheer polls, which were 4 feet above her rail, and tons of water was sweeping aft. All the vessels were burying their bowsprits and shipping water to their hatches as they heeled over. Tom McManus was on one of the racers, and he said afterwards, "Another quarter inch, and she would have filled and sunk." A passenger on the *Steele*, Dr. William Hale, an experienced yachtsman, wrote about it later: "During the long thrash to windward, every vessel sailed on her lee rail, with deck buried to the hatches . . . the brave, labouring craft would roll under the surging seas to the second or third ratline, then would follow awful moments of suspense as the unflinching crews with teeth set and hands clenched watched to see if their craft would stagger up again, or go down under grievous load. Desperate as the chances were, not a vessel luffed or reefed, as to be the first to reef would make her the laughing stock of the town, and there was not a skipper in the fleet who would not carry away both sticks rather than be branded as a coward."[10] But when Sol Jacobs broke his jib, Charlie Harty had had enough, and he and the *Steele* headed for home, along with pretty well all the race and spectator boats. A few minutes later another entrant, the *Blaine*, followed them in.

The race came down to just two vessels, the *Belden* and the *Rowe*. They both plunged together through the narrow final turn off Davis Ledge (though the race committee had warned everyone who would listen that there was only room for one vessel between the buoy and the Ledge), and *Belden* edged past and headed for home, her crew up to their waists in green water but exultant. What a yarn this was going to make!

And yarn it was. Nothing could have better demonstrated the grit of the fishing fleets, and their superb skills, and that the *Belden* had won with a load of mackerel was altogether too delicious. Even the Boston papers were full of it. One of them had sent out a reporter to cover the races, and he'd perched on the cliffs at Marblehead to see what he could see, but after they made the first turn he went back to his office.

"I thought I sent you down to cover the fisherman's race?" an irate city editor demanded.

"I went down there, but there was no race. All I saw was a lot of foolish fishermen trying to drown themselves." If that didn't make Gloucester crow, nothing could.

It was the most famous race until the start of the Dennis Cup series, until the looming, irresistible, relentless, apparently unstoppable presence of the *Bluenose* put the *Belden* out of mind, at last.

After that there were no races for a few years. Perhaps the fishermen had enough yarns to last them a decade; more likely the fishing was good, and that was much more important than fooling around close to shore. Racing didn't earn a man an income.

In 1906, Thomas Lipton, the British tea magnate who had spent huge sums of his own money in a vain attempt to wrest the America's Cup away from New York, was persuaded by Thomas McManus to put up a cup and some money, and he did so. Since $2,500 in prize money was a nice inducement, twenty-seven schooners registered for the race, but when race day came around, only five showed up. The rest had gone fishing. Still, the race came off and Provincetown's Marion Perry, who (or so the fisherman's yarn goes) had only entered because his wife had thought the cup would look pretty decent on the mantel, beat his closest rival, the "Portygee" Manual Costa. Everyone assumed the Cup would be an annual event and that Perry would defend it again the following year, but the event fizzled. Neither Perry nor his cohorts took such racing at all seriously and saw no need to "defend" something that was now an old story. "Sportsmanship ain't in it," he told Connolly. "Man's gotta make a livin'." Perry became something of a folk hero in the fishing ports when he was invited by a presidential envoy to come and meet President Roosevelt, in Provincetown to lay the cornerstone of the Pilgrim Monument. Perry was busy checking his rigging at the time, and said so. When the envoy insisted that the president really did want to see him, he finally relented. "Tell the president if he wants to see me he knows where to find me," he said, and went quietly back to work. The other skippers loved that. It perfectly reflected their own view of life's priorities. If they didn't like something, they would say so, and if someone wanted them to do something they didn't feel like doing, they'd simply not do it and be damned to anyone who tried to insist.[11]

The Canadians held fewer races. In fact, before the run-off races for the Halifax Herald Trophy in 1920, the only formal races were the 1871 Aquatic Festival races won by *Flash*, and those held at Digby, in 1911 and 1912, under the chairmanship of Digby's mayor, Harry Short, along with Captain Howard Anderson, who managed the Maritime Fish Corporation's local plant, and O.S. Dunham, who not only ran the local newspaper, the *Digby Courier*, but was commodore of the Southwestern Nova Scotia Yacht Club. That the fishermen didn't just hold the August races themselves, but were sponsored by the Maritime Fish Corporation, which was based in faraway Montreal, was a sign of the times, but nevertheless the fishermen's reunion of which the races were a part was a great, if rather provincial, success: lobstermen and trawlermen in gear-mending and rope-splicing competitions, oyster- and clam-shucking contests, crews of sturdy Banksmen, stripped to the waist in the summer heat, pulling mightily on two-man dories, clambakes and lobster-broils and great big pies made of summer fruit, peaches and plums and early-season apples. The town was covered in bunting and filled with throngs who had arrived by train, car, buggy and, occasionally, ox-drawn cart, coming from all up and down the Fundy Shore.

The Digby "fishermen's regatta" started at seven in the morning at Tiverton, 35 miles away, with a race by a whole flotilla of motor fishing boats. This opener was followed by teams of trawl fishermen in sharp-hulled open motor boats, unmuffled, roaring around the bay, the air vibrating from the din. Then came Mi'kmag birchbark-canoe races, but the Indians scorned to pull hard, preferring to let their chief paddle comfortably into the lead, and all shared the prize money later.

The main event, a race between two all-sail fishing schooners, was held later in the day. The contestants were the 93-ton *Dorothy M. Smart*, tied up at the Maritime Fish Corporation wharf, and its rival, the *Albert J. Lutz*. The *Smart* would be skippered by Harry Ross, then only a boyish twenty-four, who had already acquired a reputation as a fish killer, and a "driver," fearless and daring. He was only twenty-one when he took his first command, going Banks fishing out of Digby. The *Lutz* would be skippered by John Apt, who lived at Port Wade across the Annapolis Basin; he was both skipper and part owner, and what John Apt didn't know about handling vessels wasn't worth knowing.

Both vessels were round-bowed McManus semi-knockabouts that had been built at Joe McGill's Shelburne yard, but Apt had incorporated some ideas of his own into the *Lutz*, based on his long experience with sail plans, and after she was launched and went fishing she swiftly became Queen of the Digby Fleet, which to Digby people essentially meant Queen of the Nova Scotia fleet or fleet anywhere else for that matter; and for two years his prowess rankled in Digby hearts, he not being a native son and all, but a "Port Wader." So it was no surprise that when *Smart* was built it was at least partly for the purpose of taking the breeze-born John Apt down a peg or two.

The race was a fine romantic tale, two splendid boats, their black hulls glossy in the summer sun, their copper-plated underbodies smooth and fresh with new paint, decks and rails newly varnished, the boyish Harry on one vessel, the tall, spare, stern, moustachioed fortyish John Apt on the other. The reason we know as much as we do about the race is due largely to Frederick William Wallace, who sailed aboard the *Smart* and left a fine account of the affair in *Canadian Century* magazine, and later in his memoir, *Roving Fisherman.* Wallace, along with James Connolly and Rudyard Kipling, was one of the great romancers of the fishing life. He was both a novelist and a journalist, with a fine ear for dialogue and an observant eye. He spent most of his working life as editor of the trade journal *The Canadian Fisherman*, but his memoirs of his days sailing with fishermen and his many stories and novels were best-sellers in their day, and contributed no small amount to the reputation the intrepid "iron men" enjoyed at large (Wallace did not invent but was largely responsible for popularizing the phrase *Wooden Ships and Iron Men*, the title of one of his memoirs).

Both the *Lutz* and the *Smart* made a good showing around the Digby course, carrying a full press of sail, and Harry Ross beat John Apt by a mere ninety-six seconds. Wallace records the reaction: "One of the crew jeered from the deck of the winner as they sailed by after the finish, but the skipper was furious. 'Shut up you lunkhead!' And then to the others, 'Come on fellers, three cheers for the Lutz! By gorry she deserves it!'"[12]

The *Smart* had won the Brittain Cup and was Queen of the Fleet, but both Howard Anderson and Harry Ross knew that John Apt had been unlucky. He had sailed the best race, they both believed, and would be back. Anderson had years back been dorymate with Apt, and was sure: "He won't take this lying down. Next year, if he gets a chance, it may be a different story."

Indeed, the races were held again the following year, this time in even more of a celebratory mood. The Governor General, the

Duke of Connaught, came down on a special train from Ottawa, a delegation of yachtsmen came up from New York, and the town was jammed with revellers. Apt was taking no chances. Wallace reported, "Carpenters were set to work planing off any projecting butt ends below her waterline. Putty holes were filled and rubbed smooth and after the bottom was painted it was given a coat of tallow and blacklead. Rigging was set up and new halyards and sheets were rove off. Fifty yards of additional canvas was let into the head of the mainsail until the hoist of the gaff could carry no more; a bonnet on the jib brought the foot of that sail almost to the bowsprit, ballast was trimmed anew and every unnecessary item of gear was put ashore, dories, gurry-kid, the two 600 pound and 700 pound anchors, the chain cable and riding hawser . . ."

The *Smart*, too, had been "skinned to the ballast" and was in racing trim.

In the end, the *Lutz* won by thirteen full minutes, and the race for the Brittain Cup was over, and John Apt's triumph was never to be contested again in his day. It was not until eight years later, in 1920, that racing between fishing schooners was revived, this time across the province in Halifax and Lunenburg, in preparation for the challenge to the Gloucestermen. The *Lutz* didn't last much longer; she was sold to fishing interests in Catalina, Newfoundland, and capsized in a squall off the town of Renews, drowning one of her crew, William Johnson. The *Smart* found a new career, albeit briefly, as a rum-runner, before she was seized by U.S. Revenue agents and sold at a U.S. Marshals' auction. She too ended up in Newfoundland and was wrecked in a storm on the Grand Banks in 1930.

CHAPTER NINE

H E R

T A N G L E D

P O L I T I C S

*I*n the spring of 1922, before the races resumed, a
schooner passed the *Bluenose* as she was riding her sea
anchor on Sable Bank. It was a fine day, for the spring—
wispy clouds were scudding across from the southwest, and there
was a steady 10-knot sea breeze. The temperature was hovering
around the zero mark, and the dories were just ready to go when
the other vessel came up. Nothing so surprising in that; there were
plenty of vessels around Sable on a good day when the wind was
fine, and the watch had spotted her and called down her heading
so the old man would know what she was at. But she was still a nov-
elty for all that. Most of the men had heard her before seeing her,
for one thing; her topmasts had been struck and she was flying no
sails at all, but she was moving well through the sea, a plume of
black smoke trailing her, an evil wake, almost as though she was
herself on fire. They could hear the thumping of her diesel a few
miles off, and everyone stopped what they were doing to watch,
even Angus himself. After a few minutes she passed by with a wave
from the wheelman and what crew were on deck, then she was

gone, grumbling away to the horizon, and the *Bluenose*'s dories were set out in their sequence, as they always were. No one said anything, not that anyone could remember.

A few years before, when the gasoline motor and then the diesel had first started appearing on the Banks, the older hands had been upset. The noise, it was said, would frighten off the fish, and no one would catch anything. Of course, this turned out not to be true—fish were stupid things—which was obvious when these "auxiliaries" came back to port with their holds stuffed, just like regular vessels.

And just a week earlier the *Bluenose* had watched as an auxiliary caught fire and her dories fled in all directions while the vessel burned to the waterline and sank. All her men got away, though two were scarred from the fire, and one of them never sailed again. They were not safe, these motors, and there was no future in them, was there? Wind was free, and it was always there, and what would you do if you ran out of fuel, out there in the middle of the sea?

It took no skills to drive one of those things, did it? Only luck.

The *Bluenose* was built, and the International Fishermen's Races were staged, in a rapidly shifting industrial and political context. Everything in the fishermen's world was changing, which perhaps explains why they clung so fiercely to their sense of themselves and the merit of their very considerable traditions. The early fishermen's races and their intense competitiveness, and all the tales of wreck and ruin at sea, of rescue and recovery, yarns told in the fo'c'sle and in the waterfront taverns and the wharves on shore, helped create and maintain a "unique working-class culture, as distinct and real as that of any other group,"[1] in Michael Wayne Santos's words. This working-class solidarity was enshrined in the familiar tales of great runs to the Banks, of great catches by famous fish killers, of great vessels and the great sail carriers, men to whom it was a matter of honour to "crack on," to carry every scrap of muslin in a great gale, men who would drive a vessel for all she was worth. The names of the best skippers became a kind of shorthand for the legends themselves. The yarns were reinforced in turn by need—by an industrial context that was radically transforming, and threatening, their way of life. They needed all the solidarity they could achieve. Everything was indeed changing, and not at all for the better.

It is a deep irony of the International Fishermen's Races of the 1920s and 1930s, the races in which *Bluenose* remained gloriously pre-eminent, that the men who instigated them (among them newspaper publishers and corporate leaders from Halifax to Boston) and the men who encouraged and financed them (among them captains of industry summering at Chester or at Eastern Point and Cape Ann outside Gloucester, millionaires taking a break from their labours), that these men became entranced with the romance of the fisherman's culture just as they and the corporate ethos they represented were destroying it.

The changes were coming in three ways: technological, industrial, and political.

The political context is of course obvious. The First World War had convulsed the world in an orgy of bloodshed of appalling scope, on a scale made possible only because the mass media and the workers in the new industrial classes fed on each other, demonizing the enemy and whipping up a fever of false patriotism. These workers were vulnerable because their lives in the newly created factories and reorganized farms of the new order had stripped from them much of their dignity and independence. The battered economies of Europe were themselves vulnerable to the siren calls of Bolshevism echoing from Russia; not for nothing did Lenin confidently predict the falling first of Germany, then France and Britain and their empires, and ultimately the capitalist bastion, the faraway United States. Indeed, the brutality of the American captains of industry and their goon squads almost did Lenin's work for him before unionism took hold and helped to save capitalism from itself, and the wild and woolly Wobblies, the Chicago-based International Workers of the World, made their brief inroads into newly strike-prone factories of the industrial east with their hymn, "Solidarity Forever." As we know, Trotsky's revolution consumed itself in self-hatred, as Robespierre's had done before it, and failed to root outside Russia, and workers' rights in the West took a different turn, but this was far from clear as the Depression loomed.

The purely industrial context is a little more complicated, though of course linked to politics. The nineteenth century was really the end of artisanal labour in the West; until then, skill-sets were often inherited, the apprenticeship system was endemic, and craftsmen took considerable pride in what they did. By the early twentieth century the main job of skilled and unskilled workers both was the mind-numbing one of tending and coddling machines. Manufacturing went first, then mining. At first, farming and fishing seemed immune—catching fish from an unstable dory in a high sea took great skill, and such men could not easily be replaced—but this immunity was illusory. In the end, as Santos put it, schooners and dories were workplaces like any other, just as farms were, and someone more distant came to own what Marx called the means of production, which then needed to become ever more efficient just to survive.

The fishermen attempted to head off the changes, but their efforts were doomed to failure. The change was only drawn out, not stopped, when the fishing way of life became entrenched in the popular imagination through romancers like Connolly and Kipling and Wallace. It was against this backdrop that the fishermen's races took place.

The technological changes were represented by the motorized auxiliary passing the *Bluenose* that spring day in 1923. It was not that the fishing industry hadn't already changed. I've already recounted how the transition from small schooners with a couple of men aboard handlining over the side to dory trawling had taken place in the 1850s, and how even then Lunenburgers had resisted it, on the no doubt correct grounds that it was too efficient and would deplete the stock—exactly the same argument used against purse seiners, beam trawlers, steam trawlers and, in the late twentieth century, deep-sea draggers with GPS systems and fish-finding radar. Still, the transition from a few men with a brace of handlines to each man setting a thousand hooks four times a day and then to trawling was not such a large step. The real change began twenty years before *Bluenose* was even conceived, around the turn of the century, when Sol Jacobs, another Maritimer, launched the *Henry Miller Gould* out of Gloucester. She was schooner rigged, and 117 feet long, bigger than most but not grotesquely so. Her main difference was her propulsion—she had sails, but she used a single 150-horsepower gasoline engine. The launching was widely ridiculed wherever fishermen congregated, but Sol came back highliner that year and each sharesman earned $863, a record.

The *Gould* only lasted a year—she was gutted by fire in 1901, a major hazard for early motorized vessels—but others had seen what she had done and soon followed suit. Some of the early writers had some fun with these cumbersome vessels with their clumsy engines, not always taking them seriously. Frederick Wallace recorded the departure from Canso, Nova Scotia, of an early auxiliary-powered vessel:

[They were not easy to start] . . . The engineer had torches blowing on the cylinder heads to preheat them before starting—necessary in crude oil engines of that vintage. Advised by the engineer that he would be ready in a minute, the skipper was at the wheel ready to go.

"Are you ready!"

"All ready!"

"Heave up!" shouted the skipper to the men at the forward wind-lass. The anchor was broken out and the order was given to start the engine. There followed a series of muffled explosions. Then came a halt. A few more coughs, then silence. The big schooner was swinging in the tide and the wind and the skipper was anxiously glancing at the vessels around him in the restricted harbour.

He hailed the engineer again just as that individual came running up from below with an oil can. "Where the hell are you going?" cried an excited skipper.

"I got to get some gasoline for the air pump, cap'n. She won't start."

"But we've under way, man. The anchor's up."

"Sorry, cap'n, you'd better let it go again."

The skipper exploded and in a roar that could be heard all over Canso. "Damn and blast you and your jeesly blank blank engine! I'll take her out under sail!"[2]

But it was no use. Gasoline engines were expensive (they could cost more than $7,000, burned 30 gallons an hour and required an engineer at a salary of at least $75 a month), unreliable (see Wallace's story, above), and unsafe (they tended to explode easily and caused many a fire), but they could drive a vessel at a steady 12 knots, and do so while towing two seine boats and a dory, and do it regardless of the wind direction—no more beating about uselessly trying to make harbour, no more fearing a lee shore, no more weather-driven delays getting product to market. The *Bluenose*, when she was launched, turned out to be brilliant beating to windward; these engines made her ability pointless. The new schooners designed by Tom McManus, the knockabouts with their tucked-in sterns, lent themselves well to inserting auxiliary engines, and the unsteady gasoline motor soon gave way to the dirtier but much more reliable diesel. By 1910 no more boats were being designed that didn't take into account the addition of a motor at some point; and by 1921—when the *Bluenose* was already in the water—the *L.A. Dunton* was launched in Gloucester, the last big schooner without a motor, excepting those that were specifically designed to conquer the engineless *Bluenose*. By the time the first few racing series were over, Gloucestermen hardly ever used sails, and only a few carried them at all. Sail lasted longer in Lunenburg, by about a decade, and longer still in Newfoundland, but even there, by the 1930s, dorymen were a dying breed.

Few skippers and crews—even owner-skippers, who were more budget conscious than most—adapted to the new reality as easily as Sol Jacobs did. Indeed, they often remained "belligerently ignorant of motor power," in Santos's phrase. Engineers, the "black gangs from the factories," made a skipper's expertise and all his skills useless; it was the engineer who now got you to market fastest, and all your skill at sail-handling was suddenly redundant. The crews resented the engineers too. They took no apparent risks—never went out in a dory—but took a double share of the revenue anyway. Technical prowess, skills—here Santos again—"gave way to a place in a hierarchy," and it rankled.[3]

It's true that dorymen were not infrequently exploited in the "older days" (that observant English traveller John Josselyn described as early as 1638 how merchants trapped men in a web of bondage caused by drunkenness and indebtedness[4]), but the new wage slavery meant that no man could count on work, for all were replaceable at the whim of the owners. There should be no outcry over the ending of a way of life. Why should there be? Other industries had gone through the same thing, and no one had regretted their passing, had they? Progress was inevitable.

Actually there *was* an outcry. This was at least partly because schooners did not at all resemble smokestack industries, no matter the theoretical similarities—they were, not to put too fine a word to it, beautiful. And partly because writer after writer had romanticized the fisherman and his family until they became obscured in a thick varnish of schmaltz. The outcry that resulted was sustained by the attention given to the fishermen's races. It's just that it made no difference at all.

To add to their powerlessness, the men found their livelihoods being reordered without their knowledge, as the grinding weight of industrialization changed the way the fishery was organized. In the 1840s and 1850s, single-vessel owners were still the norm in New England; but by the turn of the twentieth century most of the vessels sailing out of Gloucester or Boston were owned by an increasingly small group of fishing companies. At the same time, the power shifted from Gloucester to Boston, and as it did so the size of the proprietors grew ever larger. In 1884, when the industry essentially relocated to T Wharf in Boston, landings of fish at Boston totalled 18,514,086 pounds worth $383,973, only 18 per cent of the tonnage and 13 per cent of the value of Gloucester's take. But by 1887 Boston was already getting 93 per cent of the tonnage and 72 per cent of the value of Gloucester's take.[5] There were still large fishery operations in Gloucester, such as the venerable Gorton-Pew, but their focus was increasingly selling their produce in Boston and beyond.

In 1905, financial men from Boston formed the Bay State Fishing Company, one of the earliest attempts to translate to a resource industry the notions of integration and consolidation that were emerging in manufacturing, along with all its ills—union bashing, the breaking up of guilds, the almost alchemical translation of traditional skills into mechanized process. Their intention, if not their methods, is easily recognizable to a modern eye—it is no different from a corporation like, say, Sony, which makes movies and then attempts to control the medium through which they are distributed and shown. The Bay State managers wanted to control every aspect of the fish business, all the way up the line. They would catch their own fish, process them, and then sell them. In the first year of its existence the company built the steel-hulled trawler *Spray*, and within a year had turned a profit and was launching five more vessels. There were attempts to head off the inevitable by banning landings by trawler, on the modern-sounding grounds that they would destroy the resource through overfishing, but to no avail.

By 1912, the trawlermen had already gone out on strike, with no good outcome. In 1915, there was another walkout, and an attempt to get a union recognized. Not successful. In 1918, they struck again, this time for a wage increase and an increase in crew size. The following year, in a significant sign of the changes that had been wrought, the remaining sailing vessel crews struck too, marking the final change from worker autonomy to collective action. Even the skippers weren't immune; they were told when to go out and when to come in, and were always reachable and therefore accountable and therefore vulnerable, by radio or telegraph, to a subsequent port of call.

By 1917, thirty-seven independent fish-trading firms in Boston and Gloucester had consolidated into two, and the remaining independents were under threat. Five years later, when the *Bluenose* races were already under way, the U.S. Supreme Court convicted the Boston Fish Pier, which operated a fleet of steam trawlers, of conspiracy to monopolize the market by buying up the remaining twenty-five small independents.[6] At the same time, vessels got bigger, and more efficient, and by 1925 only a third of the landings were from schooners, including those with auxiliary engines.

Things changed more slowly in Canada, where owner-operated vessels remained the norm until the end of the century and beyond. Nova Scotia had been lagging behind the technological changes too (its decentralized shipbuilding industry, once its great strength, found the transition to building the more demanding steel vessels too difficult), but fishermen nevertheless kept abreast of what was going on. Lunenburgers particularly were watching carefully, and as early as 1912 were lobbying hard to ban mechanized trawling. Nova Scotia had outlawed trawling within the 3-mile limit the previous year, mostly to protect its inshore fishermen, and now the Banks fishermen were looking for protection too, so Nova Scotia was trying to persuade the federal government in Ottawa to extend the ban to all trawling. But the industrialists were against them, and money from Halifax soon financed trawlers out of Port Hawkesbury and Canso, most of them dealing in fresh fish.

A sign of the times was that two dozen schooners were sold to trawling companies by 1922—none of which then used Lunenburg as home port because it had no facilities for handling fresh fish. It wasn't until four years later that Lunenburg Sea Products (later National Sea Products and now Highliner Foods) built a cold-storage facility, and the first dragger was based in Lunenburg a few years after that.

Still, "steam trawling" and dragging remained controversial, if inevitable—there really wasn't any way for the Canadians to avoid going through what the Gloucestermen had already experienced. But in 1928 the cumbersome machinery of the federal government lumbered into action anyway, with the classic Canadian solution to any social conundrum: appoint a commission to study it. The commissioners duly interviewed everyone they could and were besieged with angry fishermen, operators of small fish plants, boat-builders and other interested parties, none of whom agreed with each other except to condemn the menace of steam trawling and dragging. They paid visits to what were still the major fish-catching ports: Shelburne, Lockeport, Lunenburg. The claims most often made were that even beam trawling was severely damaging the industry and the viability of small fishermen, and was also damaging the fish stocks on which they all depended. The main point made was that the vaunted efficiency of draggers was illusory. They were efficient for their operators, perhaps, but at ruinous cost. In dragging, particularly, the wastage of stock was immense—for every 350,000 pounds of fish brought to market, another 200,000 were simply thrown away—wrong species, wrong size, too much damage. Schooners, on the other hand, caught only good-quality fish—the dorymen's habit of knocking dogfish and skate off the hooks and throwing them back conveniently forgotten—without cost to the resource itself. Auxiliary power, they pointed out, made fishing schooners more efficient but not at the same cost to the resource. They could amply supply the local market with fresh fish. Draggers were, not to put too fine a point on it, just not needed, except to make money for their owners.

Perhaps disappointingly for the government, the commission's final report was trenchant: they recommended banning all mechanized trawling. The government's first response was a partial ban. Trawlers would not be allowed to work in winter.

This paltry solution of course satisfied no one. Trawling was still to be allowed, which annoyed almost everyone except the trawling interests. But trawlers were not to be permitted to make their industry profitable, which infuriated them; in their view, the government was simply subsidizing inefficiency. No one yet spoke for the fish, soon to be victims of the new industrial sin called "surplus efficiency."

The trawling industry proposed a compromise: allow trawling all year but limit catches and especially landings to Canadian-owned vessels. The government accepted this proposal but added a revenue wrinkle of its own: very high licence fees were imposed on trawling and dragging vessels. This was promptly denounced as a tax on efficiency. Again, no one was satisfied.

Just as in Gloucester, the changing ownership structure of the industry exacerbated the problems. Impersonal corporate money replaced personal financing from small investors.

In March 1930, *The Atlantic Fisherman*, in a report from Lunenburg, outlined the key issue—that the Canadian fishery was

organized into smaller units that depended on amiable cooperation between owners and fishermen: "The fisheries of Nova Scotia . . . have skilled seamen who cooperate with each other and
firms of long standing who are scattered over the rural parts of
Nova Scotia. The beam trawler implies corporation control. Its
appearance in numbers means that the skilled fishermen who are
able might secure jobs as coal heavers for a monthly salary or [have
to] leave the country to seek opportunity in other lands."[7]

For the fishermen themselves, the issues went beyond the business of wage slavery versus sharing. In all the dozens of small communities that had practised boat-building and fishing, there were
small fish plants that processed stock brought in by local people.
Not just Lockeport and Yarmouth and Lunenburg, but Pubnico,
Port Medway, Dayspring, Port Mouton, Petite Riviere, Big and Little Tancook Islands, East Ironbound—small communities utterly
dependent on a certain way of doing things, with its consequences
for community, cooperation, self-reliance, and an interdependent
way of life. As an old fisherman, quoted by Peter Barss, put it,
". . . it's just an endless chain—goes right around. These fellers
on the draggers here think they're doin' good fishin' on Sundays,
but they're not. They're losin' on t'other end." Losing that meant
losing control over the pace of their own lives, a certain quality of
living, and implied becoming cogs in the industrial machine, a
proletariat. It was an evil choice.

For the skippers, who had worked their way up from throater to
doryman to second and then first hand, the change was even more
profound. Steam trawling made their skills irrelevant. Dragging
was worse. No point in learning to think like a fish, or to understand the sea, or to have a feel for your living vessel and her skittish
ways . . . All you had to do now is drag a net or a bucket along the
bottom, catching everything that swims and ruining everything
you touch . . . It took no skill to drive a bulldozer across a front
lawn with the blade down, did it? Sure, it mowed the lawn, but

then the lawn was gone, wasn't it? Dragging was the fisheries equivalent.

They were right, of course. It's why they invested so much emotion in the international races. Those took nerve and skill and deftness and strength which could never be replaced, or so they believed; they were a showcase for what had been and what could still be, given the chance. The public and their surrogates, the newspaper writers, sensed some of this too, and invested the races with a romantic attachment to the notion that skill could still somehow trump "the system." Not that it made any difference in the end. Except to postpone the inevitable.

CHAPTER TEN

HER

FAMOUS

VICTORIES

*I*f the run-up to the 1921 races had been rancorous, the races themselves had generated little controversy. The following year, though, it was different. The elimination series in both Canada and the United States went off with hardly a hitch. It was the races themselves and the way they were organized that became the problem.

In Canada, the *Bluenose* had not yet assumed the status of an unassailable icon, and faced challengers who thought they could beat her to become the Canadian contender. *Canadia* still thought she could win, for she seemed to be sailing better than the year before, and so did two other vessels, the *Mahaska* and the *Margaret K. Smith*. *Mahaska* was built for Captain Paddy Mack, who in 1908 had built the Canadian version of McManus's *Clintonia*, also called *Clintonia*, whose graceful line and attractive sail plan had taken his eye; she was an exact copy, built at the Smith and Rhuland yard in

Lunenburg. The *Mahaska* had won several hook-on races during the season, and Mack was confident she would do well against any rival. The *Margaret K. Smith* was another Smith and Rhuland hull. She had entered for the fun of it, because she wouldn't be eligible to race against the Americans, only having been launched a few months earlier.

Only one race was needed, as it turned out, but it did serve to illustrate the *Bluenose*'s legendary speed. Ironically, she needed to show her speed mostly because of two rare errors of seamanship by Angus Walters. First, he was "caught in irons" at the start—that is, headed so directly into the wind he could move neither to starboard nor port—and had to wait agonizing minutes for an errant breeze to swing him about. The *Bluenose* was a full five minutes late crossing the start line. But with the wind closing in on 20 knots she began hauling in her rivals, and within half an hour was in second place behind the *Margaret K. Smith*. With his eye on his rival, he paid less attention than he should have to the course, and as he roared past the *Smith* he also roared past the Inner Automatic Buoy—on the wrong side. The *Smith* followed him. Both the *Canadia* and the *Mahaska* swept by on the correct side, and took the lead.

As the *Toronto Telegram*'s Jerry Snider put it, Angus roared out his orders to come about, and "thirty oil-skinned figures jumped like scalded cats to their stations." The big vessel swung about to repass the missed buoy on the proper side. By this time the *Canadia* was almost a mile ahead, with the *Mahaska* close behind her. "Spit on your hands and never say die, boys," Angus Walters yelled. "I got us into the hole, but the *Bluenose* will get us out." Indeed, the *Bluenose* was not to be denied; she headed up into the wind, sailing as close as a canny skipper could, and with spume flying and green water racing along her sail with a great hiss she passed the *Mahaska*, caught up with *Canadia* and forged ahead, crossing the finish line a full seven minutes before any of her rivals.

There were no other races. The wind had disappeared and none of the vessels finished the next day, or the day after that. The race committee had no hesitation in opting for the *Bluenose*, and got no dissent from the others. She was escorted to Gloucester by the destroyer *Patriot*.

Gloucester, for its part, was busy changing its mind. Having gamely lost the trophy with the venerable but outclassed *Elsie*, Gloucester's considered opinion began to shift. Clearly, nothing currently afloat, except perhaps *Mayflower*, had any chance of beating the formidable *Bluenose*, and the town's antipathy to purpose-built racers-that-fish (and to a lesser degree to Boston itself) melted quietly away.

Within a few months three new keels were laid in Gloucester and Boston: the *Puritan*, the *Yankee*, and a still-unnamed boat rising on the stocks at the famous Arthur D. Story yard in Essex, designed by Tom McManus, to be skippered by Clayton Morrissey.

The *Yankee*, financed by a group of Boston racing enthusiasts, was smaller than the other two, a pretty little vessel that turned out to be a good all-round fishing boat. But she drew much less public attention than the other two, and when she was eliminated in the American preliminary series, she didn't race again.

The public face of the *Puritan* was a well-known Gloucester fishing skipper, Jeff Thomas, but the real driving force was Ben Pine, a Newfoundlander who had built a Gloucester junk business into a formidable fishing fleet. Pine was a bluff man with equal amounts of charm and ruthlessness; he was known for his charity to indigent seamen and lost boys on the wharves of his adopted city, but also as a man who didn't scruple to bankrupt his opponents. He moved easily between the working fishermen and the moneyed elite at Eastern Point. He wasn't a fisherman himself—he'd been to sea, though never as a working man—but he loved the life and was caught up in the romance of the races. He'd actually borrowed a boat, the *Philip P. Manta*, from Manta himself so he'd have something to sail in the elimination races in 1921. He came last, but then the *Manta* was old and a little hogged, and everyone agreed Pine had handled her competently.

The conception of the *Puritan* followed *Elsie*'s loss by only a matter of hours. Pine had crewed on the *Elsie* to get a feel for the races, and so was in Halifax anyway; that night he met with Thomas and a couple of other businessmen, including at least one banker, and by October 25, the Pine–Thomas syndicate announced their intention of building a contender. They called themselves the Manta Club, and hired Starling Burgess to design it for them, the same Burgess who had designed the elegant but rejected *Mayflower*. The money was Pine's. The expertise, the "driver," was to be Jeff Thomas.

Burgess's instructions were clear: build another racer that could be disguised as a fisherman, make her as fast as *Mayflower* but avoid the gaudy elements that had led to *Mayflower*'s disqualification— make her look like a fisherman, at least. And so he did: the result was a little smaller than *Mayflower* but still a big boat, 123.9 feet on deck, the longest fishing schooner in Gloucester, and with the tallest main mast, 89 feet. Her lines approached those of a true fisherman, but everyone agreed she was quick and nimble, "a flying fool," able to reel in 15 knots in a good breeze. On her maiden voyage she ran away from a sub-chaser steamer, and on the one occasion she "got into a hook" with *Mayflower* she beat her handily.

But she was never to be tested against the mighty *Bluenose*. On her third fishing voyage under Jeff Thomas, carrying a full press of sail in a thick fog, she ran aground on Sable Island's northwest bar, and was completely wrecked, with one man drowned. The legend was that she was "so fast she had gotten ahead of herself," overrunning her course by 20 miles, her skipper not expecting that Graveyard of the Atlantic for another hour or so. The story on the Gloucester waterfront and in the skippers' clubs, though, was somewhat less flattering. Jeff Thomas had supposedly had too many snootfuls of rum, and was said to be more or less comatose when she ran aground.[1] Be that as it may, Jeff Thomas came home from Sable and never raced again.

The Manta Club had no comment, but Ben Pine announced he would build yet another vessel for the following year, a new *Puritan* that would no doubt trim the sails of anything then afloat. Fishing was nowhere mentioned in his announcement, only winning. Fishing was most definitely not the point anymore. It was just one of the rules of engagement.

For 1922, Pine chartered the McManus-designed knockabout *Elizabeth Howard* from its New York owners, the revised rules under the Deed of Gift making her newly eligible, and having been infected with the racing bug, decided to skipper her himself. He refitted the *Howard* as a semi-knockabout with a short bowsprit, and set her up for fishing.

Meanwhile the boat at the Story yard was being planked up and was almost ready for launch. Gloucester legend has it that the skipper, the taciturn Clayton Morrissey, had mortgaged his home to see her built, against his wife's explicit wishes, and it may be true, although most of the money came from wealthy Eastern Pointers, who didn't care if she ever made a penny fishing—they wanted her to win.

The vessel wasn't named until late in the building process, and to everyone's surprise Clayt decided to name her the *Henry Ford*, after the Detroit tycoon. If he hoped that Ford would therefore be persuaded to put up some money he was disappointed; all he got was a polite letter from Detroit saying that Ford agreed to have his name used, wished him well, and would be following the vessel's activities with interest.

The aging Charlie Harty, who had only recently declared *Mayflower* to be the finest vessel ever built, now came out for *Ford*: "The nearest thing to perfection of any fishing schooner ever built," the old man declared. Gloucester was no longer irritated, only amused.

At 138 feet on deck, the *Ford* was shorter than the *Bluenose*, though she carried almost as much sail, something that would soon ensnare her in the increasingly meticulous regulations governing the races. She was also damaged on launch and missed her deadline for fishing, but the American racing committee decided to qualify her anyway.

As they did so—and because they did so—the *Mayflower*'s owners once again applied, arguing that though she had been disqualified the year before, she had since put in a summer and winter fishing—unlike *Ford*, they pointed out. At first the Gloucester committee accepted her. After all, she had been highliner of the Boston fleet that year, bringing in 116,000 pounds of fish on her last voyage, and it was now hard to argue she wasn't a bona fide fisherman. But the Canadians once again rejected her, and in a testy response Gloucester said they'd insist on her eligibility should she win the elimination series. When that got no response from Halifax, they suggested postponing the races for a year pending a discussion about revising the rules. When this offer was also ignored, Gloucester yielded and banned *Mayflower* once again. Too much was now at stake to see the races cancelled.

The Canadian argument for not accepting the *Mayflower* was essentially the same as the previous year's, that she had been designed for racing and in no way conformed to the ideal of a schooner wholly adapted to the industry. In any case, they argued, it was unfair to race an American fresh fisherman against a Canadian saltbanker, because fresh fishermen were designed for speed and saltbankers for cargo. This was even more specious a reason than before. Not only was the *Bluenose* "designed for speed," but the given reason rather ignored that the *Mayflower* had been salt fishing since her launch.

The miffed Mayflowers, as the owners called themselves, immediately challenged the winner of the next international series to a single winner-take-all race. To this, they got no response.

With the *Mayflower* disqualified and *Puritan* pounded to pieces in the Sable Island surf, four boats entered the elimination races around the Cape Ann triangle: the *Henry Ford* under Clayt Morrissey, the *Yankee*, the *Elizabeth Howard* under Ben Pine, and the *L.A. Dunton*.

The McManus-designed 123-footer *Dunton* was also built at Essex's Story yard in 1921, and her skipper, another Newfoundlander called Felix Hogan, although not known as a racing skipper, decided to have a fling and entered her in the elimination races. There, she was badly outclassed, and returned to fishing. (She was sold to Aaron Buffet of Newfoundland in 1934, cut down to a ketch rig, and fished the Grand Banks until the 1950s, when she was sold as a coaster. Mystic Seaport acquired her in 1963, and restored her to her original condition. The *Picton Castle*'s Dan Moreland was one of the restorers; and the *Dunton* is still at Mystic, the last of the saltbankers still afloat.)

The actual races were something of an anticlimax. Ben Pine's *Howard* had her trestletrees give way in a gust soon after the race started, and the main topmast tumbled to the deck, putting her out of the running. *Dunton* trailed far behind, and the *Yankee* didn't fare much better. *Henry Ford* it would be, with Clayt Morrissey at the helm.

Like Marty Welch before him, Clayt was from Nova Scotia, hailing from Lower East Pubnico down near the southwest of the province, a part of what is known as the French Shore. His first command, at the age of nineteen, had been his father's schooner, the *Effie M. Morrissey*, another vessel now at Mystic Seaport as the *Ernestina*, but he soon made his way to Massachusetts like so many of his fellows. He was an experienced mariner and a well-loved captain with a daring streak. He skippered many vessels in his time, but his favourite was always the *Arethusa*, a boat named after one of his daughters. Once he used her to outrun a Canadian Coast Guard cutter, the *Curley*. The *Arethusa* had been fishing within the Canadian territorial limits off Cape Breton, and Clayt had just sent his men ashore in dories to buy what bait they could, when the *Curley* steamed toward him at full speed. Clayt hurriedly up-anchored and sped away, rapidly outpacing the cutter. (The next he saw of his men was at St. Pierre, to which they had hitched a ride. He took them aboard, acquired new dories, and nonchalantly resumed fishing.)

Clayt was a tall, gangly man, taciturn and unsmiling, so much the prototypical fisherman that the sculptor Leonard Craske used him as a model for the fisherman's statue that now stands on Gloucester's Western Avenue. He was a reluctant racer and even more reluctant celebrity; he agreed to take part in the races because it was the only way he'd get his vessel built, but he never found the races fun, and rejected any notion that he was a sports hero, despite the popular press's sporadic attempts to liken him to people like Jack Dempsey and Babe Ruth, working-class heroes who did, in the end, play to the stereotype.

The actual races didn't go well. In an ill omen, Clayt Morrissey was told less than twenty-four hours before the first start that his mainsail was too big. The sail-size provision in the Deed of Gift's rules had come back to haunt him. ("Vessels shall race with the same spars and no greater sail area than used in fishing, but the sail area not to exceed 80 per cent of the square of the waterline length as expressed in square feet.") The scrutineer (another innovation of the yachting crowd, and an MIT professor to boot) had measured and hemmed and hawed and finally declared that two 20-inch strips had to be cut from the mainsail. Tom McManus, who had started the whole thing with his no-rules, anyone-can-enter fishermen's races and who had designed the *Ford*, was outraged. He called it butchery, and so it was. Clayt Morrissey's feelings weren't recorded. He hauled 'em down, cut 'em off, and showed up at the start line the next day. At least he and Angus respected each other. He could still make a contest of it.

At race time, there was barely a breeze. So light were the winds that the race committee decided to postpone the start by thirty minutes, and a Canadian destroyer was dispatched to tell the skippers. Neither of them paid any attention, to the destroyer and its message or to the tiny black ball hoisted on the judging boat that was supposed to denote a postponement. Both Angus and Clayt naively believed they were the masters of their own destiny, and both agreed to start anyway. In the end, *Ford* finished ahead, but the race took longer than the six hours allotted, and the race committee declared the result null. Both contestants had made false starts, the judges declared.

Both skippers protested. Angus had said right after the finish that "it's a race for Clayton. We'll take him tomorrow." To McManus he said ("in a rare show of grace," as McManus's biographer, W.M.P. Dunne, put it), "she beat me fair and square, and she beat me plenty." Clayt Morrissey, who hadn't wanted to race in the first place, and who had nothing but contempt for yachtsmen and their poncy rules, said the hell with it and decided to go fishing instead. What made it worse was that the official who had measured the *Ford*'s sails declared, again, that they were still too big and would have to be trimmed yet again.

Had it been Angus, he would have done exactly what Clayt threatened to do, upped his anchor and gone fishing; indeed, in a later dispute that was very similar, Angus did. But Clayt couldn't. In theory it was "his" boat, but the Eastern Pointers who had put up most of the money wanted him to stay the course. When their pleas for him to stay on "for the honour of Gloucester and in the spirit of sportsmanship" fell on deaf ears, they brought in the secretary of the navy, who appealed to the crew's patriotism and, shrewdly, to Clayt's Nova Scotia origins: "Never let it be said," declared the secretary, Edwin Denby, "that the men of the Pubnicos and Clark's Harbour were the ones to trail Old Glory in the dust."

The second race was just more of the same. There was hardly any breeze, and the two vessels drifted around the course, moving at the speed of a dinghy. At each mark, the *Ford*, the better boat in light winds, was a few seconds farther ahead. The *Bluenose* sailed under a protest flag (the vessel had settled on a rock and had gashed her keel, and Walters wanted time to inspect the damage), but the protest was disallowed, and it made no real difference. At the finish, the *Ford* had won by a short margin, but again, the committee decided to declare the race void. This time, though, the vociferous protests of both skippers was heard. Chalk one win up to Clayt.

Once again, he prepared to sail for the Banks. In his view, he'd won twice, and that was that. The cup should be his. Once again he was bullied by his owners into staying on. His wife told him to quit; it wasn't worth it. Worse, their son lay deathly ill and he should be home. The races were a travesty. He should get out.

Jerry Snider recounted her dramatic appeal. "Think of my boy lying at death's door," she told Clayt and his crew. "Boys, think of your own mothers and wives. Why should you go out at the point of your lives for the pleasure and the profit of a lot of miserable millionaires who have money on this race? Angus Walters says he is willing to call both races you won yours, and let it go at that."

Miserably, Clayt wandered over to the *Bluenose* to talk to Angus and find out what he thought. But Angus wasn't about to make the decision for him. "We're good friends, Clayt," Walters said, "but there are people around here trying to make us bad friends. If you lay to the wharf I'll lay to the wharf, and if you go out, I'll go out."

Clayt went back to his vessel to tell the crew to get ready. To his wife he said, "Go home now. I must go, they've got me."

The public sympathized with Morrissey, "and were quick to blame the yachting crowd. But if he really had gone fishing he would have been vilified," as Santos put it; he would then no longer have been a working-class hero, living up to the middle-class fantasies generated by the press, a perception based on a supposed earlier and more heroic time that had made America great.[2]

As Claude Darrach points out, and as Nova Scotians know in their bones, off the eastern seaboard light winds are merely known as weather breeders, and in due course the real breezes returned. Both the next two races were sailed in squally 25-knot winds.

Both vessels hit the start line of the third race together, only seconds apart, but Angus had the weather gage and Clayt had to hang back to escape his wind shadow, and fell a length or two behind. The *Bluenose* rounded the first marker a minute or so in the lead, but in the heavy swells of the open sea they were so close they might have been cabled together, tacking in unison and shouting insults at each other across the narrow gap. *Ford* pulled ahead for a minute or so, but the *Bluenose* slowly reeled her in, and as they passed the second mark she was well in the lead. When they got to the last and windward leg, the *Bluenose* pulled steadily ahead. Even Clayt remarked on it. "I don't mind saying that in a breeze of wind she is too much for us going to windward," he said afterwards.

The *Bluenose* crossed the finish line more than seven minutes in front. The series was officially tied, one race each.

Before the start of the 4th and final race, an emissary from *Ford* appeared to ask for a postponement. A gale was blowing, 4-knot winds. But Walters refused. "I didn't come here to sail until Christmas," he said. "I'm going to the line. If you're there, fine."

On the second leg of the race, *Ford* broke a topmast in a strong gust, and Walters won comfortably. Some of the yachting crowd complained that weather fit to break a topmast wasn't fit for racing, but Clayt scorned to adopt that view and conceded the race. Angus was typically acid: "The *Ford* was kind of tender-sided," he said. "I never could figure it out, but something the Gloucestermen never seemed to learn was not to over-canvas their vessels. Practically all I saw carried too much sail and that made them tender weather boats."[3] He'd already said something similar about the *Mayflower*, that "they've bent every bloody bed sheet in Boston onto her!" Running and reaching before the wind, the *Ford* was fine, he said. "But the last leg was to windward. She fell over and damn near stayed there. Thank God it was the last leg or they would have called it [the race] off. Around the last turn we were no further apart than from here to the corner. At the finish, they were so far to loo'ard you could hardly see them."[4]

Even the most grudging Americans conceded *Bluenose*'s magical ability to windward. "[She was] not much handicapped by Angus's rare sportsmanship in shortening sail when the *Ford*'s foretopmast broke," Joe Garland wrote.[5]

Tempers were so high in Gloucester that Angus Walters refused to let his crew ashore. His nephew, Bert "Boodle" Demone, went anyway, and was found dead the next morning, battered and bruised, floating in the harbour. Angus believed he'd had a few too many and was shoved. "They had no use for our fellers," he said. The *Bluenose* sailed home with the cup and with her flag at half mast.

"Angus Walters reneged on his promise to meet the *Mayflower* in a match race after the Dennis Cup races, and the *Bluenose* surreptitiously departed for Nova Scotia under the command of her mate." Thus an influential American view.[6] This despite Boodle's death—and despite that the *Mayflower*'s cheeky challenge had never been accepted by anyone from the *Bluenose*. Tom McManus called the races "a bungling mess, disgusting," and said the *Ford* had been robbed. Members of the race committee were accused in the Gloucester press of having rigged the races; the race committee chairman, George Peebles, was forced to combat rumours that he had bet money on the *Bluenose*. Gordon Thomas, grandson of Captain Jeff Thomas of the *Puritan*, was more measured: "The races should have ended in a tie. *Ford* was like a gull with clipped wings. She proved she had the better of *Bluenose* running before the wind, but was no match for her beating against the wind. During the races she was frequently hove down until the solid water came up to the lee hatch coamings, or about nine feet inboard, and the sheer poles of her rigging eight feet above the deck were buried."[7] Everyone recalled the days of the early races, when fishermen just showed up to go racing, and almost everyone urged that the races be restored to the fishermen to whom they belonged.

But it was too late for that. The races were public spectacles. In Canada, the fishermen still had a piece of them. In America, by contrast, it seemed that the fishermen had become actors in a screenplay written by others, obliged to do whatever the script said they should.

The *Bluenose* slipped out of Gloucester quietly, her flag at half mast. No horn or bell marked her departure. The crowds that had lined the wharves had gone home.

CHAPTER ELEVEN

HER

ACRIMONIOUS

DUEL

with the

GLORIOUS

COLUMBIA

*I*n the months that followed the *Bluenose*'s hurried departure for home waters, a good deal of harrumphing and
posturing could be observed in Boston and Gloucester,
much of it aimed at their cousins up north. In order "to show Halifax how it should be done," Gloucester organized a regatta for its
300th anniversary (finessing the interesting fact that this 300th
anniversary in 1923 came exactly thirty years after the town had celebrated its 250th in fine style), and set in motion a race between
fishing schooners deliberately designed to be reminiscent of the

great events of the past, especially the Race It Blew of 1892—that is, no rules, no fuss, no restrictions on size or ballast or rigging. Under these circumstances, Clayt Morrissey came back with the *Ford*. Ben Pine raced the *Elizabeth Howard*, his new boat the *Columbia* having collided with a French vessel and being laid up for repairs in St. Pierre. In the end, the race was run in a fine breeze and Clayt won by a whisker and everyone said again how she was robbed in her races against the *Bluenose*.

In Nova Scotia the Bluenosers paid no attention. The cup was still on display in the Silvers' store window on Lincoln Street in Lunenburg, and that was proof enough.

Robbed or not, Ben Pine had considered the *Ford* good, but not good enough, and had gone back to Starling Burgess, the designer of the disqualified *Mayflower* and the speedy but jinxed *Puritan*, for more. The result was *Columbia*, considered by Angus Walters and many others as the finest challenger of them all, and by many as one of the most beautiful boats ever built—James Connolly wrote of her that "to see her sail coming bow on in a smooth sea and a fresh breeze—to see her so, viewing her from under her lee bow, and the way she had of easing that bow in and out of the sea—well the beautiful lady was poetry, then."[1] She was 124 feet long, some 20 feet shorter than the *Bluenose*, with a mainmast 93 feet tall and a boom stretching aft 80 feet. She had a short straight keel, a great raking stern, and a long bow that swept through the water. Silver Donald Cameron wrote that "a photograph of [her] just after her launching reveals her to have been one of those ships so sweet in her lines, so well favoured in her bearing, as to seem slightly unreal, like something beyond the capacity of mere men to create."[2]

Beautiful or not, she still had to be accepted by the Canadians as a contender. The rancour between Nova Scotia and Gloucester hadn't yet cooled down, and a new telegram from the committee in

Halifax brought it up to simmering point again. The telegram, peremptory and suspicious in its tone, as though the Gloucesterites would *put one over* if you didn't watch them closely, demanded that the Americans submit to Canada the plans for any vessel they planned to enter, so they could be matched against the new rules. This was too much. The American race committee responded within a few hours: take what we send you, or no races.

For a few days there was no reply, which only made things worse. Clayt Morrissey, this time with the backing of the *Ford's* owners, went fishing. So did the *Elizabeth Howard*. The comely *Columbia* kept her sails furled and remained at wharfside. Pine was furious. Tom McManus was heard telling everyone who would listen, *I told you so*. Was this to be *Mayflower* all over again? He urged Gloucester to put an end to it, to pretend the Canadians didn't exist, to consign Dennis and his cup to the trash can. But the races were by now too important to Gloucester to cancel so casually, and another exchange of telegrams followed. Gloucester demanded submission, or else. The Canadians said, well, send us only the *Columbia's* plans. The Americans sent them up but for "advisory purposes only"—there were to be no disqualifications. The Canadians said they'd disqualify any vessel that didn't meet the specifications.

But *Columbia* was not, after all, *Mayflower*. She was beautiful and fast, but she was clearly a fisherman, had already been to the Banks, and had done well there. Many of the fishermen on the Banks found out for themselves how fast she was, trying vainly to match her speed, whether she was empty-hulled on the way out or with a hold jammed with cod and haddock on the way in. To everyone's relief, the Canadian committee gave her the all-clear. Her mooring lines were let go and she was towed round to the yards to be hauled out and have her bottom scraped. To make sure she was the right choice, however, Gloucester decided to hold a series of elimination races after all. The *Howard* came back from the fishing grounds in plenty of time, and Clayt Morrissey arrived home in the *Ford*, loaded with 1,800 quintals of cod, mere hours before the first race was to begin, just as Maurice Whalen had, before he went on to come from behind and win the great Race It Blew. But Ben Pine spoiled the script by outsailing both his rivals to become the American contender. Tactlessly, he invited Clayt to join the *Columbia*'s crew for the races, but Clayt decided a winter fishing trip was more important. He had, finally, done with racing.[3]

There was one more hurdle to cross.

Ben Pine, strictly speaking, wasn't eligible to compete. The rules said the skipper had to be a man who had himself fished the Banks, and though Pine was acknowledged a fine helmsman, he was no fisherman. The Canadian committee asked Angus Walters what he thought. "Ben'll be fine," he growled, and that was that.[4]

The *Bluenose*, again, was to be the Canadian contender. She'd not been idle in the past year. She'd made two winter trips to the West Indies, each time bringing back cargoes of salt and molasses, had gone fishing both spring and summer but was back in Lunenburg in plenty of time to be scraped and painted. The *Canadia* had by now given up the challenge and was herself fishing. A new challenger, the 125-foot schooner *Keno*, was being constructed at the McLean yard in Mahone Bay, but she was not finished in time. (She never got a chance to race, then or later; on December 31 she left Louisbourg in Cape Breton on her maiden voyage to get frozen bait in Newfoundland, and vanished without a trace, drowning her skipper, Albert Himmelman from Lunenburg, and all seven crew members. In a revealing sidelight on the hazards still experienced at sea, one of the lost crewmen, Gabriel Demone of Lunenburg, had himself already lost two sons at sea, Elburn on the schooner *Cape Alert*, and Ivan from the *Halhawk*; another unlucky family was that of Heber Miller, whose young wife lost not only her husband on the *Keno* but a few years later four of her brothers—on the schooner *Mahala*—and in later years a son, Ronald, on the *Flora Alberta*.)

The *Columbia* ran aground on the way to Halifax, but was not seriously damaged. She turned back for repairs, and finally, on October 23, 1923, she swept into Halifax harbour.

The first two races, and there were only two, were rough affairs in the take-no-prisoners style of earlier contests. *Bluenose*, no longer a green vessel, had settled in the water somewhat as her wood absorbed seawater, and travelled under lighter ballast than before.

The start of the first race was in moderate westerlies, lighter than Walters would have liked, but he was first across the line and the boats stayed close to each other for the next few hours. As they turned the third marker to head back to Halifax harbour, the wind freshened to the southwest, and a "luffing match" ensued. *Columbia* was under the lee bow of the *Bluenose*, and kept nudging her to windward, a good tactic if it can be made to work. As they passed the Bell Rock Buoy to landward, the tactic became more dangerous. *Columbia* was crowding the *Bluenose* out of the channel and dangerously close to the shoal waters of Sambro Ledge, an ugly jagged thing that had ripped the belly from more than one hapless sailing craft.

Both craft were now boxed in. Ben Pine found himself with an awkward choice of his own making. He could swing away and let *Bluenose* through, but he'd risk losing the race. Or he'd risk crowding *Bluenose* onto the rocks proper, which was clearly against any rules of the sea, race rules or not. Angus, too, had a bad choice: swing away with the risk of collision and hope Ben let him through, risk running aground, or slow his vessel and finish a poor second.

Throwing the race wasn't an option, so it came to striking *Columbia* or striking the rocks. In the end, that wasn't much of a choice either. He yelled over to the *Columbia* to give him room.

"I'm swinging and I'm swinging fast!" he yelled, and swung over, his massive boom catching *Columbia*'s fore rigging, ripping off her sheer poles, and stretching her wire stays. For a while it looked as though the *Bluenose*'s main boom would leave its saddle and be torn free; for a heart-stopping minute it hooked a bight of rope at the bow and actually towed the *Columbia*, then she broke free and ran for home. She won by a mere eighty seconds.

All night the controversy raged. It was illegal to put another vessel on the rocks. It was also illegal to deliberately collide. American opinion was that Angus had blatantly fouled his rival and should be disqualified; opinion in Halifax was that Ben should be penalized for his dangerous tactics. The only two men whose opinion counted said nothing. Neither Walters nor Pine lodged any protest, and the result stood. Chalk one up for the *Bluenose*.

The racing committee, trying to head off such tactics in the future, changed the rules overnight. The ruckus had been caused by forcing Angus to pass Bell Rock Buoy to landward. Henceforth all buoys must be passed to seaward. This was a sensible enough notion, but they didn't trouble to consult the two skippers, and Angus at least didn't take the admonition seriously. He'd pay attention to race course marker buoys, of course, but he'd treat other navigation buoys the way he always had, as sometimes useful advisories. No one could tell him how to sail his own boat, after all. As Claude Darrach wrote later, "The committee would have done well if they had spent the intervening time playing golf, instead of . . . messing around with the rules."[5]

Columbia passed the night making repairs. The *Bluenose*, having seen *Columbia*'s ability, retrimmed her ballast. In Angus's view, his was still the better boat. *Columbia* was fast, but only in some wind aspects. *Bluenose* was still better to windward. He remained confident.

Moderate winds delayed the next race by two days, but they woke on November 1 to a gusty nor'easter, and at the start line the scuppers were awash. *Columbia* crossed the line a few seconds after the gun but a few lengths ahead of her rival; Angus started on the extreme east end of the line, and as a result he passed Light-house Bank Buoy to starboard instead of to port, as *Columbia* more properly did and as the revised rules stipulated. Otherwise there was no interference and both vessels sailed well, *Bluenose* coming in first by less than three minutes. As far as Angus was concerned, he had won cleanly, the cup was his, and the celebrations could begin.

It was not to be. Just before the celebration banquet was to start, both skippers were called out and told that the race was to be awarded to *Columbia*. Ben Pine had protested, as was his right under the new rules. Angus had indeed passed a buoy to landward, in violation of the new instructions. It was not considered relevant that by doing so he had actually crossed more water than *Colum-bia*, or that it would have made no difference at all to the outcome, or that it was a customs buoy and not even a course marker. A rule was a rule.

"Ben knows as well as I do that that there buoy don't mean nothin' in this race course," Angus protested. "Ben very well knows he couldn't beat us, so what's all this talk about buoys?"

He turned to the other skipper. "Ben," he demanded, "did I gain or lose anything by my passing the buoy on the side I did?"

Pine was noncommittal, and the committee was adamant. *Blue-nose* would be disqualified, and the race went to *Columbia*. Angus made a counterproposal that the race be disregarded instead, and was scathing about Pine, whom he otherwise liked. "I wouldn't have been so damn small as to accept a race I didn't win," he said. "But he never said a word. So I told them to go straight to hell, and we left."[6]

And leave he did, doing what Clayt Morrissey had wanted to do a year earlier but couldn't. He told the committee and whoever would listen that he was going back to Lunenburg to get ready for fishing. Who needed this aggravation, after all? Who was master of this vessel? Arthur Zwicker, director of the Bluenose Schooner Company, tried to dissuade him by appealing to his sportsmanship,

an oddly clumsy choice of words, for to Angus sport really had
nothing to do with it. Zwicker then called in the premier of Nova
Scotia, but this had no effect either; Walters was not Clayt Morrissey, to be bullied by his owners or embarrassed into an act of patriotism. He acted as the skippers of old would have done, as his own
master, subject to no man's whim. Zwicker instructed the Halifax
port tugboats to leave *Bluenose* at the wharf while he frantically cast
around for another crew to finish the series. But he had forgotten
that Angus was the managing director and could do what he liked,
and the still-furious skipper spied a passing coal heaver from Lunenburg (some accounts say a Halifax water boat) and persuaded it to
give him a tow out into the harbour. He raised sail for Lunenburg
and didn't come back, ending the international races for another
seven years.

The committee told Ben Pine all he had to do was sail around
the course by himself and he'd be given the trophy. This Pine
declined to do, by now rather chastened by the fuss, and set sail for
Gloucester. The series was declared a tie, the prize money divided
into two shares, and the cup stayed in Lunenburg.

The reactions in the two ports was sadly predictable. Pine received
a hero's welcome in Gloucester, where his virtue in declining to
take the series by default was contrasted to Angus's poor sportsmanship. W.M.P. Dunne put the Gloucester point of view baldly:
"The *Bluenose* won the first two races, but the Americans protested
the result of the second one when the Canadian boat intentionally
sailed on the wrong side of a mark. When the international committee failed to resolve the issue to his satisfaction, an already sulk-
ing captain Walters tossed a tantrum, packed up the *Bluenose* and
went home to Lunenburg in a state of high dudgeon."[7]

The Boston *Globe* was even more prissily disapproving: "All
racing off for 1923," its yachting editor cabled from Halifax. "And

no winner in the international fisherman's match. This is a result of the action of Capt. Angus Walters and his all-captain crew from Lunenburg, who when Thursday's race was awarded to the *Columbia* on a protest refused to race any more. Rather poor sports and cry babies, who when they were beaten at their own game would not play any more."[8] There were hints, always conveniently vague, that the affair of the buoy had only been the last straw, and that Angus had cheated and manipulated dozens of times before and had gotten away with it. Appalling poor form and all that, blathering on about the dreadful damage done to international sportsmanship, sounding more and more like something out of P.G. Wodehouse. Dash it, Walters didn't live up to the golden-hearted captain of Kipling's uplifting novel, what a shame.

Ben Pine's virtue in declining the series on a technicality was rather less well thought of in Lunenburg, where there seemed very little difference, morally speaking, between claiming a race on a technicality and claiming a series on the same flimsy grounds. In that view, Pine was a whiner, a loser who brought his rival down by invoking a silly rule that neither of them had accepted in the first place.

Back in Lunenburg, the Bluenose Schooner Company board met in Arthur Zwicker's office. The meeting was dominated by Angus Walters, who was still seething about the outcome of the contest. The company's minute book duly authorized him to take whatever action he needed to protect the good name of himself and his vessel, and reaffirmed that he had the power to do so without consulting the board itself. The wording was forthright: it declares that the *Bluenose* and her crew had "won two of the three races and proved . . . her and their superiority in sailing ability and seamanship over the other competitor . . . and by reason of the so-called protest lodged with the sailing committee certain disputes and differences arose and the Trustees of the said Trophy failed to award it and the winner the prize money." Angus was duly authorized to invoke a solicitor.

The lawyer's response also appears in the minute book: "It is elementary that the term and conditions of a contract cannot be changed by one party," the legal opinion said in its hectoring lawyerly way, ". . . and that the [racing] committee could not make any alteration to the conditions contained in the Deed of Gift and the Blue Folder handed to Captain Walters without his consent." This Blue Folder contained, among other things, the "courses of the series, and these could not be changed without consent, which was not forthcoming; his appearance for the start of the race did not constitute an acceptance of the changes made. He is therefore entitled to the trophy and the prize money. Further, the Deed of Gift itself mentions no Sailing Committee, nor does it empower the international committee to constitute such a body without express consent."

The solicitor's letter then abandons its judicial tone and becomes openly partisan: ". . . those responsible for the actions of the master of the schooner *Columbia* did not hesitate to resort to such measures [the idea of deciding the outcome of a sporting event by a resort to legal technicalities] to obtain a technical victory for *Columbia* which on her merits she did not deserve, and then placed themselves before the public as heroes on the grounds that they refused to take the trophy on a technicality, my clients do not feel disposed to tolerate such inconsistency without making a counter-move . . . Therefore this letter is being sent also to certain press correspondents having seen fit to severely criticize Captain Walters actions in withdrawing *Bluenose* from the series . . ."

These "certain press correspondents" included the yachting editor of the Boston *Globe*, and James Connolly. Neither of these parties changed their minds, and the letter had no effect on the official outcome.

But it made Angus feel better. His honour had been impugned, and he had struck back. He could go back to fishing.

A more sympathetic American view was that "the public really didn't want a genuine fishermen's race if it involved real fishermen.

They wanted Ben Pine, who was at home behind the wheel but also at Eastern Point. The races were the result of marketing and public relations, and Walters was not [Kipling's] Disko Troop."9

There was a curious footnote to the affair that has not been mentioned before, and which rather fights the romantic view of Angus's lifelong attachment to his beloved *Bluenose*. The microfilmed records of the Bluenose Schooner Company in the fisheries museum archives contain a note, dated December 1923, that the board, with Angus assenting, authorized Angus to put the *Bluenose* up for sale by tender. It's not recorded why. But if the *Bluenose* had been built to race, and the races were over . . . who needed the *Bluenose* anymore? On January 7, a cryptic scribbled note in the minute book said the vessel had been sold to one Mr. E.C. Adams for $18,000. Edwin Adams owned a clothing store in Lunenburg, and it's unclear why he wanted the *Bluenose*, but the price would have been a bargain, since *Bluenose* had cost $35,000 to build, and was insured for $20,000, "hull only." Presumably the sale didn't go through, because Mr. Adams was not mentioned again, and the Bluenose Schooner Company didn't disband.

CHAPTER TWELVE

HER

DISPIRITING

LIFE

in the

GREAT

DEPRESSION

Bill Roué, who was building a solid career as a skilled naval architect, was not particularly sentimental about the *Bluenose*. He was proud of her, but if he could build a boat to beat her he would, especially after being stiffed by her owners for his expenses, and having to set a lawyer on them to get his fee. So when he was approached to build another and better *Bluenose*, he didn't hesitate.

The money came from a group of Halifax yachting people fronted by H.L. Montague. They never admitted it publicly, but it seems clear they were prodded by the Halifax racing committee, who had finally realized that Angus Walters was not a man to do their bidding, and wanted a backup, just in case. It was no secret that the new vessel was meant to beat the *Bluenose*. Prudently, they had her built not in Lunenburg at the Smith and Rhuland yard, but down the coast in Shelburne, at the Shelburne Shipbuilders Ltd. yard under the direction of master shipwright James Harding. She was smaller than the *Bluenose*, 128 feet on deck, which most people agreed was anyway a better size for a fishing boat. She was a sleek and elegant vessel, as most of Roué's designs were, with *Bluenose*'s long racehorse taper but lower forward than *Bluenose*. (Roué didn't have the irascible Angus standing over his drawing board making changes; and at her launch celebrations he made a point of congratulating the builders and her skipper on how faithfully they had followed his designs, everyone present acknowledging this as a dig at Angus.) She was also strong. The *Shelburne Gazette and Coast Guard* noted that "her materials were stronger and better than those of an ordinary fisherman. Her keel, her sternpost etc. were of oak, her decking of spruce and Oregon pine; her iron work was particularly admirable, and the blacksmith, Mr. Spidel, received many compliments on his work."[1]

The vessel was named *Haligonian*, and launched on March 25, 1925; with schoolchildren given a day off to watch her slip down the ways in unusually warm late-winter weather, it was from all accounts a wonderfully festive and celebratory occasion. The skipper was a Lunenburger, Moyle Crouse, who knew Angus well— he had sailed with Angus in the races against *Elsie* in 1921—and believed he could clip him when the time came.

Like most schooner skippers, Crouse was confident of his own ability. None of them were awed by the success of *Bluenose* and Angus Walters. They knew Angus was a pretty good sail carrier, but so were they. And they had good sound vessels. In their view, the *Bluenose* was just another fine schooner produced in Nova Scotia yards. More than a hundred of them were still afloat when she was launched, after all, including a dozen or more that they believed were every bit as good. Crouse sailed *Haligonian* for a few years before turning her over to George Himmelman, who fished her out of Lunenburg for four years. That was after the Halifax people had lost interest, and the ships' chandlers, Henry W. (Harry) Adams and Alexander Knickle of Lunenburg, had bought her at a sheriff's auction. "A & K" were colleagues and sometime business rivals of the Zwicker family who were co-owners of the Bluenose Schooner Company. They had founded their family firm as out-fitters in 1897, and were moving into the fishing business them-selves—later, they introduced deep-sea scallop dragging to the port of Lunenburg—and were not reluctant to have a fast and able schooner of their own. For his part, Crouse himself got out of the fishing business and into the more lucrative trade of supplying thirsty Americans with the whisky they craved; in the mid thirties his vessel *Cadet* was seized off Nantucket by revenue agents and Crouse was arraigned in New Haven, Connecticut. Nothing came of it, and he raced again with Angus Walters in the last international series, in 1938.

Plans were laid for the *Haligonian* to race the *Bluenose* later in the year, after the summer's fishing on the Banks, but it was not to be. With a hold full of cod, the *Haligonian* stopped in at Canso to rebait, but the fog held visibility down to less than 50 yards and she ran aground on a gravel shoal; she was refloated and seemed sound, but there were some fears her hull had been twisted. Less than two weeks later *Bluenose*, too, ran aground in Placentia Bay, Newfoundland, and was holed, spending four anxious days on the rocks before being taken to Burin for refitting and repairs. No fish-ing, no racing that year.

The following year, 1926, was a difficult one for the fishing fleet, and an almost fatal one for the *Bluenose*.

In April she got into a savage spring nor'easter with blinding snow and hurricane-force winds. Most of the accounts of the storm simply assert that Angus had himself lashed to the wheel throughout and sent the crew below to safety, but it was a little more complicated than that. He was, indeed, at the helm, but he wasn't always alone.

The *Bluenose* had been anchored 16 miles off the west light of Sable Island with a thousand feet of cable down and the treacherous island invisible under the horizon, in 27 fathoms of water. Then the cable broke and she began drifting. That was the "cheap" cable Sam Whynacht had warned Angus against: "Well," he recalled years later, "I'd looked at the cable he took on board an' I told him that wasn't a very good lookin' cable. He says, 'That's a new cable.'

"I said, 'Hell, all right.'

"So we went out . . . an' we got in a hurricane off the sou'west bar on Sable Island an' first t'ing the anchor was off—cable parted. The vessel was adrift and blowin' towards the island. Angus said we should try to heave the cable in. Well, we was heavin'-hovin' a little while an' I said there wasn't much sense in that because we had to condemn the cable anyway. So I went back an' told him and said, 'Why not cut that cable off? I just seen an outside trawl buoy go past up this side. That's one mile from where we was anchored. We're driftin' in here pretty fast.'

"'By t'under,' he said, 'I wouldn't like to lose that cable.' You see, the cable parted right down close to t'anchor. That's what made that a bad t'ing.

"I said, 'I wouldn't give two cents for that cable. Cut the damn t'ing off.'

"He said, 'How much cable did you heave in yet?'

"'Not too much,' I said. 'We should cut it.'

"'No, make it if you can.'

"So I said, 'We can get it in for all that, we can. But we should've chopped it long ago.' A bad sea was on and I was scared it would take someone o'erboard, you know, o'er the side. It was howlin' like a bull, the wind. It was howlin', I could hear it howlin' t'rough the riggin' an' everywheres.

"Well we was heavin' that damn old t'ing in an' all the time it was breezing up. We finally heaved in the rest of it, what was left. I didn't t'ink much of the situation, I tell you that."

Angus didn't think much of it either, as it happened. "I kept sounding until I got only eleven fathoms," he said later. "When I got that I sounded no more. We had no chance, really, after it had shoaled to fifteen. The seas break from the bottom then." Clem Hiltz, who was on board as a young lad, remembers Angus yelling at him to leave the lead alone, to "t'row the damn t'ing on t'deck and leave her be," and he did and went below.

Around midnight, the wind began to shift, to "haul." Sam Whynacht, whose watch it was, went back to the helm to talk to Angus. They yelled at each other, Sam recalled:

"'The wind's haulin',' Angus told him.

"'Well,' I said, 'how's the wind haulin', old man?'

"'Nor' to nor'west.'

"'Well,' I said, 'that's haulin' in our favour. All you have to do is veer the vessel an' go t'other way.'

"'Take the lead and have a sound,' he says, I took the lead an' sounded. It was [still] eleven fat'om. We was gettin' in closer. I could see the sand in the water then . . . the water was right white wit' sand. I went back an' I looked at the compass. Sizin' up the situation, you understand. I seen she was headed right into the nor'west. I told him again, I said, 'Why don't you veer the vessel 'round and let 'er go down t'other way, down past the island? You're not going to get acrost the bar because the wind is haulin' that way. That's the way it's startin' to haul an' that's the way it's going to finish up an' you can't make it.'

"He said, 'You t'ink we can veer her?'

"I said, 'Do you t'ink we can veer her! Why not? Either veer her or let her tear herself to pieces. One or the other. It's as bad as that.'

"'All right,' he said, 'stand by,' and he swung 'er off. I'd say that vessel went two miles. She went off to the side o' the wind . . . down . . . around. With the sea heavin' in there on the island . . . she done good. She headed up almost to the sou'east. It was the only t'ing we could do."

Then, indeed, Angus had himself lashed to the wheel and for the next six hours he kept her head up into the wind, biting into the gale, sailing almost parallel to the shore, gaining just a few yards with every tack.

"I never expected to see Lunenburg again," he said. "I stayed to the wheel because I didn't trust anyone else. They might have been as good as I was, but I knew the vessel. But I never knew all through that night when we was going to scrape bottom. You couldn't see the seas coming. Just the white capping up. Half the time you couldn't even see the white, it was snowing so hard. You could hear 'em coming. Got your feet planted, not that it would do any good. You'd get a grip but the sea would knock it out. Sometimes I was all under, just come up to get my breath."

Angus stayed at the wheel. By early morning, the watch crew were back on deck. "Alby, my brother was wit' us," Sam Whynacht recalled. "It was bein' his watch, first watch. An' he said, 'Don't keep us too full.'

"'Yes,' I said, 'hoist the jumbo yet.' Forestaysail is the right name of it, but we called it the jumbo. An' we hoisted it. Then we had the fores'l, stormsail, an' jumbo on.

"An' he said, 'Don't keep her too full.'

"'You go down below and we'll watch her.' First t'ing, I seen the water come o'er an' right down the stairs to the companionway an' strike my brother. He come up—soakin' wet—an' said, 'You're keepin' her too full.'

"Well, she took a couple of old wallows while she was goin' off. But she done famous . . . she done famous. An' she never drifted off any, you know. She held her own, see. That's the beauty of it. I knowed she could do it.

"When we were off an' our watch was up, I said to Alby, 'You get the lead tub and I'll take the lead ahead.' Well, I took the lead ahead, like you would to the foreriggin' for to t'row it o'erboard tryin' to get a plumb sound, you know. An' a sea broke. I heard it . . . couldn't see. It was dark. I heard the sea roarin'. An' I sung out to Alby, 'Watch out, there's a sea comin'!' An' I jumped for the riggin' an' I lost the riggin'. An' the next t'ing it picked me up . . . I was goin' over the cabin there . . . an' old kind of bait boards we had—big planked bait boards. The sea tore them right off. It was me an' the bait boards going' t'rough the sling lift on the main gaff. The bait boards went t'rough, but I caught the sling lift. When she was up—come up out o' the water, the water run off her—I called to Alby, 'Alby, you all right?'

"'Am I all right! Am I all right! You got too much damn sail onto her!' He was down in the cabin. He'd jumped down into the companionway. He was safe enough. See, that's all I was feared of, was him . . . that he was gone. We got the lead cleared out o' the mess an' took it up an' sounded. We had thirty fat'om o' water, thirty fat'om. We were out o'er the edge, startin' to get out o'er the edge of the bar. That was around two o'clock in the night."

Just before dawn, another massive sea struck. "I don't know when it struck 'er . . . but it woke 'bout everybody up. Struck 'er for'ard . . . smashed the rail off. Tore everything off her from the bowsprit right back to the break beam, cleaned 'er right off, you. When daylight come, then we had to look for gear. An' we got all o' the gear back—about all. But that old rotten cable—we still had that.

"Bent another anchor onto it an' t'rowed it o'erboard. An' there come a little blow again. First t'ing, the anchor was off again. Then we lost a set o' gear that time. Lost a set o' gear . . . the whole damn works—two seas o'er the deck an' it was gone. An' still we hove that cable in."

Angus stayed at the wheel throughout. "I was about all in, to be honest wit' you. Worst gale I've ever seen on the Banks. But she kept heading up, biting her way into the gale. Don't know as any other vessel could have done it."

Sam Whynacht often disagreed with the master, but not about that, though he couldn't resist one more dig: "Well, we condemned that cable—it wasn't no good an' I knowed it. I told the old man that but no, he wouldn't listen. That damn t'ing got us into a nasty old mess, but the *Bluenose*, she done famous. She pulled us out, you . . . an' I was onto plenty o' vessels that couldn'ta done what she done. She done good . . . She done famous, you."[2]

The morning after the gale there was Sable Island sand on the deck, and the taffrail log, towed behind the vessel, had its splices choked with sand. Clem Hiltz, who was below for most of the storm, believed for years that she had actually driven herself across Sable's fearsome bar. In any case, he says, "Angus lashed himself to the helm and sent us below. All night long we listened as he beat her to weather. Green water would crash over her and we'd wonder if the old man was still there. She had the deep-reefed fore and jumbo on her, and she'd make a little to weather like that. Not much, but I guess it was enough."

He was still a boy, though, with a boy's preoccupations, and Angus later remembered him asking, a little timidly, "Cap'n, you t'ink we'll be home time to get our Easter eggs?"

Later in the year, on August 7, an early-season hurricane struck the Banks, Sable, Quero, and the Grand Banks. It was only a Category One hurricane, but it appeared with no warning and was slow to pass, lasting all night and much of the next day, fourteen or fifteen hours of high drama, terror, and destruction: *Sylvia Mosher*, lost with all hands, *Sadie Knickle*, lost with all hands, *Mary Pauline*, lost two men overboard. The *Mary Ruth*, the *Golden West*, and the *Silver Thread* miraculously survived, having been driven, or having saved themselves, by sailing right across Sable Island's sandbar. On the mainland, just a hundred unreachable miles away, it was a beautiful day.

Three days after the storm, the *Mary Ruth* limped back into port, with nine of its crew seriously injured; its captain, Harris Conrad, had a broken shoulder, its sails were torn, all dories were gone, and even the cabin stove was smashed to pieces. The storm had driven the vessel onto the northwest bar of Sable Island, and the surf had swept it clear of everything that was left on the decks. Then, as though by a miracle, it was lifted by a massive wave and hurled free of the sandbar into clear water on the other side. There it lay to, "until the crew could sufficiently recover themselves to set sail for their home port, which they reached in a most exhausted condition."

The *Golden West*, from the LaHave River, was fishing on the south side of the island, several miles off, when the storm struck. It was one of the three vessels to save themselves by the desperate means of deliberately sailing over the bar into deep water beyond. Herbert Getson was the mate, and his brother was skipper. "The bar runs out there twenty miles and we crossed it in two places. My God, it was an awful sea. It was breaking on the bar and breaking right over the vessel—we lost 11 dories out of the 21. She only struck the one time and then the sea lifted her clear, and being a brand new vessel it didn't hurt her any. Then we got clear of the bar, got clear of everything and it was some better."

Getson's other brother was the master of the *Silver Thread*, and, although the vessel was thirteen years old and loaded with fish, it also managed to cross the bar into the relative safety of the deep water beyond, having first calmed the sea by throwing barrels of fish oil through the scuppers. As they approached the bar, the mate went down to the fo'c'sle and stood in the doorway. All hands looked at him standing there. "You got any friends home," he said, "now it's time to t'ink on 'em. Everybody on deck, if she strikes the bar we're all hands gone. It's every man for himself and the devil for us all."[3]

Neither *Bluenose* nor *Haligonian* were caught in the hurricane, and life goes on. In October the two boats finally faced each other over a course in Halifax. The first two races in a bare breeze were called because neither vessel finished in the time allotted, the *Bluenose* easily winning the next two.

Gloucester, and Ben Pine particularly, were watching all this with interest. There were dissenting voices. McManus's biographer, W.M.P. Dunne, asserting sourly that "following the *Columbia* series, Gloucester did itself proud by ignoring Walters for the next eight years; during that time, Gloucester held three agreeable and gratifying races for some of the last of the topmast-rigged fishing schooner breed."4 In fact, the city made several attempts at reviving the international series, to little enthusiasm from Canada; apparently Angus hadn't overcome his "sulk." In 1925, Ben Pine issued a challenge directly to Angus himself, but the telegram went unanswered; Angus was fishing and couldn't be bothered to reply. Still, when news of the *Haligonian–Bluenose* races was received, it was assumed this was an elimination race for a new challenge to Gloucester, and in the fall of 1926 there were two races between *Columbia* and her old rival the *Ford*. There was talk that the *Mayflower* would be invited too, but she declined. Invitations were issued to both *Bluenose* and *Haligonian*, neither of which showed up; Angus responded he'd only appear in Gloucester when they paid him the money owed from his having so clearly won the last international series. In the end, Ben Pine outsailed the *Ford* both times, the last time to an immense cheering crowd on Columbus Day. He immediately sent another telegram northwards. This time the Halifax committee answered. If Angus wouldn't race—which he should, having beaten his challenger—perhaps the *Haligonian* would. She'd be good enough for *Columbia*, no doubt of that.

It looked as though the races would resume after the season's fishing in 1927.

Again, it was not to be. There was another hurricane in August. A much, much worse hurricane.

In all the long and bleak history of the saltbankers, there was no storm that took a more terrible toll than the August Gale of 1927, a Category Two hurricane that struck so suddenly and without any warning that experienced seamen had no time to prepare, and many went down with their ships. A few survived, and their testimony of improbable escapes from the raging seas now fill to overflowing the file drawers in the archives of Lunenburg's fisheries museum. The granite monument on the Lunenburg waterfront to the men who died at sea shows the lists of names from the years 1926 and 1927 much longer than any other, more than 150 men and boys, from just a handful of tiny villages. One woman alone, Mrs. Granville Knickle of Blue Rocks, lost her husband, three brothers, and two brothers-in-law in that single 1927 storm.

Fred Crouse, who was "second hand" on the fishing schooner *Partana* out of Lunenburg under Frank Meisner, recalls the story. "Frank said to me, 'We're standin' a poor chance. Fred, there's only one t'ing that I would know that we got a chance . . . to swing her off and run her on the bar. Maybe if we run her on, she might jump it . . . can you get two men that will volunteer to take the wheel?'

"An' two fellas, Johnny Knickle and Billy Tanner, said they would take the wheel, and I lashed 'em to the wheel and they swung her off. We sailed I'd say 15 minutes or somet'in' . . . well then there was a sea boarded us. How much water went over that can never tell but when he swung her he told the crew, he said, 'It's every man for himself. . . . you can go below and shut the companionway, you can go in the riggin' or you can stay on deck, but it's every man for himself.'

"After the sea went over we got across the bar an' it was smoother. One fella on the wheel, he was as black in the face as the stove. It must 'a been where the sea hit him so hard. We carried him in the cabin an' got him on the floor and worked with him an' he come to. It blowed that night, you couldn' walk from one end o' the vessel to t'other, you couldn' walk agin' the wind. We had a rope run and the only way you could git from one end to t'other was holdin' on t'the rope an' pull yourself along. Because we had boards, bait boards we used to call 'em, on the cabin house for cuttin' bait on an' they were two-inch spruce planks nailed right solid on the cabin house an' I had sixteen five-inch galvanized spikes in 'em, nailed solid, an' the next mornin' after that sea hit us, the boards was gone. . . . the sixteen spikes was drawn right through the boards, drawed the heads through."[5]

Those were some of the survivors. Others didn't make it through the night. But it was many days before the real toll was known. Weeks later the *Halifax Herald* finally produced an issue detailing the grim news. In a headline style normally reserved for the beginning or ending of wars, the paper blared: "Over Eighty Lives Lost in Great Disaster. Lunenburg Fishing Fleet Suffers Most Appalling Tragedy." The subtitle was as charged with emotion as the headline: "Pall of sorrow spreads over fishing communities as captains and crews of four gallant vessels are given up as lost— Pathetic loss of bread winners in Nova Scotia towns and villages— In some cases lives of three members of households are blotted out—Pathos Unutterable—Dread toll of Sable Island sands."

Lost with all hands were the schooners *Clayton Walters*, whose wreckage was never found, the *Mahala*, the *Joyce M. Smith*, and the *Uda Corkum*, all grounded on the south side of the west bar. The vessels that made it home were the *Marshal Frank*, which reported two men lost at sea, the *Alberfolite*, the *Andrava*, which survived by going over the bar, the *Partana*, which also found safety by driving over the bar, and a dozen others. Eight out of ten Newfoundland boats fishing on the Grand Banks were lost in the same storm.

The *Bluenose* was on the Banks at the time but was anchored in deep water prudently far from Sable Island, and managed to ride out the storm at anchor. This time her cable held.

The *Columbia* wasn't so lucky. Perhaps she was on the wrong side of that treacherous island; perhaps her dories were too far out and couldn't get back, perhaps she was hit by a rogue sea and knocked over. No one ever knew. She sank, and all hands were lost. Ben Pine, her owner, wasn't on board.

On October 11, the Boston *Globe* reported the grim news: "Captain Iver Carlson, of the Boston schooner *Acushla*, reported this afternoon on arrival at the fish pier that he had located the last resting place of the schooner *Columbia*, which was lost in a hurricane on August 24th with her captain and crew. The wreck, Captain Carlson states, is 23 miles northwest of Sable Island. In this location last Saturday he saw a spar sticking out of the water which in type and timber was similar to the *Columbia*'s boom. Carlson steered his vessel as close to the spar as he dared hoping to find a mark on it which would definitely identify it as coming from the lost vessel. But he was unable to get close enough to it to note any such indications. Captain and crew of the *Acushla* watched the spar with feelings of awe as they reflected that beneath it might be the sleek hull of the vessel now a tomb for Captain Wharton and his courageous crew of a score or more of fishermen. Early Sunday, by use of boats and considerable effort this spar, which proved to be that of the ill-fated schooner, was secured. It was brought here by Captain Carlson. After tying up at the pier, Carlson went to the Government Hydrographic office where he reported the location of the wreck and said it was a menace to navigation. A government cutter will be sent to the spot and the wreck will be blown up."[6]

The following year, the *Henry Ford*, too, was lost in a gale off Martin Point, Newfoundland.

None of this stopped Ben Pine from wanting to resume the rivalry with Nova Scotia. There was another fishermen's regatta in Gloucester in 1929, which was a huge hit despite the absence of either *Columbia* or *Ford*; and within weeks he put together a syndicate to build a new challenger to the aging but still formidable *Bluenose*.

Fishermen and fishing captains weren't even considered for this one. Pine and his buddies (among them Joe Mellow, who ran a transportation company, and Louis Thebaud, who had retired as chairman of a New York insurance company) commissioned a firm of yacht builders to come up with a contender. Oh, she'd need to be able to fish—there was still a generalized desire to conform to the original rules—but she didn't have to fish very hard. She should look good, be nippy, and be ready to take on the *Bluenose* when the time came. The result was a pretty little vessel, a 134-foot semi-knockabout, named after Thebaud's wife, Gertrude. The boat was well turned out, with beautiful mahogany fittings in the captain's cabin and the most modern electrical systems throughout. She carried a powerful diesel motor that was easily removable when the need arose. She was launched to great acclaim, and on her maiden voyage in the waters around Boston carried a great press of socialites from Boston and Eastern Point. She could carry a piffling 175,000 pounds of fish, and cost $73,000 to build, a ludicrous sum, but no one cared. "She was," declares Dan Moreland, "a pisspoor fisherman all her life and never made anyone any money, but people loved her anyway." The only time she ever hoisted sail was to race against *Bluenose* or to enter and depart from harbours, where crowds would actually notice. The rest of the time she relied on her motors.

The Massachusetts Bay Tercentenary Committee said it would sponsor an international racing series if it were held to coincide with the anniversary, in the fall, the Mass. Bay's (and Boston's) 300th being conveniently different from Gloucester's, which as we have seen was not so very different from Gloucester's 250th. The old reliable Thomas Lipton was again persuaded to put up a cup, and the Deed of Gift so worded that outside vessels would be eligible to join. *Haligonian* and *Bluenose* were on the Banks, fishing (they "got into a hook" on the way home, and *Haligonian* outsailed *Bluenose* and made it back to port first). When he got home they apprised Angus of the challenge. "Let 'em come here and I'll race," he said. Let's finish what was started and never ended, he implied. Besides, *Bluenose* was in battered condition, in no shape to race. It would take thousands of dollars to fit her out for racing.

Then, always one to needle the Americans, he told the Bridgewater *Bulletin* that he didn't think he'd race Americans anymore, "unless of course," he added mischievously, "we take the mainsail off her first, and maybe we'll tow an anchor alongside as well."[7]

Pine didn't give up. The Lipton Cup would carry the same prize money and expenses as the Dennis Cup, and he offered to finance *Bluenose*'s refitting. Walters met with his board, and they passed a resolution, recorded in the minute book, that "the Board agrees to the forthcoming races in Gloucester, on condition that the $10,000 that had been offered for the refit is paid in full ahead of time, and that the event does not count as an International Series but only as a special fisherman's race."

Before this happened, *Bluenose* and *Haligonian* met again, in an informal series of races to coincide with Lunenburg's Fisherman's Reunion and Picnic. The *Bluenose* had just been commemorated by the government of Canada with a special 50-cent stamp, but Moyle Crouse, *Haligonian*'s skipper, declined to be impressed and thought he could beat her. Two other schooners, the *Margaret K. Smith* and the *Alsatian*, competed. The *Bluenose* was not sailing well; she was looking badly battered. She lost to the *Haligonian* both times; the first races she had lost at home, and the first series she ever lost.

Still looking battered, but with a new suit of sails, she set off for Gloucester.

The press coverage in that city reached hysterical proportions. Every mansion in Eastern Point had its tercentenary party. The races were to coincide with Lipton's perennial challenge for the America's Cup itself, and the press sometimes found it hard to say which race was which. Both were big news on the society pages as well as the sports pages.

The course was to be a short triangle whose every point could be seen from shore.

The opening race was held in light winds. *Thebaud* was in fine trim and Ben Pine sailed her well. *Bluenose* manoeuvred awkwardly, and her new sails were slack, looking like ill-cut circus tents, as one reporter put it. It didn't feel at all like his *Bluenose*, Angus said afterwards. "My god, if I may say so, she was in hard shape." *Thebaud* won by fifteen minutes.

"Bear in mind," Dan Moreland says, "that the *Bluenose* was ten years old and by any measure, and especially from a racing point of view, would have to be past her prime. Not a rotten boat by any means, but she had soaked up a lot of water. The match-up was a little like Muhammad Ali coming out of retirement . . . I mean, you still didn't want to be punched by the guy, but he's not really a fighter any more."

There was next to no wind for a few days, and the races were held off. *Bluenose* used the time well, hauling out for some keel repairs, recutting her sails to tighten them up—Walters trimmed 5 feet from the mainsail alone—and removed tons of ballast, and after a time she seemed more like her old self.

Ben Pine fell ill, and was replaced by Charley Johnson.

After another day of calm, a Canadian reporter named Agnes McGuire was said to have flung all the change from her purse into the sea to call on the sea gods for wind[8]—an old New England custom called "buying the wind," whose lesson is usually invoked to explain hubris confounded, for skippers who tempted fate that way usually got far more than they bargained for. Whatever the reason, October 15 dawned with a squally southwest gale, 30 knots gusting to 50, causing choppy seas. These were conditions in which *Bluenose* thrived, and Angus was delighted. The two vessels crossed the line together, and *Bluenose* pulled steadily ahead. After the second marker, she was a good 2 miles ahead. But rainsqualls made the marker buoys, really just little flags on staffs that Angus called "baby buoys," very hard to see.

Just before the turn, a gust tore the boom off its "jaws," a housing attaching it to the main spar, and threatened to tear the 4,000-square-foot mainsail right off. The men managed to haul it back and lash it tight, and they lost barely a few hundred yards.

But the weather got worse. The Coast Guard cutter that carried the judges, and the press boat, lost sight of the racers altogether. Angus had trouble finding the 18-mile baby buoy. So the judges called the race off.

Angus was furious. Races called for too little wind, races called for too much wind—what was this? Did the wind have to be perfect for a vessel to venture out at all? Had no one ever been to the Banks? "Let's take our chances," he said. "If something carries away, that's our hard luck. We're satisfied to carry on." Hadn't the original intention of the races been to produce vessels that could stand a real blow and come through unscathed? This race, It Didn't Blew. Charley Johnson prudently said nothing.

The second race was finally held three days later, on October 18, in a light but erratic wind. The *Bluenose* was sailing well and took an early lead, and was five minutes ahead at the second mark when Angus made one of his rare navigational blunders, "splitting a tack" and heading farther inshore to look for a steadier wind, which turned out not to be there. Angus blamed himself, mostly for following the advice of a Gloucester pilot aboard. "He told me that if I stood in under the land I'd catch a favourable wind from the nor'west. Well, I did it, but instead found light winds from the sou'west and dead ahead, and me on a lee shore with trouble on my hands . . . Still, it was my mistake and *Thebaud* made the best of it."9 *Thebaud* won by eight minutes, and took the Lipton Cup; *Bluenose* had lost her second series of races within a few weeks. "But *Thebaud* didn't beat *Bluenose!*" Walters protested. "She beat me!"

Within a few days newspaper reports had escalated the single Gloucester pilot's advice to two Gloucestermen on board, and then three, one of them at the wheel itself; there were also reports that *Bluenose* had hit bottom not once but three times on Round Rock Shoal and that Angus was using that as an alibi. But all these notions seemed to have happened only in the excitable minds of the reporters, and Angus never blamed anyone but himself.

Everybody could live with the outcome. Gloucester was thrilled that it finally had a contender able to beat the hulking presence from the north, even if she was really from Boston; the Lunenburgers took comfort from the fact that the series didn't really count for anything, and besides, the *Bluenose* had handled well when it counted, heading to windward in rough weather. So nothing was settled.

Within a few weeks Ben Pine, having recovered from the illness that prevented him from personally thumping the *Bluenose*, challenged the champion to a race for the main prize, the international Dennis Cup. *Bluenose* accepted. There wasn't anything else to do.

Because outside the rarefied world of Eastern Point, the world was looking much grimmer. The Great Depression had spread like a hemorrhagic disease through North America and both countries were bleeding unemployment. Seven million people were unemployed in the United States, and that number was climbing steeply. It would soon reach 12 million, then a quarter of the population.

In Canada it was, if anything, worse. In 1931, the Labor Department in Washington, responding to intense pressure from what unions survived, sent foreign workers home, from whatever industry—from opera singers (my father-in-law, in Boston) to steelworkers to the fishing fleets. It didn't help American unemployment—there were not enough skilled Americans either to sing the arias or to do the dory-handlining work, and two out of three of the remaining schooners were tied up and idled when the Canadians went home.

The same year the Lunenburg Board of Trade sent an urgent communiqué to Ottawa once again demanding the abolition of trawling. This time they had a more compelling argument: trawlers put 20,000 independent jobs at risk, a whole industry that threatened to go broke and become a charge on the public purse.

They once again argued that factory trawling was damaging the resource on which they were all dependent. Foreign trawlers, the communiqué pointed out, were now fishing the Banks, especially the Grand Banks, because they had already ruined their own.

Once again, in a pattern that has persisted until modern times, the pleas were ignored.

In June 1930, the United Maritime Fishermen was formed under the prodding of Father Moses Michael Coady of the town of Antigonish, Nova Scotia. Coady was one of those hundreds of mostly unsung men and women who were such beacons of light in the deep darkness of the Depression; he helped develop what became known as the Antigonish Movement that brought together the poor and the undereducated in so-called kitchen meetings to "learn to read, think about the causes of their poverty, and act together to solve their problems." Out of these meetings streamed a wide variety of clubs and societies based on the philosophy of cooperation that Coady espoused; among them were more than 200 small fishermen's cooperatives in the Maritime provinces and the Magdalen Islands, which belonged to Quebec. (St. Francis Xavier University in Antigonish has since set up the Coady International

Institute whose aim is to do similar things for the peoples of under-developed nations.)

The United Fishermen, being a Coady creation, was not quite a union, for though it represented more than 3,000 fishermen it also happily found a home for Fisheries Department officers, fisheries inspectors, and their supervisors and had as its prime aim the settling of disputes between members and the promotion of "social inter-course, a higher standard of community life and the study of eco-nomic and social questions bearing on our interests as citizens and fishermen." But all this high-mindedness took a back seat at their 1931 meeting to a ringing denunciation of trawlers and trawling. They demanded the "complete and immediate abolition of the trawler."

Which of course they didn't get. The industrial juggernaut was by now quite beyond their capacity to derail. The price of the fish they were catching dropped, and then dropped again, partly because people were too poor to buy more than they absolutely must, and partly because events turned out as they had feared—the vaunted efficiency of the trawlers was just that, and they effortlessly glutted the market. The Atlantic fishing banks had become the Maritime equivalent of the Great Plains or the Canadian Prairies, where mountains of unsold wheat and corn were piling up at rail-road sidings; the draggers were catching too much fish but they couldn't even cover their costs. Making a living dory-trawling became almost impossible, and as we shall see even the *Bluenose* spent years tied up, or making a depressing spectacle of herself at expositions and in the tourist trade.

With all this as background, Ben Pine's challenge to the *Bluenose*, and the *Bluenose*'s acceptance, counted as good news. Or at least better news, diverting attention for a while from the much grimmer stuff that had spread from the business pages to the news pages and from there to the society pages. To the working men, almost all the news was awful, and the disparities in wealth enormous; as Sterling Hayden put it, ". . . kids cast loose in the dismal thirties, on the shores of a world so civilized a man could starve to death in a flophouse while less than a mile away the poodles wore matching booties and jackets when they were taken for a ride."[10] But even Eastern Point and the wealthy of Boston were caught in the Depression's snare. Joseph Kennedy, JFK's millionaire father, was heard fretting that he'd soon be reduced to "nine children, four houses and no cash at all." The international series could even be run early: the *Bluenose* had gone out to the Banks but had come back in a few weeks; they couldn't sell what fish they caught anyway—at those prices every cod cost them a penny instead of earning them one. In Gloucester, the *Elsie* had been chartered to the Sea Scouts. *Haligonian* was tied up at Canso, and her skipper, Moyle Crouse, had taken to the seas in his swift little cutter: the American Volstead Act, which ushered in Prohibition, was still bringing in a little money to Lunenburg County. Even that was ending though: the dozens of Lunenburgers and Tancookers who had kept their families alive by running rum, by transporting it from large freighters on the open sea to hidden rendezvous inshore, were now seeing even that source of revenue coming to an end; by 1931, speed, not stealth, served the rum-runners best, and cunning seamanship was replaced by diesel power. Tancook's boat-building dried up, and small yards all up and down the coast laid off their workers.

There was no need for elimination races—the *Thebaud* and the *Bluenose* were the only all-sail vessels left fit to race. Still, the venerable little *Elsie* was stripped of her engines and refitted borrowed topmasts to give *Thebaud* a workout before she left, and ended up giving the *Thebaud* people a fright when she almost won. The challenger redeemed herself on the way north, clocking in at 15 knots for long stretches, and her crew approached the races with a confident air.

The races were held off Halifax in mid-October. The *Bluenose* had been hauled and sanded and painted; she was waterlogged but sailing well. The *Thebaud* had cut her sails to conform to the Deed of Gift, but seemed sluggish; Ben Pine had loaded her with ballast, expecting heavy weather, but the winds were light. So light that neither vessel finished the course the first day, and the race was cancelled. Just as well for the *Thebaud*: the *Bluenose* had sailed well and was more than 4 miles in front when they called the whole thing off. Despite the light winds, there had been a nasty chop to the water, and *Thebaud* had seemed as inelegant as a grampus. It didn't bode well.

The moderate winds held, and the second race took place in a dead-calm sea. In the end, it wasn't much of a contest, for Angus pulled ahead before the first marker and ground out the yards all the way to the end. The only drama was whether he would be able to finish in the requisite six hours, and he made it, but only just—by six minutes. *Thebaud* trailed in thirty-two minutes later. The Boston *Post* reported glumly that maybe she had forgotten to pull up her anchor.

The following day, in a fair breeze but still dead-calm seas, she performed a little better. The two vessels were dead even by the third marker, but when they turned into the windward leg, the *Bluenose*'s strengths became ever more evident, and she came home a comfortable twelve minutes ahead of her rival.

Ben Pine sailed home without the cup to a muted reception in Boston. *Yachting* magazine opined that "Gloucester had sent a boy to do a man's job, and a boy with his pockets full of pig iron at that." Angus Walters agreed, and was ungracious in victory. He had only contempt for *Thebaud* anyway, calling her useless in hard weather, impossible to tack in a heavy breeze for fear of upsetting her, a tender vessel, a toy. "I'm sorry it can't be arranged we have company on these schooner races," he said sarcastically. "*Thebaud* wasn't company . . . an' a feller don't get much out o' racin' the clock all the time."

Pretty well everyone assumed that the international schooner races were now over. All new vessels had diesels, even in Canada, and the lifespan of a wooden boat hard used by the Banks was not much more than a decade anyway; soon there would be no vessels left to race. The *Bluenose* tied up at her berth in Lunenburg, and Angus Walters went home.

The *Bluenose* made a profit in 1931, but she lost money fishing. The prize money helped.

Her balance sheet for 1932 was bleaker:

Receipts:	$21 (sails and gear sold)
Expenses:	$775.07
Cash on hand	$40.32

Angus couldn't say her future was bleak. She didn't seem to *have* much future.

H E R

Y E A R S

a s   a

D O W N H I L L

R A C E R

he Depression only got worse. *Bluenose* had been built to race, but there were no longer any races. She was an adept fisherman, but the market for salt fish was poor, and all-sail schooners found it impossible to compete with mechanized draggers. She was a fast sailing boat, but not fast enough for the fresh-fish market, what little of it there was. Still, her owners kept her going, hoping like everyone else that the economy would somehow miraculously improve, that life would be breathed back into fishing, that she would be able to resume at least part of the life she had been created for.

The last racing series had been a disaster as a sporting event, but the notion of beautiful schooners under full sail, abetted by the newspapers, and by the Canadian post office with their *Blue-nose* stamp, had by now entered the public imagination, and the schooners become popular tourist attractions. To keep afloat, literally and financially, the *Bluenose* installed cabins and took on paying guests for cruising. In 1933, Angus and the board accepted an invitation from Chicago's Century of Progress exposition (a nice piece of whistling in the face of a bleak economy, that) "to operate as a concession" at the fair, and duly sailed to the Great Lakes. The *Gertrude L. Thebaud* had been invited too but wasn't there; Ben Pine had taken her down to Washington to help publicize the plight of New England's fishermen. Moored on the Potomac, she drew large crowds and even President Roosevelt, who brought along British prime minister Ramsay MacDonald to meet Pine, but Roosevelt's New Deal held little immediate comfort for the fishing fleet, and none at all for sailing vessels.

There were boat races in Chicago too, but for yachts and smaller vessels, and the *Bluenose* was too big to compete. Still, one of the races, for the Mackinac Cup, allowed all vessels to compete as long as they did so outside the competition itself, the prize being a massive wheel of cheese, which the *Bluenose* duly took home. Angus Walters confessed to a reporter afterwards that he didn't know whether to be dispirited at the nature of the race or pleased at the chance once again to lay on a press of sail and put the old girl through her paces. A few weeks later she was chartered for a cruise, Angus got into an argument with the charterer, was sued, and departed for Canadian waters.

Bluenose remained in the Great Lakes for the summer of 1934, spending some months in Toronto. In July, there was an exchange of messages between Angus in Toronto and the board members in Lunenburg. "We could get $20,000 if we sold her as is," Angus wrote. The board was clearly skeptical, for at a special meeting the other directors passed a resolution to sell the vessel by tender, with a reserve price of $15,000. Angus sailed her back to Lunenburg. There were no takers.

Her income for 1934, almost all of it from Great Lakes charters, was $7,534.74, for a net profit of $1,863.63. She was keeping her head above water, but not by much.

The following year, 1935, she was invited to England to take part in the flotilla sailpast marking the Silver Jubilee of King George V, and a yacht race around the Isle of Wight. In the regattas that followed, she kept up valiantly with the best of British racing yachts, to their evident astonishment, having remarked on her heavy cotton canvas sails and sturdy rigging fit for an Atlantic gale. She did so well that the king gave her a lighter and a special stitched mainsail from the royal yacht *Britannia*, and invited Angus to come aboard for a chat. Also aboard his current yacht, the *Victoria & Albert*, were the king's three sons, the Prince of Wales and the Dukes of York and Kent. "He was a very nice, ordinary sort of fella," Walters recalled of the king. "Though if I may say so I thought he looked a little frail. Well, we chewed the rag for a while. He had heard some of the *Bluenose* and he was very interested in knowing about herring fishing. Then the Prince of Wales, Edward, leaned over and explained to him about cod fishing. Then he told me to come and stand by while they took our picture . . . After we'd chewed off a little more fat, I went back to the *Bluenose*. The king later sent word he'd come aboard, but was recalled to London instead. I was kind of sorry about that. I didn't carry any liquor aboard that trip, but I decided I should offer him a drink . . . So I sent ashore for a bottle of King George whisky."[1]

On the way back from England the *Bluenose* became entangled in a murderous hurricane, a storm that had maintained its ferocity all the way northeast from the Caribbean and then had merged with another storm front at high latitudes, which had intensified it dramatically. Angus believed it was worse than any storm he had encountered, even including the storm of April 1926.

From the *Bluenose* logbook: "Vessel labouring very hard and terrific seas running. Laying now under bare spars. Impossible to do anything. Continued pouring oil through toilets and by oil bags.

At 10 p.m. a terrible sea hit the vessel heaving her almost on beam ends, breaking for'gaff and for'boom, smashing boats, deckhouse engine box, throwing cook stove over on side. Tons of water going below doing other damage and causing vessel to leak very bad. Had to keep continuing pumping. Vessel opening up aft by pounding heavy. At 3 a.m. kept off and ran her under reef jumbo."[2]

When she was hove over, her keel showing and tons of water pouring down her hatches, Walters yelled, "Get up, you black bitch, get up!" and slowly, slowly, very slowly, she heaved herself upright. He was prepared to cut her rigging and even her masts if he had to, but she did what schooners in the post-McManus era were built to do, she shook the water off and slowly righted herself.[3]

On board was a naval commander, Ian Black, who said it was "the most terrifying sea I have ever encountered" in his seventeen years afloat. Once again, the *Bluenose* had proved her wondrous abilities in hard weather. Some said she had just won the greatest race of her life.

Angus got full credit for saving the vessel, though the mate, George Corkum, was at the helm throughout the storm, and later would grumble angrily into his rum at the stories of "Angus's miracle," and at the way the skipper's legend grew at the expense of a poor working stiff. Nobody paid him any mind. And in any case he was wrong: it really was the vessel they remembered, not her master.

The following year, 1936, the board of the Bluenose Schooner Company once again authorized Angus to sell the vessel if he could. Once again, he agreed—indeed, it was partly his suggestion—but once again there were no takers. In the spring he sent a memo to the other board members suggesting that they install engines to make it possible for *Bluenose* to engage in fresh fishing. He'd grown fed up watching the increasingly reliable steamers beating him to port;

in his usually blunt way, he said he didn't see why he should "piss around in the fog when others weren't, and not do so well as plenty of 'em who weren't so good fishermen as me." It wouldn't necessarily ruin her, he said, not if the engines could be taken out if she were ever to race again. The board wasn't averse, but was wary of the costs. Angus was asked to come back with estimates.

Retrofitting motors in a vessel not designed for them is not so easy. Roué had made no provision for shaft timbers or propellers; they simply hadn't been in his mandate. If he had planned for engine power, one single-shaft engine would have been best; as it was, Angus wanted to be able to remove the motors when necessary, and this meant two engines with a single propeller each, with shaft timbers through the hull planking on either side of the sternpost. It was neither a cheap arrangement nor particularly efficient, but Angus didn't tell the board that.

The estimate he got from the marine engine company Fairbanks–Morse was for $11,459 for two 90-horsepower diesels. The contract was signed June 16, 1936. Balance sheet that year: Revenue of $12,726, mostly from sailing parties and insurance claims; expenses of $12,446, including crew salaries of $3,908.40 and a payment of $5,000 to Fairbanks–Morse. Net profit: $280. Debt load: $6,500.

As part of the refit, the topmasts were struck down and their sails stored ashore. Concrete and pig iron ballast was installed, and she was outfitted with twelve dories for winter fishing, and fished all winter in trips of ten to twelve days.

Even so, there was little market for the fish they caught.

The few vessels that attempted trips to the Banks in 1935 and 1936 found it very difficult to recruit crews—why go, if you come back to a net loss? In 1936, Angus Walters himself took home less than $10

from a three-month trip; one of his union members made $6.98 for the season. "You made a penny and you sucked it for a week before you spent it," Angus said.[4]

In 1936, the fishermen had coalesced into a true union, the Fishermen's Federation of Nova Scotia. In December the following year, Captain Angus was elected president of the Lunenburg chapter. One of his first acts as president was to officially support the dorymen's demand for a quarter cent per pound rise in the price of landed haddock, a change the fish processors were resisting. "The dealers say they can't afford to pay more for fish," he declared. "I ask them, did not fish bring them wealth? Dealers always argue that it was a poor year. I ask them how can they afford to buy up vessels and draggers at the cost of hundreds of thousands of dollars? I'd like to ask some of them who complain most loudly how much money their fathers left them—money that was made by the sweat of the men who sailed to the Banks?" In response, the fish wholesaler Wallace Smith was widely quoted as saying, scornfully, "Why, if they get their quarter cent or half cent all the fishermen's wives will soon be wearing mink coats!"

The wholesalers, primarily the Maritime Fish Corporation of Montreal and General Seafoods of Halifax, refused to give in, and the fishermen struck, tying up not just their own vessels but the dragging fleet too, and shutting down the big processing plants.

The strike lasted three weeks before the provincial government forced through a compromise and got everyone back to work, but the outcome scarcely mattered. Michael Wayne Santos is right when he says that it was the fact of the strike that was important, not its outcome: "With it, Lunenburgers' worst fears were realized. Impersonal business dealings, threat and class strife had replaced labour-management cooperation, personal integrity and a sense of mutual responsibility and respect. It was a bitter pill to swallow for people whose values were grounded in generations of a close-knit community."[5]

The same year Angus took on the presidency, 1937, Ben Pine

once again took the *Thebaud* to Washington to press for some relief. Once again it wasn't forthcoming.

Towards the end of the year the Canadian mint produced the first dime bearing "a two-masted fishing schooner," which for some bizarre reason they never identified as the *Bluenose* until "revealing" this ill-kept news in March 2002. The year the dime came out, the *Bluenose* made a net loss of $746.67.

It was in 1937, too, that MGM issued their version of Kipling's *Captains Courageous*, starring the Essex-built schooner *We're Here* as herself, Spencer Tracy as the noble-hearted Portuguese fisherman Manuel Fidello, Lionel Barrymore as Captain Disko Troop, and Freddie Bartholomew as the insufferable little rich kid whose education in the ways of the sea stitches the whole improbable story together. The screenwriters knew what they were doing, and set their story firmly in the American tradition, no different in kind from the big-hearted cowboys who settled the American West. They even killed off Manuel (noble-hearted but *foreign*, after all) to give the story more pathos, but pathos wasn't really the point. The point was to portray the fishermen as hard-working, courageous men, taciturn but fair, tough but sentimental, with a stoic pride in themselves and their work. Their way was of course the American way, and their spirit of fair play and inborn justice the American spirit . . . And so on and so on, and it worked—the movie was a big hit and it rekindled interest in fishermen and their traditions.

Which is where we pick up the story half told in the prologue: Gloucester's Master Mariners Association, taking full advantage of the unlooked-for publicity, declared itself in favour of one more series of International Fishermen's Races, and Ben Pine was duly dispatched to Halifax to issue the challenge, for a best-of-five series raced off Gloucester and Boston.

As recounted, Angus was reluctant. Partly for himself: he was fifty-six years old, his wife Maggie had died two years earlier and he was now somewhat secretively engaged to Mildred Butler, whose nickname around town was "Dimples," who would become his second wife in a few months. (He had met Mildred in a tavern in Halifax, where she worked as a barmaid. The family didn't approve; his sons referred to her ever after as "that woman.") His life was changing. He wasn't going fishing much. He was ready to retire from the sea, and was casting around onshore for a job to do, perhaps as a harbourmaster somewhere. He was involved in union affairs and in the town of Lunenburg, and he wasn't sure he wanted to tear himself away for yet more races that were bound to be acrimonious and uncertain. The *Bluenose* was old, at eighteen very old for a working vessel.

But after Ben Pine promised the refit money, Angus assented and made the run down to Gloucester, where the first race was to be held, Angus and the crew full of foreboding for the fate of their beloved vessel.

The racing committee had hoped to attract Spencer Tracy as a crewman aboard the *Gertrude L. Thebaud,* but he declined. Still, they had what everyone agreed was the next best thing. Sterling Hayden, not yet a big Hollywood star, was the real thing, a home-grown fisherman who had spent some years as a maintopman aboard working schooners; that he was six feet five inches tall and "a fine masculine specimen," as the Boston newspapers rather embarrassingly called him, surely didn't hurt. Nor did it hurt that he was a romantic who could express himself eloquently about his experiences aboard.

Here's Hayden on the *Thebaud* sea trials before the races began: ". . . Out of Gloucester . . . forty men and one tall ship bound on a trial run. Pitted against the clock. Against some wind as well, brawling wind blowing a southeast gale. Storm warnings fly beneath a dull grey sky, and leaves skirmish. (But on the Banks no dories will work this day, and up in Boston girls clutch skirts and hats go tumbling to leeward.) Half past ten says a belfry clock. Captain Ben Pine stands by the wheel. You would swear he is part of his ship—in spite of the blue vested suit, the brown felt hat, and a red bow tie. More like a coach he looks than a racing-schooner skipper . . . With a thrust of his fist, Ben orders a man aloft. Up he goes on the run till he reaches the masthead, where he heaves himself over the hounds, breathing hard, and goes to work with the topsail. 'Stand by!' Ben's voice betrays his calm. One final look—full circle—with an arm flung wide for balance. Now he claws at the wheel, fighting it over. 'Helm's alee!' For the first time he really yells out. She slashes into the wind. Canvas booms and sheet blocks dance under the booms. Straight into the eye of the wind. 'Leggo your main sheet boys.' Ben is right where he wants to be. 'Clear that coil—now let her run to the knot.' The sheet runs out till the knot fetches up in the block . . .

"Up aloft you hang on. Beyond the breakwater the wild Atlantic growls. Plumes of spray bounce on lighthouse windows. Your mainmasthead is six feet higher than where Jack Hackett lives, thirty feet away. His voice is high and loud. 'Oh dyin' Jaysus boy, if she catches one o' them seas just right she'll pitch us clear to Newfoundland!' Up here you feel the motion more. You feel her reach out over a sea and hang; then down she goes with a sickening rush, and the second after the crash your mast goes bucking forward with a sideways motion. You wonder how wood can take it.

"Boudreau comes up from the galley, wiping his lips, leaning into the weather rail, shoulders hunched. His yellow oilskins shine. He rests one knee on the deck and jams one booted leg out stiff against a hatch as he watches the vessel go. Low in the water she flies; two feet of sifting water conceal her rail. Her long bow threads through breaking seas, reaching high, plunging down, always with the roar in the shrouds. He thrashes his arms and screams: 'Fourteen, god-dam it, boys, fourteen she goes, or I hope to die with a hard-on!'"[6]

The first race went off as described. Angus was outmanoeuvred by Ben Pine, split his bowsprit, and lost.

The second race finally took place on the 13th, after several days of light winds, and the *Bluenose* won by a comfortable eleven minutes.

The conventional script says that race was followed by almost a week of . . . well, nothing very much, which is what the prologue said. But it wasn't quite true; or at least it was true but far from the whole truth. The second race was barely over when there was a furious challenge from the *Thebaud* people. The *Bluenose* was still not right on the waterline, they said, and needed to be lightened up. The engines had already gone. Now out went the fuel tanks, generator, lighting plant, and whatever else Angus could think of. Once more the story-poles and plumb bobs came back, but enough was enough as far as the irascible skipper was concerned; when the busybodies were forward, Angus had the crew, who were down below, walk aft to raise her bow; when they moved their measuring tools aft, the crew sprinted forward. But the real uproar was about ballast. Rule 9 of the Deed of Gift specified that "no ballast shall be taken on or put off the competing vessels during the series, and no ballast shall be shifted after the fifteen minute preparatory gun is fired before each race."[7] Angus, however, had been installing and removing ballast in the night—taking some off when light winds were expected, putting it back on for heavier breezes, and he'd been caught—a *Thebaud* crewman had marked where the ballast lay on the wharf with innocent-looking sand, and when it was disturbed they had their man. The press demanded the *Bluenose* be disqualified. Angus brazened it out. As far as he was concerned he'd been told to get the boat in trim and at the proper length, and how he did it was his concern. It was his ballast, and he'd use it as he saw fit. Besides, he said, the *Thebaud* was carrying too much sail.

The uproar built through the next few days, in which there were no races, five days of fog and light winds following monotonously one on another. On October 20, they tried again, but the committee ended the race with the *Thebaud* in the lead, to that boat's fury. The following day Cecil Moulton, who was now skippering the *Thebaud* for Ben Pine, who was ill, once again protested: Angus had taken on ballast the night before, again. What was the race committee going to do about it?

Nothing, as it turned out. Captain Charles Lyons, the committee's head, supported Angus, despite the shellacking Angus has given him earlier. As it happened, the extra ballast would have worked to the *Bluenose*'s disadvantage in light winds. Besides, he said, again echoing Angus, he'd told them to get to the waterline length specified in the Deed of Gift and he didn't care how they did it.

The third race, as described, went to the *Bluenose*, the fourth to the *Thebaud*.

Two races each.

And so indeed it came down to the final race, the final race of its kind that would ever be, and the two glorious vessels, breathtakingly elegant, beautiful artifacts at the very pinnacle of boatbuilding craft, breathing easy in an 18-knot breeze, sailed round the course for the final time, and at the last, as the script said it should, the *Bluenose* surged ahead and halfway through the run home into the wind she was almost four minutes ahead. Then, as recounted, with just one short tack left, the main foretopmast staysail halyard block broke as she came about, jamming the halyard and leaving the staysail flapping noisily, a little heart-stopping moment. But in the end it didn't matter. She was too far in front. Dipping her bow into the waves, she ran for the finish line, crossing two minutes and fifty seconds ahead of her rival.

Which led in turn to the lyrical passage from Silver Donald Cameron, already quoted: "The great black schooner from Canada stormed over the finish line . . . An awesome sight, a legendary ship at the moment of her final and greatest triumph. The crowd was silent for a moment. And then the bells and whistles and horns of Boston burst on the air, mingling with the cheers of crew and crowds alike in a thunderous ovation. She had won the regard of a foreign city. She had won the race, the series, and the trophy. And she would keep them forever."[8]

In fact, the city of Boston was largely silent; no bells rang, no whistles blew, no horns blared, no cheering crowds were waiting at wharfside. And the boats hadn't tied up more than a few minutes before the carping and the acrimony began again.

The ever-ungracious Cecil Moulton announced to the press that "the *Thebaud* was not beaten by the *Bluenose* but by Captain Lyons. He sent us out day after day when there wasn't enough wind for a real race and kept us in port when there was a good wind." Ben Pine, usually a bigger gentleman than this, added his two bitter cents': "We took two races sailed in a good breeze. The *Bluenose* took three in weather I don't consider fit for a fisherman's race." Perhaps both men had forgotten how tender the *Thebaud* was in heavy weather, and that *Bluenose* was at her best in a gale. Even if they had forgotten, which is unlikely, it would have been more civil to button their lips, especially from men who complained about the cantankerous and "unsportsmanlike" Angus Walters ("the bellicose bantam," as the Boston papers called him).

Late in the afternoon there were "victory" celebrations; the crewmen of both vessels gathered in the *Bluenose* fo'c'sle and holds

with a barrel or two of rum and the tuneless music of Fred Rhodenizer, the *Bluenose* topmastman, and refused to go on deck to hear
the governor and the mayor blathering away about honour and
glory and sportsmanship. That night, at the awards banquet, the
prize money was "not ready" and even the trophy had mysteriously
disappeared, some say the victim of pranksters, but to the *Bluenose*
crew and master just another sign of Yankee boorishness. It showed
up a few days later wrapped in newspaper at an orphans' home (the
New England Home for Little Wanderers; Mrs. Elizabeth Meyer,
as principal, professing herself "completely mystified at the pack-
age's deposition") with a piece of doggerel pinned to it:

> *Here's to Angus good old sport*
> *Whose challenge sort of takes us short*
> *Send us a gale that blows at Thirty*
> *And we'd bet our shirts on little Gertie*

The Bluenosers replied with their own, even worse, doggerel:

> *And here's to Gertie who tried in vain*
> *The Fishermen's Trophy to regain*
> *The Bermuda Challenge she also shirks*
> *So make better use of your Yankee shirts*

The Gloucestermen had promised the *Bluenose* $8,000 in refitting
money should she agree to participate, but it never came. In the
end, but only after Angus sent them a lawyer's letter, they paid half
of what they had promised, and accused Angus of being cheap
when he complained. That was a nerve! They had demanded he
come, and they had offered the money to make it happen. He wasn't
rich, as he was quick to point out.

The business of the "Bermuda challenge" in the retaliatory
doggerel referred to an exchange of telegrams between Angus Walters and Cecil Moulton. Apparently too angry to actually speak to

Angus, Moulton had fired off a telegram almost as soon as the two vessels reached shore: "I hereby challenge you to a race in Massachusetts waters over your own course in any breeze of 25 knots or over, you and I put up $500 each and race vessels under Deed of Gift. Please advise immediately. Put up or shut up. Winnings go to the winning crew." This was ungracious even by Moulton's practised standards, and it drew a contemptuous response from the peppery Walters. He had better things to do, he said—and he did, he was going home to be married to Millie Butler, his second and last wife. To a crowd of reporters he said: "Five hundred dollars! Huh! That's only pokerchip money. Let's get this thing settled once and for all. Let's race for $5,000 from Boston to Bermuda, around the island and back to Halifax, winner take all. Let them think that over instead of spouting chicken feed." It was not enough, said Moulton. How about $20,000? said Angus recklessly. There was no response. Cecil didn't put up, but he did shut up.

Angus said he'd be damned if the *Bluenose* would ever race in United States waters again, not as long as he was master. Ben Pine said he'd be damned if he'd ever challenge again, anywhere. Angus said he'd better sail for home right away lest the *Bluenose* disappear just like the trophy did.

And he did. And so it ended.

The *Bluenose* sailed into Lunenburg to a rapturous welcome from that small town, with speeches and bunting and a parade of "decorated automobiles," and Angus tied her at the dock.

A short while later Howard Chapelle wrote that the racing schooners like the *Bluenose* and the *Thebaud* were "an aberration, a late and mutant flowering of a tradition that was outdated when they were conceived . . . The racer was no more than a special and technically minor adaptation . . . She had no relation to the fishing-schooner design, whether as a descendant or as a parent . . . And she was generally an economic failure."

This wasn't quite true. The *Thebaud* was an economic failure, but then she had been built only to race. The glorious *Mayflower* was always profitable. And the *Bluenose* paid dividends most years, at least until the Depression. At the end, the board estimated that she'd paid back her investors about 150 per cent.

In 1938, the profit for the year was $6,953.14, of which $5,397.43 was from racing.

The Americans didn't pay what they owed until March 29, 1939, and then they only paid some of it, niggling to the last.

CHAPTER FOURTEEN

HER

FINAL

ADVENTURE

*I*n 1939, the year after he won the International Fishermen's Races for the last time, Angus Walters finally "swallowed the anchor" and retired. But what to do with the *Bluenose* herself? She went fishing that year, and made a profit, albeit a small one, but she was old and she was obsolete and she needed to retire too, with dignity if possible. The best thing was to find a maritime museum to take her on, with government funding, to keep her tied up and in good shape, a memorial. Perhaps the province itself would take her on? Or the federal government? A stamp and a coin—why not the vessel itself? But no one seemed interested. Lunenburg didn't even seem able to work up enough enthusiasm to make the case to Ottawa.

Worse, the engine makers Fairbanks–Morse still hadn't been paid. They had been patient, but were now determined. They were owed nearly $7,000, and they sent the Bluenose Schooner Company a solicitor's letter demanding immediate settlement.

In the middle of the year Angus went back to Boston. A lawyer's note that preceded his visit pointed out that he had been promised a total of $13,000 in expenses and winnings from the series against the *Thebaud* but had received only $7,000.

While he was away, the board mulled over the depressing notion of a forced sale to satisfy the Fairbanks–Morse claim. A formal exchange of letters is preserved in the Bluenose Schooner Company files. The lawyer for Fairbanks–Morse asked that a document be sent to the sheriff listing what gear would be sold along with the vessel when the time came. Angus, back from Boston without the money owed him, was still trying to find another solution but was making no progress. After a while, his friends started to avoid him; they couldn't stand the bleak, pinched look on his face. He couldn't bring himself to plead, it was not in his nature, but his face said it anyway, and they turned away.

Some people in the town tried to help. The previous fall, on November 16, 1938, the board had discussions with a save-the-*Bluenose* committee (Committee for the Preservation of the *Bluenose*) headed by Lunenburg's mayor, Arthur Schwartz, and passed a resolution to sell the *Bluenose* to them for $20,000. The deadline for the transaction was twice extended, and then faded into history. Nothing came of Schwartz's initiative, which was related to a fundraising effort by a rich merchant of the town, a member of the Kaulbach family.

The story as it is usually told is intended to highlight the smug penny-pinching to which that prosperous little town was thought to be prone—that Rupert Kaulbach had offered to match dollar for dollar any subscriptions that were raised in town; that he had opened a bank account into which citizens of the town could place their contributions, however small, but that after several months he was obliged to close the account without a single penny in it. All very well, and a nice calumny against ordinary Lunenburgers. But what of the wealthy citizens themselves? Why didn't Kaulbach himself pony up the money? Was $7,000, the amount of the debt, really so much? The Zwickers? At one of the Bluenose Schooner Company board meetings, a shareholder called Moyle Smith suggested rather testily that since the Zwickers had received so much money by doing business with the *Bluenose* during the past two decades they might like to pick up the debt themselves; Fenwick Zwicker angrily replied that he absolutely positively and categorically would not. Well, what about Adams and Knickle? Hugh Silver and his friends in Halifax? William Dennis and his family? Why was the *Halifax Herald* now so strangely silent? Couldn't Bill Roué have done something? Truth is, only Angus still cared, until it was too late.

The conventional story at this point has Angus scraping together every penny he had to put up the $7,000 necessary to save the vessel from the debtors' auction. But it wasn't as simple as that. It's true that he made a dramatic gesture, showing up at the scheduled auction a mere hour before it was to begin, and plunking down on the sheriff's desk the $7,000 that Fairbanks–Morse were demanding. But there really isn't any evidence that he had scraped out his bank accounts or mortgaged his future, as the legend would have it; the money was in a sense a loan from him to the company. There were even suggestions at the time that the money came from the $7,000 the Bostonians had already paid him for his defeat of the *Gertrude L. Thebaud*. It's hard to see how this money would count as "his," but it is possible that he (legitimately) diverted the money to the debt instead of into general revenues, using his authority as managing director. In any case, the Bluenose Schooner Company, as contemporary newspaper accounts reminded everyone, remained the owners, with the Zwicker company and Angus the primary shareholders. Still, Angus got his licks in. To the *Halifax Herald* on November 15, he declared, "I have faith in the *Bluenose* and will have for some time to come, and I think it a disgrace that the schooner should have been threatened with the auction block." This was a pointed dig at his partners, the Zwickers. To others, he said he was "as mad as a boiled owl" over the whole affair.

A month later an ad appeared in the *Halifax Herald* offering the *Bluenose* for sale by tender, this time with Angus's assent. The first response was from Wallace Knock of Lunenburg, who offered $11,800. He was turned down. Angus himself offered $8,000, but was also turned down by his fellow directors.

In April 1940, there was another bizarre series of telegrams. A missive arrived at the Lunenburg offices of the Zwicker company from Bill McCoy, the now-retired rum-runner who had settled into a comfortable existence in Palm Beach.

"Will buy *Bluenose* condition as is $5,000," McCoy telegraphed. Angus put on his boiled-owl mien again, and scribbled an angry negative at the bottom of the telegram. It remains unclear whether his reply was ever sent, but it's unlikely. The board had rejected Angus's offer for $8,000, and a higher offer from Knock— why should the *Bluenose* go to the real McCoy at that price? Why bother to reply?

Three months later Angus did telegraph Palm Beach, this time accepting McCoy's "final offer" of $15,000, "including full racing sails and running gear but not fishing sails." He also sent a telegram to the Finance Department in Ottawa to see if selling the *Bluenose* to an American contravened some obscure regulation—maybe the mint would object. There is no record of any response to either telegram, but clearly McCoy had second thoughts, for he disappeared from *Bluenose*'s story.

The *Bluenose* went fishing again. While she was in Canso for bait, she was rammed by none other than her old rival, the *Haligonian*. A few months later a cheque came from the Chebucto Fishing Company, *Haligonian*'s owners. It was for $197.26, "for damaged rigging."

Angus needed a job but couldn't find one, so he started a dairy. Lunenburg didn't have a dairy, and he could provide a service the town would need; and indeed he worked at it until he died, still shoving around milk cans in his eighties. There's a copy of his letterhead in his old house in Lunenburg: "Lunenburg Dairy, A.J. Walters manager, Tel. 2121, *You can whip our cream but you can't beat our milk.*" His chocolate milk was a big hit. His grandson

Wayne still remembers the chocolate milks his grandfather gave him; so does Jay Langford, grand-nephew of Angus's first wife, Maggie, who recalls, "You couldn't pass by the dairy without Angus coming out and giving you a chocolate milk; he loved kids." Kids, maybe, but not the rest of them. Dairying was a good occupation, Angus said later, "but for one factor that's into it—dealin' wit' t'public."

It's at this point that the *Bluenose* legend begins to depart rather more radically from what seem to be the facts than at any other time of her long and eventful life. The conventional version is that on August 4, 1941, unable to find another solution and faced with the unwillingness of his partners to continue losing money, no matter how trivial the amounts, Angus Walters emptied his bank accounts and cancelled his life insurance and borrowed the balance from the bank to come up with the $7,000 the board now said it would take to buy the *Bluenose* outright—the second time this story of the empty bank accounts had been floated in a year, and the second time the figure of $7,000 was mentioned. Whatever the dollar amount—$10,000 was sometimes said to be the "real" number— Angus became her sole owner.

For another six months, the story goes, the *Bluenose* fished a little and traded a little and went on a charter or two, all without Angus on board, and all without making any money. Mostly, though, she remained tied up at the wharf; crew were scarce, and he couldn't afford to pay them; the hungry maw of the army sucked up every surplus body. Angus ran his dairy and plodded around from office to office, bureaucrat to bureaucrat, wealthy citizen to wealthy citizen, to see if they'd be interested in putting together some fitting memorial to the old vessel, maybe declare her a national treasure, keep her afloat. No one was. There was a war to prosecute, the Boche to beat, more important things to think about than a waterlogged old schooner, however glorious her history. Glory was a devalued currency in the days when the Wehrmacht were massing on the English Channel. Glory was for an earlier era. This war was grimness, not glory, and too much hung in the balance to worry about an old man and his old boat, no matter what miracles they had performed together.

In the end, even Angus's legendary stubbornness was not enough to keep the *Bluenose* in Lunenburg, and he accepted an offer from the West Indies Trading Company of Havana, which wanted wooden boats for the inter-island freight traffic, on the grounds that they attracted less attention from German submarines than steel. The day that her new skipper came to take her away Angus went down to the dock alone and let slip her lines himself. The legend is that he asked to be alone, to commune for the last time with the old girl he'd married more than twenty years earlier; but the truth is that nobody in Lunenburg cared enough to accompany him and had he not gone for his last farewell she would have sailed away without anyone noticing but the harbourmaster and his logbook. Angus cared, though: "I knew it was good-bye, and she was like a part of me. To tell you the goddam truth, when I walked home, it felt like coming out of the cemetery."

Well, it's a pretty story, and there is a good deal of truth to it.

These are the facts, as recorded in the various documents, especially at the Nova Scotia Register of Joint Stock Companies and in the files of the Commerce Department:

August 16, 1941, Angus Walters buys the *Bluenose* outright from her principal stockholders, mostly the Zwicker company. No dollar number is recorded. This has nothing to do with the sheriff's auction, which was two years earlier.

A month later, September 5, 1941, Angus sells thirty-three shares in his new property, still called the Bluenose Schooner Company, to a total of thirteen individual Lunenburgers.

May 7, 1942, the *Bluenose* is chartered to one Tom Higgins for six months at a fee of $2,800 per month.

June 27, 1942, Angus once again becomes sole owner.

July 2, 1942, a document filed in the Nova Scotia Registry of Joint Stock Companies says that the Bluenose Schooner Company borrowed $10,000 from Captain Angus Walters "on the security of the mortgage of the schooner *Bluenose*, which mortgage is to be dated the 2nd day of July 1942, and the principal to be repayable in the manner following, that is to say—the sum of $3333.33 on the 1st day of August 1942, the sum of $3333.33 on the first day of September 1942, the sum of $4444.34 on the first day of October 1942." Sixty-four shares are pledged as surety.

July 2, 1942, the same day, Angus Walters sells the ship to the West Indies Trading Company, for $20,000.

July 2, 1942, still the same day, a mortgage is taken out by the new owners with Angus Walters for $16,000.

November 2, 1942, just a few months later, said mortgage is discharged.

On the face of it, these documents are confusing and sometimes contradictory—how could Angus give a mortgage to a company on the *Bluenose* when that company no longer owned it? Or was he essentially giving a mortgage to the corporate incarnation of himself? But the confusion has mostly to do with a slippage of dates, and the time it took for the documents to be registered. What seems to have happened, interpreting all these events, is this: the Zwickers wanted out of a losing vessel; Angus, not yet having given up on her, wanted in. But he couldn't yet afford to buy her outright. To finance the purchase, he sold thirty-three shares for a down payment, and within a few months had struck a lucrative charter deal with Tom Higgins, which seemed to promise him the capital he needed. Higgins, as became clear later, didn't have the money to buy the *Bluenose* outright either, although his family did, but he had a friend who had the ready cash. So the Bluenose Schooner

Company, with Angus as sole owner, mortgaged the *Bluenose* to Angus himself; he in turn gave a mortgage to Tom Higgins (while still collecting charter money), and when Tom Higgins's friend came in for the rest, the deal was done: The first "mortgage" was paid off by yielding up the boat (from the company to Angus), and Higgins and his friend took possession of the *Bluenose* for the $16,000 mortgage plus $4,000 cash. Angus made a profit on the deal, but not a very big one, a couple of thousand at most. The thirteen shareholders were paid off from the $4,000 cash.

The other notion current in the legend—that the *Bluenose*'s sale, and her subsequent employment in the inter-island trade, was an altogether melancholy story and a degradation of her glorious past—quite misses the point. In fact, the "West Indies Trading Company" didn't really exist, at least not at first, and the *Bluenose* actually had rather a splendid time in her last few years. Her fate, far from being melancholy, made a gaudily romantic story, for she became entangled in the dying years of the gilded age, in the ingenuousness of the very rich, and in the sultry and decadent Cuba of Batista and Papa Hemingway and the high-society circus that surrounded the Duke of Windsor and his American bride.

The principals of the story are two preppie New Englanders, privileged youths whose families' usual social milieu was Park Avenue and the mansions of Long Island, and their story is engagingly recounted in a splendid little book called *World War II Adventures of Canada's Bluenose*.[1] The most interesting of the two, and the more active, was the aforementioned Tom Higgins, a graduate of the tony Choate school, who always seemed to feel constricted by the stultifying milieu of the New England very rich. In any case, he was too intelligent to spend his teenage summers on the beach or the tennis court with the rest of his pals, and volunteered with the Grenfell Missions, which chartered vessels to take medical care to Newfoundland outports and Labrador, and operated numerous small hospitals, orphanages, schools, nursing stations, and co-op stores. Young Higgins spent the summers of 1931 to 1934 on the hospital ship *Maraval*, and later on the *George B. Cluett*, skippered by a Lunenburger, Captain Kenneth Iverson (of whom the gossip in the shipyards was that "he knew every rock between here and St. Anthony [Newfoundland]. And who better? After all, he'd had his vessel on 'em all one time or t'other"). Higgins was only a kid, sixteen when he started, but one thing led to another anyway—Iverson knew Angus Walters, and young Higgins spent a week in Lunenburg chatting with the old man and hearing stories of the *Bluenose*'s exploits. A few years later, back in New York and bored with his life (plunked into the insurance business by his family), he married, and married well—his first wife, Julie (one of four or possibly more; the family seems to have lost count), was moneyed too, being the descendant of a governor of Rhode Island, of the Brewsters of Plymouth, and a niece of Mrs. Jessie Woolworth of the department store family.

The other principal was Jesse Spalding III, graduate of Hill School and Yale—his father had been captain of Yale's football team in 1913. Young Jesse also married well, possibly even better than Higgins; his wife was Elvira Fairchild, a glamorous young woman known as Vivi, who was chums with the Duponts, among other families.

Both young men (big surprise this, considering their parents' wealth and influence) were classified by the U.S. War Office as "4-F," which means "physically or mentally unfit for duty," and spent the early years of the war bumming around without much to do. Higgins and Julie had chartered a small yacht for cruising around the Caribbean, and fetched up in New Orleans. At wharfside they met a trader who offered them a substantial sum to transport a cargo to one of the smaller islands in the Bahamas; shipping was scarce, Nazi submarines were active, and exporters were desperate for any kind of transportation that would risk the course. The money the trader was prepared to pay was substantial, and young Tom was fired with the romantic notion of acquiring the aging *Bluenose* and using her to make the run between islands, dodging submarines, doing good work for the war effort, and making everyone lots more money . . . As a trial, as mentioned earlier, he chartered the *Bluenose* from Angus for six months at $2,800 a month, pretty good money for those days, and nicely calculated to make Angus his investment money back. That was on May 7, 1942.

Still, Tom Higgins didn't quite have the capital to buy her outright, which is where the Spaldings came in. Jesse Spalding III was then putting in his hours at the outfitters Abercrombie & Fitch in New York, and listened to Tom's impassioned pitch with a sympathetic ear. He, too, was bored with his life, and the notion of owning a legendary boat and using it for good and for profit was irresistible.

Spalding was twenty-six at the time, and in the ways of the American rich was living comfortably, though most of his inherited money was tied up in intricate trust arrangements. As Spalding put it rather artlessly at the time, he could "only" raise $40,000 in cash by selling some stocks; the rest of his money was for the moment untouchable. Still, it was enough. He wired the $40,000 to the Bank of Nova Scotia in Halifax and booked an appointment with Angus Walters in Lunenburg.

Young Jesse's memories of the events that followed were not always reliable—their plane to Halifax was diverted by bad weather, he said, to "New Brunswick, Nova Scotia," which probably meant Moncton; and the documents on file suggest the whole thing happened in summer, not the dead of winter as Spalding asserted. In any case, he maintained it took them eleven hours to reach Halifax by train, in a blinding snowstorm, arriving in the city on New Year's Eve. On January 2, the story goes, they drove to Lunenburg to meet Angus Walters. The harbour was crowded with vessels of all kinds—most of the fishing fleet was in port—and the *Bluenose* was presumably among them but invisible in the crush. The meeting with Angus took place in the Zwicker company offices, described by Spalding only as "an old fishery office on the wharf," and a meeting of some solemnity it was. They had already agreed with Angus on a price, $20,000, and had brought the money with them from Halifax in a briefcase, in cash. Angus took his mortgage back, and the balance was disbursed to the remaining thirteen shareholders, and for the rest of the day a procession of Lunenburgers, small shareholders all, Zwickers and Knickles and Knocks, Meisners and Eisners, Corkums and Crouses, Himmelmans and Hirtles, climbed the wooden stairs to the Zwicker office, to be paid off by the new owners under the watchful eye of Angus Walters. The new owners, for their part, thought the price a steal—the name alone, they thought, was worth more than the asking price.

Because Spalding and Higgins had an extra $20,000 cash in their briefcase, they also bought an old Coast Guard cutter, the *Kayemarie*, that had been idled in Lunenburg harbour. That cost them another $15,000, giving them a cargo-carrying capacity of over 200 tons for a total investment of $35,000. They were thrilled. Angus agreed to hire them crews for both vessels; the *Bluenose* was to make her first voyage to Cuba with a load of dried codfish, already in the hold. The skipper would be Edward Whynacht of Lunenburg (who was later to develop the nickname "the Crazy Captain," in Cuba, after he intentionally rammed a Spanish vessel that had annoyed him, causing considerable damage to both vessels).

There is no evidence at all for the sentimental notion that Angus slipped her lines himself as she departed Lunenburg for the last time, though he was on the wharf to wish Whynacht and crew bon voyage. Still, there's no reason to doubt the part of the story that has him walking away from the wharf feeling as though he was coming back from the cemetery; no one ever doubted his love for the old boat.

Higgins and Spalding now owned the vessel but didn't yet have a company to run it. The day after they bought her they went to Halifax, hired a lawyer, and incorporated under the name The West Indies Trading Co. Ltd. of Halifax; the *Bluenose* remained registered in Lunenburg. Later they would form a Cuban company, the Compania Inter Americano do Transporte, to manage her, thereby neatly avoiding U.S. taxes. Port Everglades, Florida, was to be her home port.

Within a few days of reaching Havana, the codfish in the *Bluenose's* hold were sold for a profit of $7,000, and the new company contracted for six runs from the islands to the U.S. mainland, carrying avocados and grapefruit; as a consequence, the *Bluenose* earned more for her new owners in the first year than she had made for the Bluenose Schooner Company in almost a decade.

But the boys—and they were still boys, for they were both just twenty-seven—hadn't bought a legend just to carry boring stuff like grapefruit around the Caribbean. They wanted more adventure than that, and back in Port Everglades they used their family connections to extend their range. They just happened to know Marshal Hemingway, the U.S. Coast Guard's man in charge, who gave them a permit to come and go as they wished, carrying whatever caught their fancy—not an easy paper to come by in wartime. This Hemingway was the son of Dolly O'Brien, famous mostly for having turned down Clark Gable's proposal of marriage; she had then married "Count" Jose Dorelis, who seems to have been from Bulgaria, though his real provenance is obscure. In any case, the count offered the boys a cool $250,000 if they would only run the Nazi blockade into the Mediterranean to pick up a cargo of attar of roses he had spirited out of Bulgaria, and which constituted his entire fortune. The Crazy Captain told them they'd be insane to accept, and in the end they considered the voyage too dangerous, and turned it down, much to their professed regret.

A short time later they contacted a member of the War Department, Admiral Land, another family friend, who obligingly provided them with an A-1 Defense Transport Permit and suggested they aid the war effort by taking dynamite to the islands to build new airfields there, and perhaps at the same time carry a few bombs for the navy. Well, and why not? Jesse went up to Wilmington, Delaware, where he contacted yet another old friend, Nicky Dupont, who agreed that Dupont's factories would sell him as much dynamite as the air force wanted. As a consequence, the first load *Bluenose* took from the mainland to Cuba was 140 tons of 60 per cent dynamite, plus another 60 tons of explosive caps, which had to be stored on deck in special crates. The cargo apparently scared the hell out of everyone on board except the vivacious Vivi, who came along for the ride, bringing with her a brand-new Plymouth convertible, just right, she maintained, for the awful Cuban roads.

For the next year or so the two young men and their glamorous wives swanned around Batista's Cuba, scoffing at rumours of the "sheep-stealer rebels" in the hills, partying at the casinos and resorts, playing tennis with the Duke of Windsor and Dwight Davis (son of the donor of the Davis Cup); golfing with Perry Como and others of his ilk, skeet shooting with Papa Hemingway . . . One day Sterling Hayden called, asking to be named skipper of the *Bluenose*, which he remembered so well from his days on the *Thebaud*. (They couldn't accommodate him at the time, but hired him for a different schooner and Hayden carried another cargo of dynamite, and made them all quite a bit of money; Hayden was still married, sort of, to the actress Madeleine Carroll, and shortly afterwards joined the marines.) The *Bluenose* herself plied back and forth under a series of captains. Crazy Captain Ed Whynacht had only lasted a few months before being replaced by Amplias Berringer, who was injured in 1942, and replaced in turn by James Meisner, her mate, and then by Wilson Berringer, her final skipper, all of them from Lunenburg. She made one more dynamite run to South America, though only after the skipper and crew had been promised an $8,000 bonus for hazardous duty. At the time, Spalding said he'd been offered $100,000 for the *Bluenose* but turned the offer down. He claimed she made almost half a million dollars in the few years they owned her, but these numbers are doubtful, and so is the anecdote that the *Bluenose* had been stopped in the

Caribbean Sea by a Nazi submarine whose skipper was supposed to have declared, in perfect English, "I'd shell you right now if I didn't love that boat so much."

Towards the end of 1944, Jesse Spalding bought out Tom Higgins to become sole owner of their companies, but already the signs were clear that the war was winding down and that Cuba, "the Caribbean Casablanca," would soon be lost to the "sheep-stealers." Jesse was already diversifying out of Cuba and out of shipping; he'd picked up a few hotel properties from family friends, the Dodges, who had made their fortune in cars. The *Bluenose* was by this time in parlous shape, only kept afloat at all by running her pumps full-time; so he took one more trip with her to Florida with a cargo of Cuban cigars, and sold her to the Intercontinental Shipping Company of Tampa, at a meeting in New York, for an amount supposed to be around $50,000. She was reregistered in Honduras as "Honduran Vessel M/V *Bluenose*." This was on December 19, 1944. At this point the *Bluenose* finally vanishes from Nova Scotia government records; the Registry of Joint Stock Companies closed its file on the grounds that the asset had been sold to non-Canadian citizens or to a non-Canadian company; remember that the West Indies Trading Company, Higgins and Spalding's creation, was incorporated in Halifax.

Intercontinental, for its part, owned the aging beauty for just about a year before ordering Wilson Berringer to Haiti on a night run. He was unenthusiastic about the prospect, much preferring daylight runs with a vessel that needed to keep its pumps going flat out just to keep afloat, and some of the ballast removed for the same purpose. His misgivings turned out to be prescient, for in a narrow channel in a "light to moderate" squall, she struck a reef and had her bottom ripped from her, her massive keel and keelson and the ribs torn and broken by the impact, and she stuck fast in the pounding surf. Charlie Akie was at the wheel, and he said nothing to anyone afterwards; the rest of the crew were all hard-case Cubans who spoke no English. No one drowned, and no one was hurt except for Berringer, who broke a bone in his hand. The ship was empty when she struck, and much too light for the conditions, as it turned out. Lloyds Register the following week contained this stark note: "January 29, 1946. Honduran auxiliary schooner *Bluenose* from Port Everglades is grounded at La Folle, near Aux Cayes, Haiti, and has been abandoned by master." Wilson Berringer wrote to Angus afterwards that he'd gone back to look at her the day after she struck and "it was a pretty hard looking sight. Everything broke over the deck. At one time, I thought it was the end for all of us . . . I was not in favour of making the trip at night, but orders are orders."

The president of Intercontinental, George Milliken, wrote a sentimental note to Angus Walters a year after she was gone. He'd flown overhead, he said, and one of her masts could still be seen, but there was nothing left to salvage. Jesse Spalding floated the rumour that she had been carrying dynamite and was a hazard to shipping and had to be bombed into oblivion by the U.S. Navy, but the reality was much more prosaic than that: she was fetching bananas, which were left to rot at wharfside when she didn't appear.

Like Higgins and Spalding, Milliken had loved the boat, and was furious at rumours he'd deliberately sent her into danger to collect on her insurance. He'd cherished both the vessel and her name, and indeed, a month or two after she went down, the U.S. War Shipping Administration issued a Bulletin, dated May 3, 1946, that another Intercontinental vessel, the *M/S Mavis Barbara*, had officially been renamed *Bluenose II*, operating under Ship Warrant 5469. No one in Lunenburg objected, but that was because no one knew about it.

For four years after "the boys" bought the *Bluenose*, Angus Walters went on with his business, "dealin' wit' t'public" and selling his milk, but from his house at the head of Lunenburg Bay he could see the wharf where the *Bluenose* had berthed, and the hole in his heart never really filled. Then, on January 29, 1946, word came that the *Bluenose* had been wrecked. (Her old rival, the *Haligonian*, followed her to the Indies in 1947 as a lumber carrier, and was wrecked in turn in May 1950.) Angus's first instinct was to fly to Haiti immediately to supervise a rescue, but he was dissuaded, and then he cried a little, and then, at last, so did many others. The Dennis family newspaper, the *Halifax Herald*, mourned her passing as "a national sorrow, the ignominy of her death a national disgrace." Angus Walters appreciated the sentiment, but his feelings were mixed. The *Herald* had helped create the *Bluenose*, yes, but what had it done to save her, there in the end when it mattered most? He didn't understand that things had moved on. Senator Dennis died only in 1954, but there was a new generation of Dennises at the helm of the paper, to whom the rivalry with Gloucester and big Ben Pine was already ancient history, far less important than the victory over the Nazis and D-Day and the transit through Halifax of millions of newly unemployed young men and women. Schooners were obsolete, of course, he understood that—even in Newfoundland, a few years after the war, there were no longer enough dorymen to fill a single saltbanker, never mind a fleet. But some things he just couldn't understand. He didn't want a memorial to himself, only to the *Bluenose* and what she had stood for, and she stood for far more than just a silver cup and a few thrilling moments in Maritime history. By letting *Bluenose* go from its collective memory so easily, Nova Scotia was letting a symbol of a large part of its history just dribble through its fingers. Nova Scotia had been *something* in the world of its time, and now it seemed to care little that it was in danger of becoming a creature only of the past, its heritage slipping away while no one even noticed. No one built ships in its coves and harbours anymore, or sailed them, or sent their sons out to the wide world to see what was there. In the end, *that* was the sad part.

Nostalgia, though, didn't die so easily. As the war receded, both Lunenburg and Gloucester felt their stars waning and their place in the world eclipsed by larger and gaudier places, and resurrecting not the schooners themselves but the idea that schooners represented seemed like a good way of recapturing at least a diluted flavour of the past.

In Gloucester the nostalgia was mixed with a generous dose of civic boosterism. Preserving the past was perceived as a good way to generate tourist dollars, after all, every day there'd been races, the hotels and restaurants and taverns of the town had been filled with paying guests from all over America, brought there by the glamour and the romance and stories of the courageous exploits of the fishermen. Perhaps that kind of excitement could be resurrected. The *Gloucester Times* ran a long series of articles proposing the construction of an "authentic" fisherman-racer, with old salts and craftsmen showing off their skills . . . It was a good idea but nothing came of it. The *Thebaud* had been wrecked the year after the *Bluenose*, also in the West Indies, but one of her builders, Joe Mellow, acquired a pretty, little fishing schooner called the *Sadie M. Nunan*, bought at a sheriff's sale in 1952. He moored her in Gloucester and tried to raise money to rebuild and repair her in the way the *Times* had suggested, but the public was apathetic and he abandoned the idea. It wasn't until 1986 that Gloucester at last acquired a vessel that her owner's gift said should be "cared for, prominently displayed as a monument to the history of Gloucester, and used for the education and pleasure of the public," and the *Adventure* has been educating and pleasing the paying public ever since.

Lunenburg was luckier. When National Sea Products, the successor company to Lunenburg Sea Products, moved away from the town's waterfront to a larger facility at the entrance to the harbour (in the Lunenburg way, the story was that the company had moved not just to accommodate larger draggers, as it said, but just beyond the municipal boundaries to escape town taxes) its picturesque old red-painted warehouses became vacant, and the Fisheries Museum of the Atlantic was installed by the provincial government. In time, the museum has acquired a wide array of fishing vessels, including the *Theresa E. Connor*, an elegant little hybrid auxiliary dory trawler, a dragger, and several others; and in 2005, they launched their museum-built Tancook schooner, whose construction on the museum premises had served admirably the purposes the *Gloucester Times* had outlined fifty years earlier.

In the 1950s, the town's tourist office frequently remarked how often tourists came to Lunenburg just to see the *Bluenose*, not even knowing she was gone. And when in 1960 the Smith and Rhuland yard was commissioned by MGM to build a replica of the HMS *Bounty* for a new movie, thousands of people came to see her being constructed. "Most everybody wanted to see the *Bounty*," the tourist office reported, "and were well pleased. If the *Bluenose* were here, she'd be a great drawing card."

Well, if the *Bluenose* couldn't be there, why not the *Bluenose II*? Bill Roué was enthusiastic, and so of course was Angus Walters. "If they build another, why, she'd pay and repay for herself . . . [But] . . . this is the last chance to build another . . . I think she should be built while the fellows are still around who know how she should go." There were a number of people still alive who had sailed in the *Bluenose*, including Angus himself, but there were only four of the craftsmen left who had actually built her: Dan McIsaac, Howard Falkenham, "Rigger Morris" Allen, and John Rhuland. The town, seeing the potential to make a little money, agreed: "If they build her it would be a wonderful thing for Lunenburg, for Nova Scotia and for Canada," the mayor enthused.

But where to find the money? As Angus had discovered, Lunenburgers were famously parsimonious, and the notion that the town of fewer than 3,000 people could come up with the sum of $200,000, which was the estimated cost, seemed absurd.

Enter serendipity. The Oland brewery in Halifax produced a lager called Schooner, and had in any case been casting around for a vessel to help promote it. So neat was the fit that they agreed to put up all the money to build her. They even promised never to use her for racing, lest she lose and the *Bluenose* name be devalued, and never to use her to promote theirs or any other beer. She'd spend as much of her time in Lunenburg as possible, the Olands said, and in any case would be there every year for the annual Fisheries Reunion and Picnic, donating the profits of that week to the exhibition. Colonel Sidney Oland, the CEO of the company, was a savvy businessman and he knew the mere existence of a *Bluenose* replica would be publicity enough.

There was one last hitch. They wanted to call her the *Bluenose II*, but neither Roué nor the Bluenose Schooner Company owned the name; and since no one knew anything about the former *Mavis Barbara*, now the *Bluenose II* out of Honduras, it was assumed the name belonged to Lawrence Allen. Allen had been both master and mate on the *Gilbert B. Walters*, and had even commanded the *Bluenose* once or twice, especially after 1938, when he sailed her home from Boston after defeating the *Thebaud*, Angus Walters having flown home to marry Mildred. Allen was building a small schooner as a personal yacht, and had registered the name. He agreed to yield his rights.

And so Smith and Rhuland was commissioned to follow Bill Roué's plans, and Howard Falkenham's son Kline was hired as foreman, and the keel was laid in the spring of 1962, with members of the Oland family and Roué and Angus Walters and a host of other dignitaries present for the ceremonial driving of the first bolt. The grainy black-and-white footage of the ceremony makes fascinating viewing: Victor Oland, a massive figure in a greatcoat and elegant hat and an expansive capitalist's smile, swings rather ineffectually at the protruding spike; a shaky Roué has a go, but then watch as Angus Walters, eighty-one years old, impatiently takes the maul away and drives the bolt home with a few crisp swings.

Lunenburg is still there, though scarcely as a working port—there are more bed-and-breakfast establishments in town than any other kind of business—and the blacksmith's shop that used to do ironmongery for the schooners has been sold, twice, with its fate uncertain. Lunenburg Sea Products became National Sea Products became Highliner Foods, but processes only the fish that others catch, and its main business is in any case packaged pastas and chicken. The town is now a UNESCO World Heritage Site, all those brightly coloured houses that had been built by trading and shipbuilding and then by fishing are still there, in better condition than ever, made over by come-from-aways, outsiders nostalgic for a touch of down-east authenticity. In 2005, the venerable Smith and Rhuland yard finally closed for lack of business. Clearwater, a major fishing company whose hyper-efficient draggers are symptomatic of the way the industry is ruining the resource on which its prosperity depends, has effectively left town, selling off its collection of six wharves and twenty-two still-picturesque shingled waterfront warehouses. In 2005 they were bought by the province and turned over to a waterfront association headed by Dan Moreland, which will try to resurrect something of a waterfront maritime industry, of what sort and with what luck is not yet known.

Only a few small shipbuilders are left in Nova Scotia—the Snyder yard at Dayspring is still busy, and John Steele's operation at Petite Riviere is thriving on a high-quality private yacht business, but Tancook's Mason yard is just a jumble of pilings, its former owners gone to Ontario to build fibreglass runabouts, and ruined also are the hundreds of other small operations that made the province a presence in the world and brought it such unexpected prosperity. Nova Scotia never did make the transition to steel hulls and larger-scale shipbuilding; the decentralization that had kept the industry vibrant in the days of wood made the transition to more massive industrialism harder when wood became obsolete. There were a few attempts—the pioneer steel ship *Mulgrave* was built in New Glasgow in 1893; and a three-masted steel schooner,

James William, 440 tons, was constructed in 1908; but when she was sold in 1927, it was the end of shipbuilding in that port. The next steel hull wasn't laid in the province until 1965. Most shipbuilders never seemed to notice their own looming obsolescence: in the early years of the twentieth century scores of Nova Scotian sailing vessels plied the Atlantic carrying oil between American ports and Europe, transporting the very stuff that was to help make them redundant.

There are no fishermen's schooner races anymore; the few precious relics and replicas in Mystic and Gloucester and Essex and Lunenburg are too expensive to risk in such foolishness and frippery. But every alternate year Gloucester fishermen come up for the Fishermen's Reunion on Lunenburg's waterfront for the "international dory races," and every other year Lunenburgers go south to pit themselves against the burliest Gloucestermen. Even this sometimes seems too much for a weary industry: in 2005, the Lunenburg town council squabbled about who should pay the dorymen's fares to Massachusetts, a mere few hundreds of dollars.

Gloucester is a bigger and brawnier town than Lunenburg, and preserves more industry, but it is also shabbier and more down at the heels, and has a harder time capturing even a faded view of its glorious past. Still, not every memory has faded, and there are annual events commemorating the old days—those dory races, for one. Every July the city holds its annual Seaport Festival at the Harbor Loop near where the schooner *Adventure* is moored, and the town holds a schooner festival around Labour Day every year, a popular event that draws tourists from all over New England.

In the nearly fifty years since she was launched, there has been much carping about the *Bluenose II*. In the early days she was often dismissed as a promotional gimmick and the Oland company unfairly accused of exploiting her name. The carpers said she looked fine enough, but then they pointed below, to the sophisticated diesels, cabins, full plumbing systems and heads, and all the trappings of a cruise ship. Partly because of her air-conditioning and other modern systems, she rotted quickly. In 1972, the Olands sold their brewery to the Labatt conglomerate and the marketing budget for Schooner lager dried up; the new owners had no use for an anachronistic sailing ship. They fired the crew and tied her up, and a few months later sold her to the province for $1. Two years later she had to be completely refitted, for another quarter of a million dollars; as a gesture, the Oland family donated $50,000, for which they got scant thanks. The *Bluenose II* had to be restored yet again in 1995. In the early years of the new millennium there was controversy over the non-profit foundation that had been created to run her, and some money seemed mysteriously to have disappeared, part of a looming financial scandal radiating outwards from Ottawa. There were some unseemly squabbles over who owned her image—do the Roués have copyright in the plans?—and some low-grade lawsuits over infringements. In 2005, the province took her away from the foundation and tucked her under the wing of the fisheries museum. Angus's grandson Wayne, who had skippered her for a while, joined the board to supervise her running. She draws tourists by the thousands, as Lunenburg's summer waterfront can easily testify, and thousands more have thrilled to stand on her deck to feel her breathe gently on the swells.

In the end, whether the *Bluenose II* is ersatz or not rather misses the point. She may be a replica, but in many ways that count she is also the real thing. She can sail, if anything, faster than her famous ancestor (same hull, better sails). On her maiden voyage under skipper Ellsworth Coggins (who had sailed the replica *Bounty* to Tahiti for the filming of the movie), she got into a hurricane, into the eye itself, surrounded by winds of 80 knots and more, enmeshed in a storm that took five days to blow itself away, sorely testing the brand-new vessel with its brand-new rigging and its largely untried crew. Angus was aboard, of course, at the age of eighty-two—he even brought his own barometer with him, mistrusting anything newer. Afterwards he said, "In all my years, I only remember one blow that might have been worse, and that was when we brought the *Bluenose* back after the Jubilee. But this ship stood right up to it. I doubt if we ever shipped a lick of green water."

Another time, heading south in January 1969, Coggins had the crew take in the mainsail after a dirty night, and while the men were furling it he saw a rogue sea coming down on the beam. "I called out to hold on, and it broke right over us, twenty to thirty feet high. It cleaned the deck. The life rafts were gone, the compass was gone, the skylights were stove in, the engine room flooded, and when the decks cleared I saw one of the men climbing back over the rail, and two more in the water." One was recovered, Craig Harding, now the senior Crown attorney in Liverpool. The other, Neil Robitaille of Yarmouth, was lost. The sea is still perilous, but the *Bluenose II* came through, again.

Anyone who sails her or even stands on her deck learns to love the living thing under their feet, for it's impossible not to sense her eagerness to move, her responsiveness, her sensitivity to wind and weather, her thoroughbred nature, her ties to her forebear and her challengers and to the many many thousands of vessels that caught the wind and travelled the world, deep back into the mists of time.

A wery good wessel, just like her mother.

EPILOGUE

*A*s to the received wisdom: she did kick Yankee ass, after a fashion, though as we have seen, patriotism was a thing imposed on the fishermen's races by others; working fishermen were competitive, but were most fiercely competitive with their own kind, and the rewards were yarns that knit them together, never flags and bunting and parades or even money. In too many ways the international races became a creature of the Royal Nova Scotia Yacht Squadron and the Eastern Yacht Club, with the real fishermen as their more or less unwitting or reluctant accomplices. And the *Bluenose* never did get to race against the best of the challengers, for whatever reason, good or venal. *Bluenose* did lose on occasion; she wasn't infallible, and nor was her master, though she was a prime vessel and he a canny sailor, and together they were very hard to catch or to match. She was a beauty, yes, but not a beauty queen; her rather lumpy fo'c'sle made her not as pretty a vessel as the *Haligonian*, the *Thebaud*, the *Columbia*, or the *Mayflower*. What it did, for sure, was to make her a "witch to windward"; no other vessel that sailed against her could catch her beating up into a gale. She was fast, yes, but there were others possibly faster, though none were both as fast and as able in hard weather. It was part of her legend that she was just a fisherman that sailed superbly well; but it's not true. She was built to race and only then to fish, and built at a time when she was needed no longer, and though many of the people who sailed her and raced her and watched her knew this, they tried not to know it too well, and this gave her every voyage an elegiac tone that at the end was hard to bear.

The *Bluenose* became a symbol not just of a way of working that had gone but of the life of an entire province that had vanished; transformed from a place that was confident of its way in the world, needing no man's help, to a place whose spirit could only be seen in the interstices, in the splendid woodwork and detailing of the old houses now restored, in the dockside warehouses standing empty, in the yarns of a very few very old men, in the businesses closed and shuttered or turned over to the tourist trade, in the tourists themselves, who come to Lunenburg and stand on the wharf, and watch as the *Bluenose II* moves gently in the water, tugging on her lines, all too obviously ready to dare what she may, a looking glass into another and tougher but simpler world. Sam Whynacht is dead now, and so is Moyle Crouse and Marty Welch and Maurice Whalen and taciturn Clayt Morrissey and irascible Angus and big Ben Pine, and this elegant creature pulling at her lines at her Lunenburg berth is their memorial. Think of the men who made it so. Iron men, in their wooden ships.

Notes

PROLOGUE

1. Silver Donald Cameron, 54ff. Permission to use quoted passages courtesy of the author.
2. Claude Darrach, 56
3. *Bluenose* crew in 1938, on six-month contracts: George Myra, 32; Borden Andersen, 22; Irving Corkum, 40; Harold Corkum, 52; Samuel Shaw, 70; Claude Darrach, 35; Clyde Eisnor, 27; Lloyd Heisler, 33; John Pardy, 39; Herbert Hardiman, 22; Thomas Black, 25; Arthur Corkum, 26; Douglas Pyke, 32; Henry Banfield, 31; Lawrence Hoover, 30; Kenneth Spidel, 62; Philip Poole, 28; Cyril Hiltz, 22; Adam Knickle, 82; Lawrence Allen, 40 (mate); Fred Rhodenhizer, 37; Horace Miller, 28; James Whynot, 50 (cook); G.C. Burgoyne, 47; Moyle Crouse; Paul Crouse; wages were $22 a month.
4. The photograph is part of the Rosenfeld collection at Mystic Seaport.
5. Silver Donald Cameron, 60–62

CHAPTER 1

1. Joe Garland, 178. From *Down to the Sea* by Joseph Garland, introduction by Sterling Hayden, reprinted by permission of David R. Godine, Publisher, Inc., copyright 1983 by Joseph Garland.
2. Claude Darrach, 15

3. James Connolly, 246, 247

4. Ibid., 246

5. Michael Santos, 17. Permission to reprint specified passages courtesy of the author.

6. Joe Garland, 178

7. Michael Santos, 89

8. Claude Darrach, 18

9. Ibid., 18

10. Michael Santos, 20

11. Ibid., 17

12. Brian Backman, 23; Tom Gallant in *Wooden Boat* magazine #170, 34

CHAPTER 2

1. *Sailing Ships of the Maritimes*, 6

2. *Sails of the Maritimes*, 46

3. Armour and Lackey, 12

4. Phyllis Blakeley, 3

5. Wallace, *Wooden Ships and Iron Men*, 12

6. Phyllis Blakeley, 4

7. Parker, 48

8. Wallace, *Wooden Ships and Iron Men*, 99

9. MacMechan, 7

10. Armour and Lackey, 6

11. DesBrisay, 482

12. B.A. Balcom, 15

13. Wallace, *Wooden Ships and Iron Men*, 4

14. Armour and Lackey, 2–3

15. Parker, 7

16. Wallace, *Wooden Ships and Iron Men*, 4

17. Phyllis Blakeley, 5

18. Wallace, *Wooden Ships and Iron Men*, 146

19. Ibid., 47

20. Ibid., 49, 50

21. Ibid., 32
22. Wallace, *Roving Fisherman*, 115
23. Ibid., 5
24. Sterling Hayden introduction to Joe Garland, xi
25. Balcom, 1
26. Wallace, *Wooden Ships and Iron Men*, 136
27. MacMechan, 117
28. Some phrases from Norman Duncan
29. Wallace, *Roving Fisherman*, 117

CHAPTER 3

1. The list of shareholders at the first annual general meeting was described in the minutes as "Angus Walters, George Tanner, Arthur and Fenwick Zwicker, Adam Knickle, Nathan Meisner, Absalom Meisner, John Walters, Captain Abram Cook, Moyle Smith, James Thurlow, Captain Richard Silver, Ralph Adams, Captain Alvin Himmelman, Dr. R. McK. Saunders, Ellison Corkum, Wilfred Knickle, Arthur Hebb, Thomas Walters, Captain Artemus Schnare, Captain Daniel Heisler, Captain John Corkum, Stewart Hirtle, Clifford Ernst, William Emeneau, Wallace Knock, George Rhuland, Richard Smith and others . . ."
2. George Bellerose, 53
3. Joe Garland, 41
4. Ibid., 37
5. Silver Donald Cameron, 2
6. Backman, 70
7. This description of the *Bluenose*'s construction came from interviews with Kline Falkenham and other workers, conversations with shipwrights, from Backman, 66ff, and from *Roving Fisherman*, 24–27
8. Dyson, 74. From *Spirit of Sail*. Permission to quote specified passages courtesy of the author and his agent.
9. Claude Darrach, 10
10. Ibid., 50, 51
11. Brian Backman, 10

12. Ibid., 29
13. Story from Martha Keddy Smith.
14. Santos and many others have made this point.
15. Quoted by Keith McLaren, as preface.

CHAPTER 4

1. Sterling Hayden, 196. Passages from *Wanderer* reprinted by permission of SLL/Sterling Lord Literistic, Inc., copyright by Sterling Hayden.
2. A hoary old joke used to good effect by Patrick O'Brian in his series of novels set in the Napoleonic wars.
3. Dyson, 34
4. Wallace, *Roving Fisherman*, 54
5. Otto Kelland, 146
6. Anecdotes from Wallace, *Roving Fisherman*, 198
7. Joe Garland, 72, 73
8. Kipling, 80, 81
9. Russell Bourne, 16
10. George Bellerose, 20ff
11. Russell Bourne, 16
12. Michael Santos, 29
13. Wallace, *Roving Fisherman*, 110
14. Michael Santos, 28
15. James Connolly, 131, 132
16. Ibid., 100
17. Quoted in Dunne, 253. Permission to reprint certain passages kindly given by the family of the late Mr. Dunne.
18. Gordon Thomas, 15. Permission to reprint certain passages courtesy of Commonwealth Editions.
19. Ibid., 109
20. Wallace, *Wooden Ships and Iron Men*, 143
21. Silver Donald Cameron, 76
22. Claude Darrach, 11
23. Jacqueline Langille, 13

24. DesBrisay, 461

25. Bellerose, 17

26. Wallace, *Wooden Ships and Iron Men*, 174

27. Bourne, 191

28. Wallace, *Roving Fisherman*, 112

29. "The Log of a Record Run" was widely published and well known at the time (1914), and was reprinted in Wallace's autobiography. It also appeared in a compilation of Maritime folk tunes compiled by Helen Creighton, who mistakenly thought it was a much older traditional ditty.

30. Wallace, *Wooden Ships and Iron Men*, 3

31. Thomas, 202, and contemporary newspaper reports

32. Thomas, 299

33. Wallace, *Roving Fisherman*, 111

34. Kelland, 146

35. Bellerose, 22

36. Joe Garland, 173

37. Michael Santos, 28

38. Feenie Ziner, 74

39. James Connolly, 97

40. Ibid., 14

41. Dyson, 33

42. Wallace, *Roving Fisherman*, 18

43. Michael Santos, 25

44. Dyson, 31

45. Santos, 30

46. Dyson, 33

CHAPTER 5

1. Randolph Stevens, Moyle Crouse, Kiah Conrad, Sam Herman, Alma Zinck, Wallace Himmelman, Lonnie Falkenham, Charles Hebb, Kenny Tanner, Albert Himmelman

2. Much of this from the Shelburne museum, but once again Santos has a clear exposition of this contretemps, p 96.

3. Santos, 91
4. Ibid., 95
5. Quoted in Santos, 95
6. Snider's piece was in the *Telegram* the following day, and reprinted in the December issue of *Rudder*. Snider died in 1971, at the age of ninety.
7. There is some doubt as to the times registered. The official version is that *Bluenose* won by 9 minutes, 13 seconds, but she was also, by the same records, supposed to have finished at 2.12.41, and *Elsie* at 2.31.12, a difference of more than 18 minutes. It is no longer known which figure is wrong.

CHAPTER 6

1. Connolly, 20
2. Sterling Hayden, 192
3. Kelland, 139
4. Wallace, *Roving Fisherman*, 43
5. Connolly, 37
6. Garland, 77
7. Phrases from Kipling, 80
8. Ernest Fraser Robinson, 18
9. Wallace, 69
10. Bellerose, 42
11. Sterling Hayden, 185, 136–37
12. Wallace, *Roving Fisherman*, 115
13. Wallace, *Roving Fisherman*, 176; Connolly, 22
14. Ibid., 34 35
15. Garland, 145
16. Wallace, *Roving Fisherman*, 38
17. Garland, 146
18. Sterling Hayden, 192
19. Kipling, 130, though Kipling's version was slightly different. He changed that "off and homeport bond" to "we're back to Yankeeland," perhaps having picked up the newly stirred Yankee patriotism, living

as he was in Massachusetts at the time. Also in later days that "fifteen hunder' quintal" (168,000 pounds) was a modest enough catch, but a song was a song and the fishermen saw no need to change it.

20. Kipling, 114
21. Garland, 173
22. James Connolly, 223
23. Wallace, *Roving Fisherman*, 3, 4

CHAPTER 7

1. Interview in Peter Barss, 49
2. Ibid., 48
3. Wallace, *Roving Fisherman*, 80
4. Lunenburg fisherman on NFB tape
5. Barss, 51. From *Images of Lunenburg County*. Specified stories reprinted courtesy of Peter Barss.
6. Ibid., 56
7. Kelland, 81
8. Blackburn's story has been published in many places. This version is pieced together from Garland, Connolly, Thomas, and other sources.
9. James Connolly, 14
10. Bourne, 16
11. Garland, 4
12. Ibid., 8
13. Ibid., 8
14. Dunne, 54
15. Garland, 9
16. Bourne, 203, 204
17. Dunne, 53
18. Ibid., 98
19. Quoted by Garland, 100
20. Garland, 17, 18, and many other sources
21. Garland, 17
22. Dunne, 99

23. Ibid., 112
24. Ibid., 95
25. Ibid., 212
26. Thomas, 122
27. Dunne, 222
28. Ibid., 243
29. Fast and Able, 176

CHAPTER 8

1. See Dunne for an excellent biography of the McManus family.
2. Dunne, 132
3. Santos, 49
4. James Connolly, 102
5. Dunne, 177
6. James Connolly, 124
7. Garland, 174
8. Dunne, 178
9. Connolly, 105
10. Dunne, 180; Garland, 173; and many others
11. This story has been told in Santos (p 59), and by Connolly and many others, differing each time in the details.
12. Wallace, *Roving Fisherman*, 9

CHAPTER 9

1. Santos, 31
2. Wallace, *Roving Fisherman*, 134
3. Santos, 64
4. Bourne, 16
5. Andrew German, 4
6. Ziner, 61
7. Quoted in Santos, 74

CHAPTER 10

1. "I knew captain Morton Selig who was skipper of the *Elsie*, and he said oh yeah, Jeff was hammered."—Dan Moreland

2. This poignant anecdote is from Santos (p 109), and is a splendid metaphor for his notion of the industrialization of fishing. See also Santos, 112

3. Backman, 43

4. Silver Donald Cameron, quoting Wendell Bradley's *They Live by the Wind*, 146–47

5. Garland, 212

6. Dunne, 339

7. Thomas, 272

CHAPTER 11

1. Quoted in Ziner, 66

2. Silver Donald Cameron, 47

3. Story told in Santos, (p 120), and by many others.

4. Backman, 43

5. Darrach, 35

6. Quote from Backman (p 44), but the story has been often told.

7. Dunne, 347

8. Quoted in Santos, 125

9. Santos, 128

CHAPTER 12

1. Shelburne *Gazette and Coast Guard*, March 25, 1925

2. From a Peter Barss interview

3. Barss, 120

4. Dunne, 347

5. Transcript of interview with Ralph Getson

6. Unattributed news clipping in Ralph Getson's files

7. Bridgewater *Bulletin*, March 19, 1929
8. McGuire story from Backman, 46
9. Backman, 48
10. Sterling Hayden, 191

CHAPTER 13

1. Backman, 19
2. Quoted in Silver Donald Cameron, 19
3. Story has been told many times, especially in Backman (p 20), Darrach (p 46), Silver Donald Cameron (p 19).
4. Ziner, 82
5. Santos 81, 83
6. Sterling Hayden, 216–218
7. Darrach, 69
8. Silver Donald Cameron, 60–62

CHAPTER 14

1. Much of the story of Higgins and Spalding that follows was sourced from this book (produced by Andrew Higgins in Newport Beach, California, and published in 1998 by the West Indies Trading Company, with an assist from Jesse Spalding III) and confirmed from Canadian and U.S. government documents.

Glossary of nautical terms

not defined in the text

But first, a note: alert readers will see that the vessel starring in this book is variously referred to as *Bluenose* and the *Bluenose*, and other vessels in the book similarly. Technically, which means in the clubhouses of yachting people everywhere, the "the" is redundant. But in real life, this "the" comes and goes, and so it is here. Pedants please direct your complaints elsewhere.

Alee—away from the direction of the wind; opposite of windward

Ballast—heavy material placed low in the hold to lower the centre of gravity and improve stability

Barque—square-rigged vessel similar to a caravel (the ships of Columbus) but larger

Batten down—secure hatches and loose objects within the hull and on deck

Beam—the greatest width of a boat; "on her beam ends"—lying on her side

Belaying pins—pins to hold fast sheets or halyards

Bilge—interior part of the hull below the floorboards

Blacklead—paint heavily laced with lead additives

Block (and tackle)—what landlubbers call a pulley system

Boom—large spar run out to extend the foot of a sail

Bowsprit—spar projecting forward from the bow

Brig—two-masted sailing vessel with square sails on both masts

Brigantine—two-masted sailing ship with square rigging on the foremast and fore and aft on the mainmast

Bulwark—side of a vessel above its upper deck; also called gunwale

By the count, by the share (*see* Sharesman)—fishing by the share means all hands share equally; fishing by the count means you get paid for the fish you actually catch

Caprail—upper part of the rail, shaped for easy gripping and very smooth

Cat-heads—a beam or crane projecting from the bow and used for hoisting the anchor clear of the bow

Clipper—sailing vessel with sharp bow, designed for speed

Companionway—stairway or ladder

Counter-sterned—flat at the stern instead of pointed

Crack on—hoist as much sail as the vessel will bear in any wind condition

Cutter—lightly armed patrol boat

Dragger—fishing method that involves dragging a net or bucket along the sea bottom

Drogue—sea anchor

Entrance and long clean run—the entrance is the shape of the bow below the waterline; the run is the shape off the hull below the waterline and above the bilges

Fashion piece—timber that frames the shape of the stern

Fathom—6 feet

Fish killer—admiring term for successful fishing skipper

Fo'c'sle—forecastle—variously a short raised foredeck, or the quarters below the foredeck

Foremast—mast closest to the front of the ship

Foresail—main sail on forward mast

Foretopsail—top sail on forward mast

Freeboard—minimum distance from the surface of the water to the gunwale

Gaff—a pole attached to a mast and used to support the upper edge of a fore-and-aft sail

Going (or beating) to weather—heading into the wind, or as close to it as possible

Gunwale (gunnel) (*see* Bulwark)

Halyard—rope or tackle used to raise or lower a sail or yard

Haul—"wind hauled around" means the wind changed; "haul her off means turn her"

Head—marine toilet

Heel—leaning over at a sharp angle

Hogged—sagging amidships

Hove over—knocked over on her side

Hove to—stopped

Jib—triangular staysail stretching from the bowsprit to the masthead in small vessels

Jib boom—spar extending the length of the bowsprit

Jumbo (forestaysail) (*see* Schooner sailplan)

Keelson—strengthening timber laid over joint where ribs or frames meet the keel

Knockabout

- schooner with no bowsprit
- semi knockabout (or round bow knockabout)—with a small bowsprit

Knot—speed equal to one nautical mile (6,076 feet) per hour

Lanyard—short piece of rope or line made fast to anything to secure it, or as a handle. Used to secure shrouds or stays

Larboard—opposite to starboard; same as port, that is, left side looking forward from the stern

Lee—the side sheltered from the wind

Lee rail—the rail on the lee side

Leeward (loo'ard)—downwind, moving in the direction away from the wind

Lowers—sails below the topmasts

Luff—to bring the head of a ship nearer to the wind

Mainsail—largest sail on after mast

Maintop—mainmast top sail

Making (as in making fish)—curing

Martingale—a rope or cable that supports the bowsprit

Pinks (pinkies)—a small vessel with a very narrow stern

Plumb-stemmed—vessel with a bow that is plumb to the water and not raked or clipperish

Port—left side of a vessel

Quintal—112 pounds

Ratlines—part of the standing rigging, used by hands to go aloft

Reach (verb)—"She could run and she could reach and she could go to windward when I had her" . . . To run is heading directly downwind; to reach is moving with the wind on the beam

Reefed—partly or wholly furled

Rigging—the shrouds, stays, and ropes of a vessel. Standing rigging supports the masts and spars; running rigging helps control the set of the sails

Risins (risens)—risings—colloquial term for bulwarks

Rove—small metal washer over which nail or rivet ends are flattened to lock a fastening

Sail carrier—admiring term for a man who carries as much sail as possible

Sailplan—the number and design of the sails carried by a vessel at any time

Salt wet—vessel with holds full of fish

Scarf—overlapping joint used to connect two timbers of planks without increasing their dimensions

Schooner—sailing vessel using fore-and-aft sails on two or more

masts, with forward mast being shorter or the same height as the
main mast

- **Schooner sailplan**—typical plan includes on the foremast:
  foretopmast staysail (jumbo), jib and jib foresail, fore gaff
  topsail, foresail; on the main mast: main gaff topsail, mainsail,
  and the fisherman's staysail (see endpapers for reference)

- **Auxiliary schooner**—schooner with or without sails whose
  main propulsion is a motor

- **Tern schooner**—three-masted schooner

- **Topsail schooner**—one or two square-rigged topsails on the
  foremast

- **Staysail schooner**—staysails only on the foremast

Scupper—a hole or channel cut in a vessel's side or waterway to drain
the deck

Seiners—vessels using large, vertically hanging weighted sails, to
catch fish while under way

Shallop—a light undecked boat used in shallow waters

Sharesman—crewman who participates in the voyage's profits

Sharpshooter—a hull with a longer and straighter run of keel, and a
schooner rig though without jib boom or foretopmast, gradually
replaced the pinkies

Sheer polls—generally steel rod that separates the shrouds holding
up the masts; usually at the lower end of the ratlines

Sheerline—the upward curve of a boat's hull as seen from the side, or
the degree to which the hull curves upward

Sheerstrake—uppermost strake of the side planking of a vessel

Sheet—rope attached to either the lower corners of a square sail or the
lower corner of a fore-and-aft sail, used to extend the sail or alter
its direction

Ship—a full-rigged ship with square sails on all masts

Shroud—a pair of ropes (though sometimes occurring singly) used to
steady a mast to the side of a hull; connected to the head of a mast
they form part of the standing rigging

Snow—similar to a brig—two-masted ship with square rigging, perhaps a bit smaller, usually two masts of square sails with a third mast and gaff-rigged sail directly behind the mainmast

Spar—general term for masts, yards, booms, and gaffs

Spreaders ("whisker spreaders")—device to separate two poles or ropes

Square-rigged—sails rigged on yards square to the direction of travel

Standing rigging—the rigging that holds up masts, spars, boom, and gaffs

Starboard—right side of a vessel when looking forward

Stay—large rope used to support a mast, leading from its head to some other mast or spar or to the hull

Stempost—vertical or upward-curving timber or assembly of timers stepped into or scarfed into the aft end of the keel

Sticks—masts, spars

Storm sail—heavy-duty small sail hoisted in rough weather

Strake—a continuous line of planks running from bow to stern

Tack—necessary zigzagging manoeuvre to make way into the wind

Tackles—the running rigging used with blocks to form pulley assemblies

Taffrail—the upper part of the stern, or the rail on top of the stern

Thole pins—wooden pins to hold oars in a dory or rowboat—wooden oarlocks

Topmast—upper section bolted to main mast to give additional height

Transom—stern cross-section of a square-sterned boat, or one of the athwartship members fixed to the sternpost that shapes and strengthens the stern

Trawl—originally a long fishing line with several shorter lines with baited hooks attached; also called trawl line; later, a large net that is dragged along the sea bottom behind a commercial fishing boat; also called trawl net; as a verb, to use or put out a trawl or setline

Treenail ("trunnel")—wooden dowel used to fasten two timbers together

Trim—fore-and-aft balance of a boat

Tumblehome (and tuck-in)—the inward upward slope of a ship's topsides

Windward (beating to)—towards the direction from which the wind is coming

Yard—a spar that supports the head of a sail

Bibliography

The Queen has had many biographers, many of them verging on hagiography and virtually all of them celebratory—and why not? She was a superbly made vessel that enjoyed many triumphs and uplifted spirits at a time in history when they seemed to need it most. Still, few of them try to tell the whole story. The back story—the culture and industry from which *Bluenose* sprang—is almost always missing in action. And it has been largely left to Americans to give the political context—that the *Bluenose* lived much of her life in a time of high economic stress and political turmoil, Depression, and acrimony. As a result, the *Bluenose* story often has the outline of legend, and as in all legends the facts often seem shaped to fit, bent and hammered and prodded until they conform. This book doesn't seek to demolish the legend—for the legend is true in its essence, if not in all its facts—but only to nip and tuck a little here and there, acknowledging the work of many writers who have been there before me.

I must acknowledge a considerable debt to Michael Wayne Santos, whose *Caught in Irons* really isn't about the *Bluenose* at all, but about the industrial fate of the North Atlantic fishermen in the last days of sail, and who has cogently and succinctly told the story of how the fishing industry was overtaken by the inexorable march of modernism, and how the International Fishermen's Races were in some way a last failed attempt to stem the tide of change from craft to hired labour. Santos lives and works in Virginia, but has caught the flavours of the Northeast as though native. He will recognize many of his arguments in this book.

My friend Bill Gilkerson, an *eminence* (though not at all *grise*) in the world of maritime painting and writing, led me to Dan Moreland, now captain of a barque, the tall ship *Picton Castle*, and both of them urged on me a copy of Joe Garland's *Down to the Sea: The fishing schooners of Gloucester*. Joseph P. Garland still lives in Eastern Point, near Gloucester, and he writes with a verve and a turn of phrase that is irresistible. The general story of the beautiful creatures that were the Atlantic fishing schooners—of which the *Bluenose* was the culmination—has never been better told.

The other indispensable reference for anyone seeking to understand the backdrop to the races of which the *Bluenose* was such an integral part is the splendid biography of Boston's most famous designer of fishing boats, Tom McManus, written for the Mystic Seaport Museum by W. M. P. Dunne. McManus's designs changed the face of the East Coast fishing fleet, making the boats safer and more productive, and his designs were widely copied all the way up the coast (and were the inspiration for one of Maritime Canada's most interesting vessels, the Tancook schooner). For Canadian readers, Dunne can be a little hard going—he is scornful of the *Bluenose*'s master, Angus Walters, and generally dismissive of matters north of the U.S. border. But this is an intelligent biography and well worth the effort.

Four other American books are worth mentioning. Russell Bourne's *The View From Front Street* recounts his travels through New England's historic fishing communities and his—largely successful—efforts to separate fact from legend. The second is *Down on T Wharf*, produced for the Mystic Seaport Museum by curator Andrew German, a book of photographs with commentary about Boston's most famous fishing quay. (I am grateful also to German for taking time to show me through Mystic's collection, especially its outstanding photo archive.) The third is Gordon W. Thomas's *Fast and Able*, useful little pen-sketches of famous schooners. Thomas is the son of Jeff Thomas, whose schooner *Puritan*, a *Bluenose* rival, was wrecked on Sable Island; the book includes hundreds of photographs from his own collection, now in custody of the Cape Ann Historical Society. The fourth is the charming tale of the *Bluenose*'s final years, a compendium of facts, anecdotes, insider gossip, and legend, called *The World War II Adventures of Canada's Bluenose*. The little book puts the lie to the notion that the *Bluenose*'s last years were ignominy, and I am indebted to it for parts of my own final chapter.

For insight into the fishing life, you can't do better than the two writers and romantics, the American James Connolly and the Canadian Frederick William Wallace. Wallace was the better journalist of the two, and his two collections, *Roving Fisherman* and *Wooden Ships and Iron Men*, offer as fine a view of life at sea as, say, Richard Dana's more famous *Two Years Before the Mast*. Wallace and Connolly were both lovely writers and spent many months at sea on all-sail schooners, and have many fine tales to tell, some of them recounted here. Dan Moreland lent me his copy of Connolly's *The Book of the Gloucester Fishermen*, but I soon tracked down my own copy of this long out-of-print classic. Sterling Hayden's idiosyncratic memoir, *Wanderer*, can also safely be filed under the "romantics" rubric. (Hayden was a crewman on the *Gertrude L. Thebaud* in her races against the *Bluenose*, before he became a movie star.)

In the same vein is Peter Barss's *Images of Lunenburg County*, now undeservedly out of print, a collection of wonderful photographs of, and transcribed interviews with, a collection of Lunenburg's old-timers, all of them long veterans of the fishing life, and all of them with colourful stories to tell. Barss has kindly allowed me to use some of his interviews here.

Of the many Canadian books on the *Bluenose* herself, Silver Donald Cameron's also out-of-print *Schooner: Bluenose and Bluenose II* stands out for the elegance of its writing, as always. It's a small book, and much of it is taken up with Cameron's own voyage as supernumerary on *Bluenose II*, but manages to cram an astounding amount of information into its 129 pages. I have quoted several of his more lyrical passages. Others worth reading are *Bluenose*, by Brian and Phil Backman, a sharply written recounting of the familiar story, and, as a change, Feenie Ziner's *Bluenose: Queen of the Grand Banks*, which though aimed at young adults is remarkable for its colourful turns of phrase. For a crewman's-eye view of the races, turn to *Claude Darrach's Race to Fame: The Inside Story of the Bluenose*.

There are a number of other niche books to which I am also indebted. The late Otto Kelland's engaging *Dories and Dorymen* is full of great yarns and tall (though true) tales (Kelland was better known for penning the wonderful lament "Let Me Fish Off Cape St. Mary's"). Two books on Tancook Island added considerably to the store of anecdotes I had picked up there over the years (my wife has a house on Big Tancook). Wayne O'Leary's *The Tancook Schooners* is a history of "the little Blue-noses," as they were called, and vividly recounted; *Facing the Open Sea: The People of Big Tancook Island* does for Tancook what Peter Barss did for Lunenburg; a lovely compilation of photographs and interviews, some of them with my wife's neighbours on Tancook.

As references on the *Bluenose* back story, I commend to you the oddly similarly titled *Sails of the Maritimes*, by John P. Parker, and *Sailing Ships of the Maritimes*, by Charles Armour and Thomas Lackey (Armour, the former archivist at Dalhousie University, now retired, was endlessly helpful in answering my questions and steering me in productive directions). The monograph *History of the Lunenburg Fishing Industry* was also useful.

Finally, for yarns of valour and endurance on the open sea, Judge DesBrisay's *History of Lunenburg County* is a grand source, and so is the little book *Sagas of the Sea*, compiled by Archibald McMechan and published in London.

Books

Armour, Charles, and Thomas Lackey. *Sailing Ships of the Maritimes*. Toronto: McGraw Hill Ryerson, 1975.

Backman, Brian, and Phil Backman. *Bluenose*. Toronto: McClelland and Stewart, 1977.

Balcom, B.A. *History of the Lunenburg Fishing Industry*. Lunenburg: Maritime Museum Society, 1977.

Barss, Peter. *Images of Lunenburg County*. Toronto: Key Porter Books, 1978.

Bellerose, George. *Facing the Sea: The People of Tancook Island*. Halifax: Nimbus, 1995.

Bourne, Russell. *The View From Front St.: Travels through New England's Historic Fishing Communities*. New York: W.W. Norton, 1989.

Bradley, Wendell. *They Live by the Wind*. New York: Knopf, 1966.

Cameron, Silver Donald. *Schooner: Bluenose and Bluenose II*. Toronto: McClelland and Stewart, 1984.

Candow, James E., and Carol Corbin. *How Deep Is the Ocean? Historical Essays on Canada's Atlantic Fishery.* Sydney, NS: University College of Cape Breton Press, 1997.

Chambers, Sheila et al. *Historic LaHave River Valley.* Halifax: Nimbus, 2004.

Connolly, James B. *The Book of the Gloucester Fishermen.* New York: John Day Company, 1927.

Dana, Richard Henry, *Two Years Before the Mast.* New York: Modern Library Paperback, 2001 (reprint).

Darrach C.K. (Captain Claude). *Race to Fame: The Inside Story of the Bluenose.* Hantsport: Lancelot Press, 1989.

———. *From a Coastal Schooner's Log.* Halifax: Nova Scotia Museum, 1979.

DesBrisay, Mather Byles. *History of the County of Lunenburg.* Bridgewater: reprinted by *Bridgewater Bulletin,* 1967.

Duncan, Norman. *The Way of the Sea.* Freeport, NY: Books for Libraries Press, 1903.

Dunne, W.M.P. *Tom McManus and the American Fishing Schooners.* Mystic, CT: Mystic Seaport Museum, 1994.

Dyson, John. *Spirit of Sail: On Board the World's Greatest Sailing Ships.* Toronto: Key Porter Books, 1987.

Garland, Joseph E. *Down to the Sea: The Fishing Schooners of Gloucester.* Boston: David R. Godine, 1983.

German, Andrew. *Down on T Wharf: The Boston Fisheries as Seen Through the Photographs of Henry Fisher.* Mystic, CT: Mystic Seaport Museum, 1984.

Hayden, Sterling. *Wanderer.* New York: W.W. Norton, 1977.

Higgins, Andrew, and Jesse Spalding. *World War II Adventures of Canada's Bluenose.* Newport Beach, CA: West Indies Trading Co., 1998.

Hobbs, Edward H. *Sailing Ships at a Glance.* Almonte, ON: Algrove Publishing, 2004 (reprint).

Kelland, Otto. *Dories and Dorymen.* St. John's, NL: RB Books, 1984.

Kipling, Rudyard. *Captains Courageous.* New York: Signet, 2004 (reprint).

Langille, Jacqueline. *Captain Angus Walters*. Tantallon, NS: Four East Publications, 1990.

MacGregor, David R. *The Schooner*. Annapolis, MD: Naval Institute Press, 1997.

MacMechan, Archibald. *Sagas of the Sea*. London: J.M. Dent, 1923.

McLaren, R. Keith. *Bluenose & Bluenose II*. Toronto: Hounslow Press, 1981.

O'Leary, Wayne M. *The Tancook Schooners: An island and its boats*. Montreal and Kingston: McGill–Queen's University Press, 1994.

Parker, John P. *Sails of the Maritimes*. Toronto: McGraw-Hill Ryerson, 1960.

Robinson, Ernest Fraser. *The Saga of the Bluenose*. St. Catharines, ON: Vanwell Publishing, 1989.

Santos, Michael Wayne. *Caught in Irons: North Atlantic Fishermen in the Last Days of Sail*. Selinsgrove, VA: Susquehanna University Press, 2002.

Thomas, Gordon W. *Fast and Able: Life Stories of Great Gloucester Fishing Vessels*. Beverly, MA: Commonwealth Editions, 2003 (reprint).

Wallace, Frederick William. *Wooden Ships and Iron Men*. London: Hodder and Stoughton, 1924.

———. *Roving Fisherman*. Gardenvale, QC: *Canadian Fisherman*, 1955.

Ziner, Feenie. *Bluenose: Queen of the Grand Banks*. Halifax: Nimbus, 1970.

Journals and Monographs

Royal Nova Scotia Historical Society, *Journal*, vol. 4, 2001, 84ff. Taylor, M. Brook. "Frederick William Wallace: The Making of an Iron Man."

Blakeley, Phyllis R. *Ships of the North Shore*. Halifax: Maritime Museum of Canada, 1963.

Wooden Boat magazine, Jan/Feb 2003, Tom Gallant, "Beyond Bluenose" (On William Roué).

National Geographic magazine. July 1921, Wallace, Frederick William, "Life on the Grand Banks."

Index

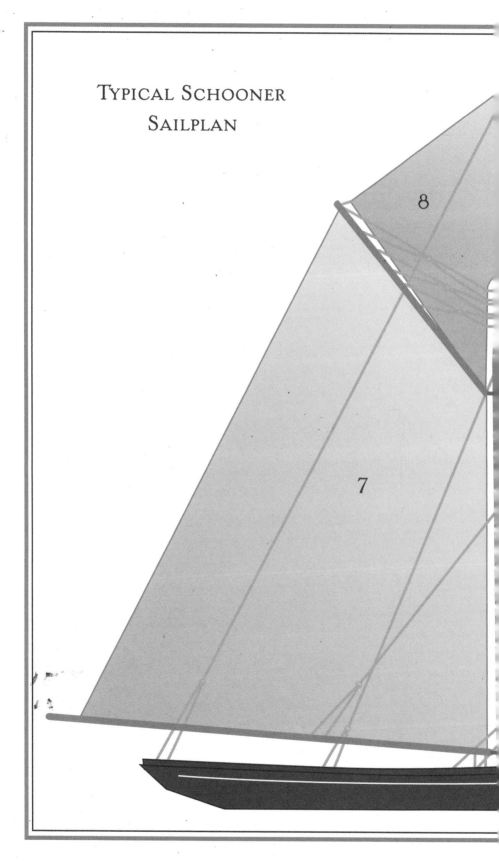

Typical Schooner
Sailplan

8

7